TO FREEDOM
THROUGH CHINA

TO FREEDOM THROUGH CHINA

ESCAPING FROM JAPANESE-OCCUPIED HONG KONG 1942

Anthony Hewitt

with a Foreword by
Sir John Mills, CBE

Pen & Sword
MILITARY

For Liz

First published in Great Britain in 1986
as *Bridge With Three Men* by Jonathan Cape

Published in this format in 2004 by
PEN & SWORD MILITARY
an imprint of
Pen & Sword Books Limited
47 Church Street
Barnsley
S. Yorkshire
S70 2AS

ISBN 1 84415 229 4

A CIP catalogue record for this book
is available from the British Library.

Printed and bound in Great Britain by
CPI UK

Pen & Sword Books Ltd incorporates the imprints of
Pen & Sword Aviation, Pen & Sword Maritime, Pen & Sword Military,
Wharncliffe Local History, Pen & Sword Select,
Pen & Sword Military Classics and Leo Cooper.

For a complete list of Pen & Sword titles please contact:
PEN & SWORD BOOKS LIMITED
47 Church Street, Barnsley, South Yorkshire, S70 2AS, England.
E-mail: enquiries@pen-and-sword.co.uk
Website: www.pen-and-sword.co.uk

Contents

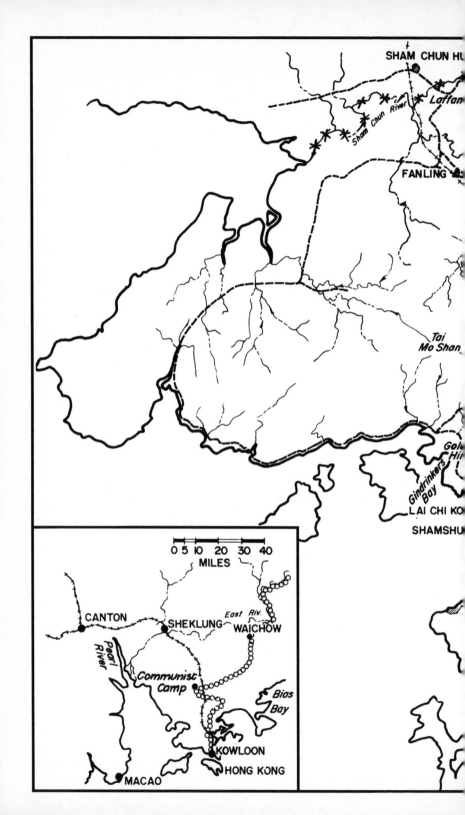

SHATAUKOK

Cloudy
Hill

Mirs Bay

Tolo Harbour

Grassy
Hill

Tide Cove

Riv.

SHATIN

Customs
Pass

KOWLOON

KAI TAK

Kowloon
Bay

ONG KONG

N

MILES

0   1   2   3   4   5   6

ooooooooooooo *ESCAPE ROUTE*

———·——➤ *RIVER*

— — — — — *ROAD*

—+—+—+—+— *RAILWAY*

✱ ✱ ✱ ✱ ✱ *BORDER*

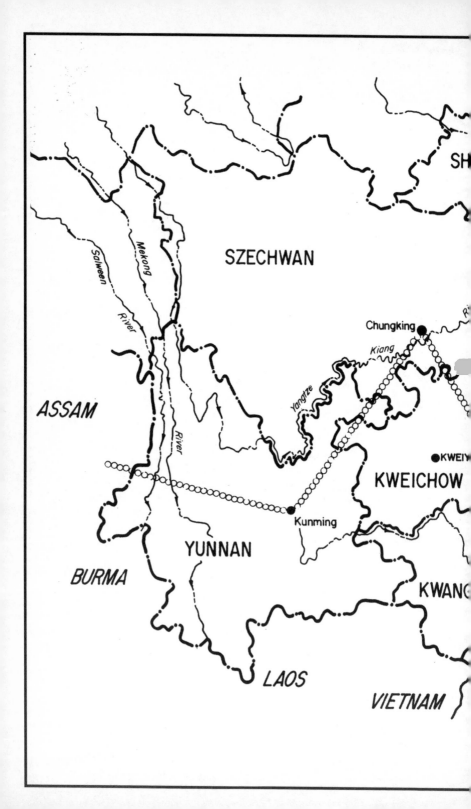

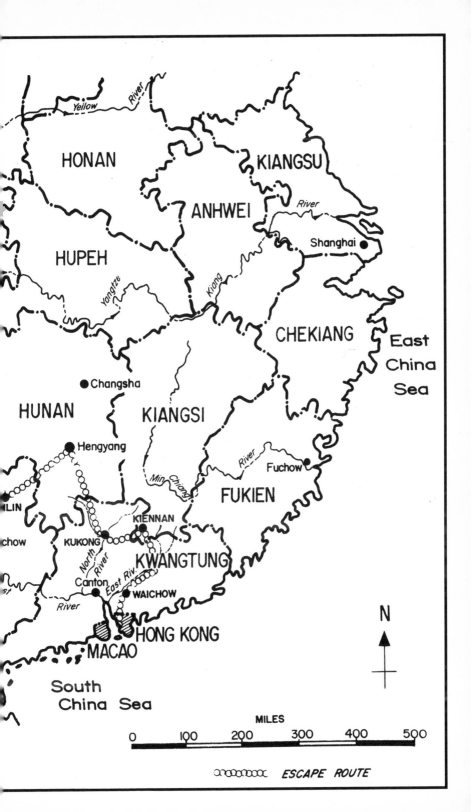

South
China Sea

MILES

0   100   200   300   400   500

◦◦◦◦◦◦◦◦ ESCAPE ROUTE

Acknowledgements

The author and publishers would like to thank Mrs Crossley for permission to include Figure 1, and the following for permission to include photographs: BBC Hulton Picture Library (no. 14), Hong Kong Public Records Office (nos 5-8), Lieutenant-Colonel Oliver Lindsay (no. 4) and Pauline Waterhouse (nos 15-18). The other photographs and Figures 2-4 are from the author's own collection.

The Route to Kweilin

Foreword

I have known Tony Hewitt for over forty years. This is not surprising, as he happens to be my brother-in-law. We seldom see each other, however, for he lives in a remote corner of Queensland, Australia, some 9,000 miles from my home in England. So it came as a surprise to hear recently that Tony had written a book about his wartime adventures, and when his publisher approached me to introduce it, I have to admit I was somewhat apprehensive.

I had forgotten all about his journey across China in 1942, although I was probably the first to hear about it when he returned. That was a long time ago. Many PoW escape stories have been written and filmed since. Indeed it is years since I personally escaped from Colditz — on celluloid! What if I found the book rather heavy going? Should I write a flattering but insincere Foreword because the author is a relation, or should I be honest and perhaps upset the family applecart?

Now that I have read the book, I am happy and relieved to find that my apprehensions were groundless. I should have thought of the extensive diaries he kept, making the story so vivid it feels as if it all happened within the past year or two, rather than nearly half a century ago. I found it utterly absorbing.

It is an amazing story. At times it seems almost unbelievable that Tony, a tenacious character, and his companions — the flamboyant Englishman Douglas, with his monocle, and Eddy, the young airman from New Zealand — could have survived what must be one of the most extraordinary escapes of the Second World War.

Tony Hewitt has written a record of a triumph against seemingly overwhelming odds. *Bridge with Three Men* is a splendid book.

February 1986   JOHN MILLS

1

The Tumult and the Shouting Dies

I do not remember making a conscious decision to escape. I simply took it for granted. Soon after the surrender of Hong Kong on Christmas Day 1941, my Colonel, 'Monkey' Stewart, suggested I should get out while I still had the chance. The battalion headquarters withdrew from Wanchai to Murray Barracks during that Christmas afternoon and shortly afterwards the Garrison Commander, General Maltby, ordered Monkey to go to the Japanese headquarters, stop the fighting and surrender. It was a highly dangerous task, for there was every chance of being shot and killed, even while displaying a white flag. Monkey returned grey with exhaustion, humiliated and distraught.

'When the Japs come here', he said, 'after we have laid down our arms and are defenceless, they will massacre us.' He was desperately tired and sad. I fetched him a mug of tea. He thanked me and said, 'You are very young and fit. There is no obligation for you to stay. Find a boat and get away.'

So I did not have to make a conscious decision: Monkey made it for me.

I left the barracks to reconnoitre along the waterfront near the Hong Kong Club and Supreme Court. The only craft I found by the shore had been damaged by shell fire and bombs. It was vital to evade capture, for it would be much more difficult to escape from imprisonment, yet immediate evacuation by sea seemed hopeless. Indeed everything seemed hopeless. My world was an empty void. We had surrendered. It was not terror, but a ghastly feeling of utter hopelessness that overcame me. There was no future. Nothing. Nothing but terrible humiliation — that and the straw to which I clung of escape, somehow, sometime, as Monkey had suggested. For the present, even survival seemed unlikely.

The capitulation of Hong Kong marked the conclusion of years of suspense brought about by Japanese aggression in China, from as far back as September 1931 when the Japanese had invaded Manchuria, and more significantly from 7 July 1937, the date of the Marco Polo bridge incident and the commencement of the Sino-Japanese War. The small British Colony had been particularly vulnerable to a Japanese attack ever since October 1938, when a Japanese expeditionary force landed at Bias Bay and occupied the country lying between Hong Kong and Canton.

Many in Hong Kong had regarded the Colony as defence-less. There was a sense of lassitude among us. Air Chief Marshal Sir Robert Brooke-Popham (the Commander of Allied Forces in South-east Asia) flew in from Singapore in 1941 in an attempt to boost morale by belittling the martial qualities of the Japanese. Myopic creatures, he called them, incapable of night fighting, lacking in automatic weapons, inferior in the air. No one was impressed. Immediately after Sir Robert's lecture, an elderly officer by the name of Freddie Guest announced loudly in the Officers' Club that if Japan attacked we would not stand a chance and would be caught like rats in a trap. Freddie was reprimanded for this prophetic remark.[1]

By 1941 Japan controlled Manchuria and coastal provinces in North China, and had advanced deep into the Yangtze valley, occupying both sides of the Pearl River Delta and Hainan Island. In Hong Kong we were surrounded by a hostile army on the Sham Chun River and blockaded by the Japanese navy in the South China Sea. The threat of invasion was constant. Yet in the perpetual cold war of nerves, we somehow managed to continue with peaceful normal lives.

---

[1] Freddie Guest evaded capture. He met me in the Grand Hotel, Calcutta. See chapter 22.

In the week preceding the Japanese attack, General Maltby dined with the 1st Battalion The Middlesex Regiment. Except for the Regimental silver,[1] some pieces of which dated back to 1757, and which had been shipped to the impregnable fortress of Singapore, the dinner was conducted with all the traditional ceremonial. The King's and Regimental Colours, presented a few years previously by H.R.H. The Prince of Wales, then Colonel-in-Chief of the Regiment, were displayed proudly on the wall. The Regimental band played 'The Roast Beef of Old England' as the officers took their seats, and later, topically chosen for the eve of war, 'The 1812 Overture'. Officers were smartly dressed in blue patrol uniforms, the extremely handsome and vivacious Colonel Monkey splendid in his bemedalled jacket.[2] It was the last time these men were ever assembled together.

On the Saturday of that same week I played rugger at the Hong Kong Cricket Club and danced all night in the Hong Kong Hotel before attending Church Parade at St John's Cathedral the following morning. Intelligence reports were indicating that war with Japan was imminent. The garrison deployed on that same Sunday to previously prepared battle positions – the Royal Scots, the Punjab Regiment and the Rajput Regiment on the mainland; the Royal Rifles of Canada, Winnipeg Grenadiers and Hong Kong Volunteer Defence Corps on the Island, with the machine-gunners of the Middlesex Regiment occupying pill-boxes through almost the whole of the Island. As Adjutant to the battalion, I was responsible for establishing the Middlesex headquarters on the north shore, close to the Chinese suburb of Wanchai.

The long-expected invasion took place next day, Monday, 8 December 1941, simultaneously with Japanese attacks on Pearl Harbour and landings on the east coast of Malaya.

British and Indian troops defending the Kowloon peninsula bravely resisted the Japanese onslaught for a few days before

---

[1] The silver survived the war in Singapore, a gold medal only was stolen.
[2] Lieutenant-Colonel H.W.M. Stewart, DSO, OBE, MC. He died in a prison camp in Japan.

retiring to Hong Kong Island. On 18 December, following continuous intense bombardment for seven days and nights, Japanese troops established a landing on the north-east corner of the Island. Quickly they infiltrated through the hills and drove a wedge right across the Island, sealing half the garrison in the Stanley peninsula while attacking with great ferocity the defenders of the western half of the Island, forcing them back into the city until they capitulated.

We had surrendered. The Colours were buried hastily in the grounds of Flagstaff House. The survivors assembled in Murray Barracks, exhausted and dispirited, and laid down their arms. That Christmas night everyone crept away into the barracks to hide in their own misery, waiting for the Japanese to come.

I could not sleep. The silence after days of bombardment was eerie. I wandered about and found myself by the barracks gates at three o'clock on Boxing Day morning when the first column of Japanese troops arrived, moving quietly in rubber-soled shoes along Queen's Road. Two soldiers seized me and an English-speaking officer questioned me. I was told to stay where I was. The party moved on, leaving me standing there alone.

As soon as I had recovered from the horror of this encounter, I ran back into the barracks to tell Monkey that the Japanese had arrived. There was nothing we could do but wait, in dreadful expectation.

Boxing Day began with brilliant sunshine and deep blue skies, typical South China winter weather. The Japanese came into the barracks, lined us up and searched us. A private soldier, attracted by the silver badge on my fore-and-aft cap, pulled the hat off my head. I appealed to the vicious looking warrant officer in charge: 'Tell him to give it back.' Immediately I received a series of hard slaps across my face, but no cap. I was a prisoner-of-war under the Japanese.

The barracks were surrounded by sentries. There was no chance of escape. From the verandah of the Officers' Mess building we could watch Japanese soldiers on the Cricket Club ground trying to play cricket. They behaved with sickening violence towards Chinese civilians in the streets. On 28 December they held a victory march, a general and officers on horses leading the victorious troops. It was demoralising. Two days later we were herded along the streets of Central Hong Kong to the ferry terminal. Bomb, shell and mortar fire had caused considerable damage to buildings and dead Chinese lay in the gutters, some only recently slaughtered. We embarked on a Star Ferry to cross the harbour — 'the fragrant harbour', as it has been described. Despite clear blue skies, the water was now green and dirty, full of the wreckage of junks and sampans, among which floated many distended corpses, the former occupants of the craft, swollen into globular form, all victims of the Japanese thirst for blood. It was by no means a fragrant harbour now.

Apart from a few ferries, the harbour was moribund. The usual continual water traffic had gone, the great junks with huge sails, the small craft, the chugging walla-wallas, all had gone. All that remained of the beauty of that great harbour were the green mountains, the magnificent Peak and the other mountains on the Island; and on the Kowloon side, the rugged Lion Rock and Kowloon Peak and in the distance the massive Tai Mo Shan. Gazing at these mountains gave me hope for escape. I knew the New Territories so well.

When we disembarked I led the battalion column with the Regimental Sergeant Major. I was glad to have with me Douglas Scriven, the Regimental Medical Officer. He carried two enormous suitcases. I had a valise, full of as much kit as I could collect in Murray Barracks.

The Japanese warrant officer in charge of the column seemed unsure where to go. Appreciating that we were probably meant to go to Shamshuipo Camp, about three miles away, I offered to show him the way, and this seemed to please him. Douglas, quick to notice that the warrant officer appeared to be a reasonable sort, ordered two coolies standing by to carry his cases and the RSM's and my kit. We were very lucky. The Japanese guards would not allow any other prisoners to have their kit carried.

It was good to have Douglas for company. He had been

with me throughout the seventeen-day battle, setting up his regimental aid post at the battalion headquarters. He was with us in the defence of Leighton Hill, where everyone took part in the fighting, signallers, clerks, cooks, stretcher-bearers, medical orderlies and Douglas. He was with us in successive withdrawals in the horrific street fighting in Wanchai. It was in this overcrowded slum, full of Chinese trying to shelter from exploding bombs, grenades and bullets, that Douglas was wounded slightly by a shell splinter which struck him just above the eyes.

We marched past the Peninsula Hotel. The building was pitted with marks made by our shells and medium machine gun bullets. We had fired many thousands of rounds to stop movement in that area. The Chinese watched us with compassion and sadness as we turned into Nathan Road, their loathing of the Japanese very apparent. Who would save them now from the harsh brutality of the Japanese?

The streets were lined with Japanese sentries, ruthless looking men, bandy-legged, monkey-like, in ill-fitting shabby uniforms, armed with rifles and vicious long bayonets. It would be difficult to slip through them into the side streets and escape. I felt sure the Chinese would help to hide any of us, but in my conspicuous position at the head of the column I had no chance of making a bolt for it. It was not even worth thinking about.

The sweating coolies carried our kit through the guarded gates into the camp and dumped it down in what had once been an officers' mess. I paid them three times more than they asked. I was grateful to them. It was the last time for a long time that anyone carried anything for me. I watched with concern to see if the guards would let them out again, but there was no difficulty.

Just as the coolies had dumped Douglas's suitcases and my kit on the floor, so the Japanese dumped prisoners into the camp, dumped them by the thousand and left them. For some days the Japanese left us alone. No food was provided, but many of the prisoners had filled their packs with tins of food collected from ration stores at the places where they had surrendered. Many had also brought in spare clothing and blankets.

That first evening in the camp I laid out my valise and blanket on the concrete floor in a room with eight other men. I shared my tin of food with Douglas, sitting despondently on the bare concrete between his two enormous suitcases. It was midwinter and very cold. Douglas asked someone to lend him a blanket.

'Why didn't you bring your own? What have you got in those huge suitcases, anyway?'

The suitcases contained no personal things of Douglas's but were packed full of medicines and medical equipment. It was a fine effort on his part. Those medicines were to be invaluable in the prison camp.

The next morning I walked about the camp with Douglas. The boundary was marked by an eight foot barbed wire fence. A few bored sentries stood about. Groups of Chinese from the slums close by were talking to the prisoners through the wire, selling food, bartering and exchanging goods, friends giving presents.

'It would be no problem to get out,' I said, looking at the widely spaced strands of barbed wire. It seemed such a simple matter to climb through and fade into the crowd. But where could you go then? I turned to Douglas.

'When shall we go?'

'When we can,' was all he said.

After what had happened recently it was difficult even to think, let alone make decisions. All the thousands of prisoners crammed into this camp were suffering from shock, from the long days and nights of ceaseless deafening bombardment, from seeing their comrades killed or wounded, many being wounded themselves. We were dazed by the capitulation, the shame, the mortifying degradation, loss of dignity. Many were suffering from personal loss, the loss of houses and property, or entire belongings. Others had lost their families, wives and children now under Japanese domination. It was an appalling situation.

I was concerned about the morale of the survivors, many of

whom were wandering aimlessly about the camp. To restore some meaning into our lives and to bring us together I held a parade of the now depleted battalion of the Middlesex Regiment. We had lost 10 officers and 100 soldiers killed; many more were wounded and some were in other prison camps. I need not have worried. Despite the loss of comrades and the hardship the soldiers endured, there was a sense of resilience among the men, mostly London Cockneys, who were always cheerful in adversity.

The battalion had been quartered in Shamshuipo camp when it first arrived in Hong Kong in August 1937. The occasion was heralded by the worst typhoon ever experienced, a bad omen for a start. Situated about three miles from Kowloon, the camp consisted of a cluster of small, low, wooden huts squatting on reclaimed land close to a smelly slum and a fetid, typhoon, junk-anchorage. There was no sewer in the area and the faecal stench was nauseating. Pungent Chinese cooking odours blew into the camp along with the fetor of bad fish and bad meat from open stalls. Merchants, thieves and prostitutes from the slums and junks used to wander in and out of the barracks at will, peddling food and other wares, followed by swarms of cockroaches. My Colonel had a barbed wire fence erected to keep the Chinese out. Ironically, it was the same fence that now kept us in. Those same Chinese, whom we had tried to keep out, rushed into the camp after the British withdrawal in the early days of the battle and stripped the buildings of everything, leaving intact the barbed wire fence.

It was an unhealthy place for prisoners; soon there was much dysentery, beri–beri and other diseases. Perhaps it was as well that the wire fence existed. In Kowloon in 1938 there occurred a terrible cholera epidemic and the people in the slums died like flies. Every day you could hear the beating of gongs and explosions of fire crackers to drive away evil spirits and devils, followed by long funeral processions moving up the Castle Peak Road to burial grounds. We needed no such epidemic in the prison camp. Now there were processions of another kind moving up the Castle Peak Road and Tai Po

Road — refugees, the inhabitants of the Colony being driven out by the Japanese. I thought it might be possible to slip through the barbed wire and join the column of refugees, but it was obvious that refugees were carefully checked by the Japanese.

At last the Japanese entered the camp. The prison guards, Japanese and Korean, had little or no idea of the ordinary humanities of civilized man; prisoners were dealt ferocious blows for no apparent reason, and any prisoners caught escaping were executed. In fact, execution would be a relief compared with other punishments that could be expected if recaptured. It was important that preparations for an escape were thorough. I could depend on Douglas as a reliable companion.

Douglas was a small and rather fat young man, with fair hair and ice-blue eyes, but you seldom noticed his eyes because the monocle distracted you. That monocle placed in his right eye did much to influence Douglas's character: it distinguished him from other men, accentuated his facial as well as verbal expression, and became a symbol of his quick wit and the cynical scathing sarcasm which so antagonised people, yet enhancing his engaging charm and flamboyant manner in dress. It also marked his recklessness with personal affairs, and made him very likeable.

He was a natural linguist and spoke French, Italian, Urdu and Pushtu. He had quickly learnt Cantonese, knew many interesting Chinese, and was accompanied often at functions and social events by a beautiful and superbly dressed young Chinese woman. His association with the Chinese was deplored in some circles of the Colonial hierarchy, but Douglas cocked a snook at Colonial society and enjoyed doing so.

2

Prisoners and Plans

'They're changing the guard at Shamshuipo.' The Japanese
guard-changing ceremony at the main gate was the entertain-
ment of the day. All the Londoners, the Cockneys, were there,
watching, laughing and shouting advice. Some adopted the
role of drill sergeants and bawled out words of command. The
attention made the Japanese nervous. Their arms drill was
very sloppy.

'Wouldn't do for the Palace,' said the Regimental Sergeant
Major loudly, 'Wouldn't do at all.'

The Japanese soldiers were getting agitated by the jeers and
derisive laughter. A soldier dropped his rifle.

'Pick it up!' someone shouted. 'Take his name, Sergeant
Major.'

The wretched soldier stood there helplessly, stiff with
fright, the rifle lying at his feet. The barracking from the
British prisoners enraged the already angry warrant officer
commanding the guard, who now lost all control of himself.
Screaming and yelling, he flew at the poor young Japanese
soldier, hitting him with great force across the face again and
again. The soldier stood rigidly still and took the savage
beating, until suddenly he slumped, falling across his rifle.
The warrant officer then started to kick him as he lay on the
ground.

The British soldiers booed and then turned away in disgust.
As I turned to go I saw beside me a young Air Force officer,
who looked about three years younger than me, with New
Zealand flashes on his shoulder.

'My word,' he said, in a clear voice, 'they're a lot of bastards. I've been at the wrong end of those slaps myself.'

Together we walked back to Jubilee Buildings, the former soldiers' married quarters, into which the prisoner of war officers were now herded. These two rows of four-storied concrete apartments with deep verandahs were on the southern seaward side of the camp, not far from Bamboo Pier, a jetty used in peacetime for delivering stores and troops.

'I didn't know we had New Zealanders here. Where are you from?'

'There's only one other, in the RNZAF. I arrived from Singapore a short time before the Japs attacked.'

'Where do you come from in New Zealand, I mean?'

'Oh, Wellington. I was born there. My father is a Veterinary Surgeon from Halifax in Yorkshire. My mother from Edinburgh.' He went on, 'I met your mate, the eye-glass doctor. I exchanged a bottle of soya sauce for a tin of bully. He's quite a character, isn't he?'

Douglas would be delighted with the soya sauce, which would help to make the foul-tasting daily bowl of rice more palatable.

'I was planning to shoot through with a couple of matelots but they've been moved to a Navy camp.'

'Oh, how did you plan to escape?' I inquired with interest.

'We were going to get a junk up to Bamboo Pier and sail to Mirs Bay.'

'Sounds too easy,' I said, incredulous.

They had sent a Chinese sailor of the HKRNVR through the wire to get a junk and bring it round for them. He did not know if the Japanese were in Mirs Bay and had no idea what they were going to do when they landed. Walk to Chungking, he thought, obviously having no conception of the distances or any knowledge of China at all.

The fact that he knew nothing about China or even what lay beyond the barbed wire and yet still intended to escape was refreshing. Many prisoners opposed escape and regarded it as ridiculously foolhardy, maintaining that a European would never get through the hundreds of miles of Japanese-occupied territories in China, and that the local Chinese would be unlikely and probably unable to help, and might even be more inclined to rob escapers and hand them over to the Japanese for a cash reward. In any case, they said, what was the use of risking your life again after surviving that disastrous battle in Hong Kong, just to be killed in some other campaign in the War? If one endured a little longer the privations of the prison camp, the United States Navy or even the Chinese National Army, would relieve us. This pathetic hope for relief was always with us. During the battle we were told often that the Chinese Army was advancing to relieve us. In the prison camp rumours that some sort of relief was on the way spread frequently.

Those of us who had been in the Colony any length of time could not have much faith in relief by the Chinese Army. In the autumn of 1938 the Japanese had landed at Bias Bay in the north-east of the Colony and rapidly drove the Chinese Army back across country in order to capture Canton. My Regiment manned the frontier between China and the Colony, to prevent the Chinese or Japanese from coming over. Many Chinese deserters got into Hong Kong and we imprisoned them. The Japanese came also, but we sent them back. Perhaps we should have arrested and imprisoned them also, but the British were always fearful of creating an international incident with the Japanese. I watched the fighting in the Sham Chun valley. The Chinese were no match for Japanese in training, weapons or command. The Chinese Army could never have relieved us.

The arrival of the Japanese in 1938 meant that we had them on our doorstep from that time onwards. When Japan made war against the British, it was a simple task for Japanese forces, which had been present on our doorstep since 1938, to cross the Sham Chun River and advance into the Colony. It was the Japanese occupation of territory north of Hong Kong which added to the difficulties of escape. Before the capitulation, weekly Intelligence Summaries stated that a huge area on both sides of the Pearl River, including Canton, and another large zone extending from Bias Bay to the East River, probably including Waichow, had been occupied. There was no information on how much more of Kwangtung Province might have been taken, but it was reasonable to assume the Japanese had been too busy capturing Hong Kong to find time to extend their territory much further northwards.

It was the state of the country in occupied areas that concerned escape planners more than the precise whereabouts of enemy forces. From peacetime positions on the Colony border, on the green hills, sheltered by bamboo clumps, sycamore and fir, we looked down on the muddy and slimy Sham Chun River, which rises in the beautiful Wu Tung mountains to the east. North of the river, in a huge valley, once lay rich rice fields, fields which had a reputation for providing the best rice in China, especially favoured by the Emperors in Peking. Gradually we had seen the rice fields left untilled and unplanted, and small villages and hamlets in the valley and in the far distance burnt and destroyed. The distraught inhabitants crossed the border into Hong Kong to seek refuge. The Japanese were carrying out a scorched earth policy to make it impossible for guerrilla forces to work against them. There would be little food for an escaper in the Japanese controlled territories.

The New Zealand Air Force Officer said he planned to make for Chungking, the only place name he knew, because it was now the wartime capital of China, where there would be a British Embassy. I knew that Chungking, on the upper reaches of the great Yangtze River, was a thousand miles north-west of Hong Kong, a thousand miles of unknown country.

I talked to Douglas about logistical problems. Where would we go once we got out of the camp? Where would we make for? How could we find the way to Free China? How far would we have to walk? Would we be able to find food on the way? Would the Chinese people help us? Could we survive a long march on little food, especially as we were already half-starved?

Perhaps it would be better to stay put in the camp, accept the humiliation and degradation imposed by our bestial

NEW ZEALAND POST OFFICE TELEGRAPHS

TELEGRAM

URGENT

Z 51 84/1 URGENT G WELLINGTON 1.47 A + CT 53 +

MRS E D CROSSLEY
53 DISRAELI ST HW +

Received at .... Operator's Initials: ....

MUCH REGRET TO INFORM YOU THAT YOUR HUSBAND
PILOT OFFICER EDMUND DOUGLAS CROSSLEY IS BELIEVED
TO BE A PRISONER OF WAR IN VIEW OF LACK OF OFFICIAL
NEWS SINCE SURRENDER OF HONG KONG YOU WILL BE
ADVISED IMMEDIATELY FURTHER INFORMATION IS AVAILABLE
THE PRIME MINISTER DESIRES ME TO CONVEY TO YOU ON
BEHALF OF THE GOVERNMENT HIS SINCERE WISH THAT
YOUR HUSBAND WILL ULTIMATELY BE RESTORED TO YOU
SAFE AND WELL +

Tel. 142. 30,000 pads/10/40—9880]

F JONES MINISTER OF DEFENCE ++

Figure 1 Telegram to Mrs Crossley

masters and wait for the Allied fleets to rescue us. Surely the
Japanese would not starve us to death or kill us in other
ways? I had travelled in Japan in peacetime before the war
and had been impressed by their politeness, kindness and
culture. Now, however, they appeared quite different.
Throughout the Sino-Japanese War, after 1937, the Japanese
committed the most ghastly atrocities, including the Nan-
king massacre. In the Colony, at Sha Tau Kok, where the

boundary ran down the centre of the village street, I had witnessed many acts of cruelty and brutality.

Prisoners of war were less than animals to the Japanese, beneath any living thing. We should not have allowed ourselves to be taken prisoner; by doing so we were reduced to nothing. We could expect little other than slow starvation and a living death. It was imperative that I escaped. The sooner I went the better. Would Douglas come with me?

As a doctor, Douglas was at a disadvantage. He was torn by a conflict of duty: was it the duty of every prisoner to attempt to escape or was it his duty as a doctor to remain with the prisoners? He could not make up his mind, although he agreed to carry on with preparations for an escape. He was anxious, however, that very few people should know that we were making plans. He wanted only the two of us to go.

'We shall be less likely to be detected. Three or more will make a crowd.'

Douglas was also concerned that there might be informers in the camp. I doubted that any prisoner would be capable of such heinous behaviour, although I supposed that under the harsh conditions there might be someone who would become an informer to gain favour with the Japanese, human frailty being what it is. So for the time being I agreed to keep it to ourselves and not invite anyone to join us.

Later I came to the conclusion that the party must consist of at least three people, and possibly four. There was an immense journey ahead in China: if there were only two and one got hurt, it would be very difficult for the other to drag along his companion alone. Selfishly, I did not relish the idea of carrying the fat little Douglas on my back across China. Knowing Douglas, I felt it unlikely he would carry me.

Suddenly, out of the blue, solutions appeared to some of our problems. Early in January, Lieutenant-Colonel Lindsay Ride, a doctor, commanding the Hong Kong Volunteers' Field Ambulance, escaped with three other men. There was no fuss, no reaction from the Japanese. That meant they had got through. Later, when asked by the Japanese what had become of the senior medical officer, Ride's second-in-command simply replied he was that person. Confused, the Japanese pursued the matter no further. There were no repercussions. I hoped, therefore, that our departure would go equally unnoticed.

The precedent set by Ride influenced Douglas enormously. Although there were a number of medical officers in the camp capable of dealing with his work, he still had to decide whether he would do more good by remaining in the prison camp with no medicines or instruments, or by escaping to participate in another campaign. In the end he opted to accept the risk of being tortured and executed if caught. I had never doubted that Douglas would come with me and I did not conceal our intention from my Colonel or the General.

We started making preparations in earnest, collecting food and equipment and walking about to get fit. The New Zealand Pilot Officer came up to us as we were standing at Bamboo Pier, gazing across the dirty water of the typhoon anchorage at the green and brown hills beyond Lai Chi Kok village.

'I believe you two are planning an escape.'

I was annoyed.

'How did you know?'

'Oh, I've watched you. It's obvious you are up to something.' He repeated the story he had told me when I had last met him at the guard-mounting ceremony.

'Oh, what bad luck,' said Douglas. 'You'll have to make some other plans now. By the way, what's your name?'

'Eddy Crossley,' he said. 'How about me going with you?'

'Not a chance,' replied Douglas. 'If we go, it will be just Tony and me. Tony knows the New Territories like the back of his hand. I can speak Cantonese. What could you contribute?'

'I've been building up a store of food,' said Eddy, rather downcast now. 'Three blokes would be better than two. I really am fair dinkum about escaping.'

Douglas would not hear of it. As Eddy walked away despondently I could see how much he wanted to go. He looked a reliable type, about 5 feet 10 high with strong wide shoulders, good looking with a firm and strong jaw, blue eyes that looked straight at you. You knew instinctively he was genuine and honest, brave and fearless, with a pleasant and humorous way of speech. I must talk to Eddy again, I thought. I found him near the barbed wire, bartering for tinned food. He looked smart in his blue RNZAF uniform, with special wings sewn above his left pocket, special because of the 'NZ' in the centre of the wings. He had arrived in Hong Kong in September 1941, to be a pilot of one of the three Vickers Vildebeeste torpedo bombers, all of which were destroyed in the first attack on the airfield at Kai Tak. Having no aircraft to fly, they were deployed to the Island. Eddy was used as an infantry man, and was placed in charge of a squad of Hong Kong Volunteers with a Vickers machine gun on a hill top which came under heavy enemy mortar fire. Years later he wrote to me:

> We were ordered to withdraw and consolidate, a decision with which we were entirely in agreement. We withdrew and consolidated about six times until we were bloody near on the Peak; there wasn't much more left on which to withdraw. By this time it was all over and we were taken prisoner.

That was Eddy's modest and pragmatic portrait of the battle — of eight frightening and bewildering days, ordered to lead people you had never met before in a type of fighting for which you were untrained, under a command you did not know, on totally unfamiliar and mountainous ground, bombed, mortared, shelled and sniped at almost continuously, seeing for the first time men killed and wounded, shocked by the horror of the terrible wounds. That was what Eddy had experienced, a mad nightmare.

The more I talked to Eddy the more I liked him. He was immature, naïve, modest, but tough. I found Douglas, in the Medical Inspection Room, tying up the finger of a soldier who had cut himself while bartering across the barbed wire fence. Eddy was with me.

'He's coming with us!' I said.

Squinting through that infuriating eye-glass, and mimicking grotesquely the voice and accent of the English upper-class, Douglas said, disparagingly, 'Oh! What ever can you provide now?'

Eddy looked at him indignantly, that square jaw jutting out: 'Two strong fists and some food!' Douglas was rather taken aback. Then as an afterthought, Eddy continued, 'But when we get into China I'll use my influence as an Air Force Officer to get us flown out to India!'

Neither of us were so impolite as to ask what influence? But almost simultaneously we realised this man was determined to go. His enthusiasm was catching. Moreover, he was the only person in the camp who had asked to join us. So, at last, we agreed to have him, happy to have made the decision.

We set to work on our plans with renewed vigour. I found an officer with a good map of the country north of the border and copied it on sheets of tracing paper with great care, writing in all the rivers, mountains and village names. Eddy, a good forager, came up with a Crown Lands and Surveys Office map with the Island on one side and the New Territories on the other, very small scale, but a great help. I found a school atlas with a map of China showing clearly the provinces, cities and large rivers. Of special interest to me was the East River, which flowed into the Pearl River. I pointed it out to Eddy and Douglas. I showed them the provinces through which we would have to travel if we were ever to get to Chungking: Kwangtung, Kiangsi, Hunan, Kwangsi, Kweichow, Szechwan. It was as exciting as wading through a travel brochure, but the distances appalled us.

Like three conspirators, we sat huddled over my traced map in the Medical Inspection Room, one of the few places where you could find privacy – a commodity in short supply in this prison camp. From the map we picked the route we should follow. Our aim, of course, was to reach Free China, and we hoped to find that freedom in the vicinity of the East

River. We did not know if the town of Waichow was occupied by the Japanese, and so planned to strike the East River further east by travelling north from the Colony and a little east for safety. Rather a vague aim, in reality. We assumed from the traced map we would have to walk about 150 miles, probably more, to get into Free China.

The map showed towns and many villages, tracks and a few roads. The Japanese would have destroyed numerous villages, but the larger ones of tactical importance, sited on river crossings or road junctions, would be garrisoned by troops. Therefore we should have to avoid large villages and towns. Douglas did not think much help could be expected from the Chinese people, Cantonese or Hakka, because those who had survived in the small villages would be women, children and old men.

'They won't be anti-British,' he said, 'but they will not want to help for fear of reprisals.'

'We ought to be self sufficient in food,' said Eddy, the now self-appointed escape-catering manager. 'How many days will it take to cover 150 miles?'

Douglas thought about ten. I felt it was unlikely that we would do as much as 15 miles a night over mountainous country.

With Eddy's foraging and bartering capabilities we soon built up a store of food, tins of bully beef, sardines, condensed milk and, strangely, Quaker Oats. The collection was hidden under the floor of the Medical Inspection Room, to protect us from awkward questions if the prison guards searched us, and against theft, which was rampant in the camp.

I insisted that we must be physically fit. Every day we walked as much as possible, all round the camp perimeter, up and down the parade ground. As we walked we observed the behaviour of the Japanese guards and the location of sentry posts. At night the guards did not come into the camp, so we could roam about at will. We discovered the exact movements of the sentries, the times when sentries were relieved, and their behaviour patterns. Off-duty the guards sat in a brilliantly lit hut and gambled all night. A newly posted sentry took some time to see in the dark. I proved this by creeping up to a sentry post, to see how close I could get before I disturbed him. Not too close, mind you. The guards were trigger happy.

At night we trained ourselves to move in formation. I was to lead, the other two were to follow ten yards behind, keeping together, the last one, Eddy, watching our rear to ensure that we were not followed. Eddy hated this role, but I had to lead because I was the infantry trained soldier and because Douglas refused to be last. In this formation it was important that both Douglas and Eddy stopped immediately I did. I tried to teach them to stand perfectly still, not to move an inch when in danger, to walk quietly, avoiding sticks and stones, how to use moon shadows for cover and many other tricks used in infantry patrolling. Douglas complained I was pedantic, Eddy thought I was demented. In the end, on the actual escape, all this training paid dividends.

I acquired an army prismatic compass for twenty cigarettes. I showed Douglas how to use it. Eddy already knew; he pointed out the Pole Star, on which we would have to march if we lost the compass.

The training went on day and night. Despite the meagre rations of two bowls of rice a day, we got fitter, though thinner. Douglas's fat little legs seemed to grow longer, even graceful. We watched the tides and timed them; we watched the state of the moon.

We had maps, we had food, a compass, we were fit and ready to go. How were we to get out?

The camp was built in a square, two sides bounded by water, two by land. Sentries were posted on the land sides; the seaward sides were covered by machine guns. In the south-west corner the jetty, Bamboo Pier, ran out to the sea. It was the obvious exit, 500 yards from the nearest sentries. It was astonishing how the guards neglected Bamboo Pier in their security arrangements.

All that changed, however, when the 38th Division of the Imperial Japanese Army, which had brought us to defeat, was relieved by a sadistic detachment of Korean soldiers. Security was tightened. We were informed that anyone found out of the sleeping quarters after dark would be shot. We decided things were getting distinctly unpleasant. We should have to go, and would swim for it from Bamboo Pier.

I found Monkey, the Colonel, in a room in Jubilee Buildings, which he shared with the Second-in-Command, the Quartermaster and the Senior Major, all good friends of mine, and asked for his formal permission. It was no surprise; he knew I had been planning to go.

'Of course, Tony, you have my permission. I know you understand you are risking your life. I know you have planned things well and you are aware of the danger. There is one chance in a hundred of you ever getting through, but if you do, it will be marvellous. Good luck to you.' The other three in the room were all very warm in their expressions of goodwill. I suddenly felt sad that I was going, leaving them, leaving the Battalion I had been with so long, leaving Monkey, whom I admired and respected.

Shortly afterwards the General sent for me. I had met him a number of times since his arrival in Hong Kong in July 1941 and had found him stiff and difficult to talk to, rather a caricature British General. He listened attentively to my plans and to my request for permission to escape. He gave me two letters addressed to the British Embassy in Chungking, which he had prepared before our meeting, and he authorised the Command Paymaster, who was with him, to give me 800 Hong Kong dollars. It was most encouraging, for I never expected the money. The General did not wish me good luck, nor did he refer to my chances, nor indicate in any way whether he approved of the attempt to escape. Perhaps he did not wish to become involved.

That evening, Sunday, 31 January 1942, the three of us were invited to a 'last supper' in the RAF mess in Jubilee Buildings. They provided us with lots of extra bits of food to make the rice more edible. They were obviously very fond of Eddy, and determined to give him a good send off.

Feeling more apprehensive than excited, I left Eddy with the RAF and went back to the room I shared with Douglas and the other men. They all knew we were going. I had given away my greatcoat, my service dress jacket, boots and everything I could not take with me. I tried to get some rest, but I could not sleep. I went over the whole thing again. Was there any chance of getting away? Could a European survive a journey through Japanese occupied China? Did I really have the physical strength to carry it through? Monkey had said there was one chance in a hundred of succeeding; almost everyone thought I was crazy to try. Should I go? Strangely, I had no doubts at all. I was certain I would make it. I had a strong intuition it was the right thing to do and despite every difficulty that might arise I would succeed. Never before or since have I been more sure of any decision I have made.

At last, at about 1 a.m., Douglas and I crept silently out of the room without disturbing the others. At the foot of the concrete stairway we met Eddy, standing in the arched doorway on the verandah. He also had been unable to sleep and had been waiting for some time, concerned that we might go without him. Beyond the doorway we could see the parade ground and the guardroom in a blaze of bright electric light. It was very quiet. There was hardly a sound from the thousands of prisoners in the barracks or from the Chinese slum houses.

Eddy had been keeping a careful watch while waiting for us. He whispered that there were no guards in our part of the camp. He had noticed also that the sentries had just been changed, which meant they were unlikely to see well in the dark until their eyes had recovered from the bright guardroom lights. Nevertheless, we took no chances. Using the darkness of the covered passageway of the building, we walked quietly in rubber soled shoes past five more doorways to the end of the building.

Ahead of us lay about 120 yards of open ground and then Bamboo Pier, where we intended to remove our clothes, slip into the muddy water and swim. It was bright moonlight. As I reached the pier I saw a sampan on the seaward side of the breakwater coming towards us. I turned round and pointed it out to the other two. We moved quickly down the ramp of the jetty. Suddenly we were stopped by a group of Chinese and Portuguese prisoners, who refused to let us go further. They said they had arranged for the boat to bring food into the camp. If it was used for escaping this method of getting supplies would be destroyed. It had been contracted to come in every night, and this was the first night. They implored us to go away.

But here was such a good method of getting out of the camp, so much better than swimming through the filthy water of the bay, that I felt enraged at being prevented from going and started to protest, vehemently. Voices were raised, joined by the sampan coolie, who seemed terrified, and then the sentry from the north-west corner opened fire shooting along the line of the barbed wire.

There was instant silence. All of us stayed there in the deep shadows of the sunken slipway without saying a word, hardly breathing. Nothing happened, and there was no more firing. The guards did not come into the camp to investigate. Eventually the prisoners moved off to where they were quartered among the other thousands of men, leaving just a few Portuguese to collect the food from the sampan.

To avoid further argument, which would create noise, we returned to Jubilee Buildings. In the dark of the passageway we sat down on the floor and held a whispered conference.

'We must get on that sampan,' I urged. 'We'll arrive on the shore in much better shape.'

'I heard them say the sampan will come again, tomorrow night,' Douglas said. 'We will have to find out who is organising the thing.'

I returned to my room, feeling upset and rather silly. The great escapers had come back. None of the others took any notice. One even returned the blanket I had given him.

After the 8 a.m. Muster Parade Douglas and I questioned a number of Portuguese Volunteers. No one knew or wanted to tell us, but in the end we found the man we were looking for in a hut not far from the so-called Hospital. He was, I think, a medical orderly. I told him that the General and Colonel Stewart had given me permission to escape, and asked him to help us to get on the sampan.

'How do I know you have permission to escape?'

It was a difficult question. I did not want to tell him too much. I said I was being sent out as a courier.

'I know you are the Adjutant of the Middlesex Regiment. I've seen you on parade. But that doesn't prove you are being sent out as a courier. You must understand if we use the sampan for escapes, our food business will be spoilt. Stopped, in fact.'

I simply had to convince him. I had to say something that would affect him personally. Then it came to me. I explained that I had proof on me but it was not wise to show it to him, in case the Japanese questioned him. The less he knew about me the better. However, if he promised to get us on the sampan, I would tell Colonel Stewart of his co-operation, and he would probably tell the General. It seemed a bit thin, but it was enough. His face lit up, he smiled, and promised to help us. We shook hands.

Later in the day, I told Monkey what had happened. He smiled and said he hoped I would make it this time and wished me good luck again. In the evening the generous RAF officers gave us another farewell dinner. We had to go this time. We could not make a practice of going and coming back.

As on the previous night, we met Eddy at 1 a.m. in the passageway of the building and, taking more care this time, in case the disturbance would cause the guards to send in a patrol, we made our way to the pier and sat down in the muddy slipway. The Portuguese whom we had met in the day joined us shortly afterwards with a few other men.

We sat in eerie silence. I knew this pier so well. I had embarked and disembarked from it so many times, in peacetime, to ceremonial parades, to guards of honour, to many events. In those days I was proud to be an officer in my Regiment, so sure of the British Empire, so happy. I was contemptuous of the Japanese. Now I was sitting in a wet and smelly slipway, cold and half-starved, running away from the Japanese, knowing that if we were caught there was only one fate.

Suddenly the sentries at the north-west corner started firing, possibly at stray dogs, but also out to sea across the typhoon anchorage, at the breakwater. I hoped the shooting was not at the sampan, but all seemed very quiet in the bay out there, and after this outburst there was complete silence. It was not uncommon for the sentries to open fire at night, to fire into shadows or at anything that moved. It probably kept them amused.

Then, in the silence, broken only by the sound of the sea water lapping against the pier and the heavy breathing of the prisoners, I heard something else. Standing up and looking over the wall, I saw a sampan approaching the slipway, very slowly and quietly. I turned to Eddy, standing and peering beside me.

'This is it!'

3

Escape

'It's this or nothing,' whispered Eddy, 'Chungking or bust!'

It was absurd to be joking at such a time. Only a slight rustling and whispering came from those who were there to collect food from the sampan.

Gradually, almost timidly, the sampan edged round the corner of the pier into the slipway and was secured to the side wall by willing hands. In the clear moonlight I could see the boat contained a coolie, who paddled it, and another man. He was the middleman who would decide whether or not to take us. Our fate lay in his hands. The Portuguese prisoners collected the food quickly from the middleman, but their leader then became involved in a protracted discussion with them. Seconds seemed like minutes, minutes like hours. I did not know if the man wished to accept us, but I was determined he would. We moved down the slipway, closer to the boat, to hear what was being said. To break the almost unbearable tension I said softly, 'Only three yards from freedom, Eddy, nothing can stop us now.' I was not going to wait any longer. I pushed Douglas forward towards the middleman and listened to him talking in Cantonese and pidgin, bargaining. This was no place to bargain. What were we bargaining for, our lives? Douglas turned to me.

'He wants $300.'

'For God's sake, get into the boat.'

Douglas jumped straight into the sampan. Eddy charged past me and also leapt in. I joined the cavalcade. The three of us pushed the sampan along the slipway wall with our hands, shoving like mad to get us out of the pier. We were away! The coolie skilfully turned the sampan and paddled it, with his single stern oar, out to sea towards the dark shadow of Stonecutters Island, and then turned again to the north-west, towards the village of Lai Chi Kok three-quarters of a mile away, travelling near the breakwater of the typhoon junk anchorage. We were well away!

I sat on the floor of the boat, tremendously excited, more so than I had ever felt before. But I also felt desperate, determined, as I had said to Eddy, that nothing and nobody would stop us. I looked up at the coolie who, despite the cold, was dressed only in singlet and shorts. He was a thin muscular man, similar to all the Chinese boat people who dwelled on the harbour. I looked at the middleman, a small little creature, dressed warmly in a thick padded jacket and long trousers, above which was a round fat face, protected by a European felt hat. I admired the courage of these two men – the almost destitute coolie and the wealthier middleman – knowing, as they must have known, that if we were caught by the Japanese, not only they but their entire families would be horribly tortured and executed. They too must have been desperate.

Boarding the sampan had been accomplished in semi-darkness, the full moon screened by thick cloud. The noise made by the prisoners and that of the sampan in the water had not been enough to attract the sentries. But once we were under way, the middleman started talking in pidgin English, saying he had been a steward-boy to some European on the Island and that he wanted people in Chungking to know he helped us to escape. Waving his hands about to explain, his little round face grew more anxious and his voice gradually increased in volume. Douglas, who had already given him the money, promised to pass on his message, but asked him to be quieter.

Just then the sampan coolie stopped rowing and started shouting at Douglas and the middleman, his voice developing to a crescendo of high pitched Cantonese words and turning into a petulant wail.

'He wants money, tea money for himself. He won't go on unless he gets his money,' Douglas explained. The middle-man joined in, excitedly.

'He want plenty money, one time.'

'Tell him to shut up. The Japs will hear. Give him the money. Tell him to get moving. We are an easy target standing still. Tell him . . .'

A shot rang out, followed by three more. The clouds had shifted and the moon shone brilliantly on the stationary sampan. The bullets hit the water, ricocheting over our heads. Crowding down in the bottom of the sampan, we swore in Cantonese and English at the boatman, to make him go on paddling, but the shooting had been enough to force him to take the oar in his thin bony hands and paddle again, guiding the vessel along and close to the seaward side of the breakwater, giving us some cover from view.

In a few seconds the moon clouded over again, but the sentries had got their machine gun into action and opened up with bursts of fire. Bullets sprayed all over the place, some bouncing off the water, some hitting the stone and concrete with an awesome crack, often a little too close for comfort. Eddy, lying full length in the bottom of the boat, kept up a steady flow of Anzac oaths, stronger at each near-miss. But the shooting was wild, the pale moon and the breakwater protected us.

The boatman paddled slowly until he came to the end of the breakwater. There were now 400 yards of unprotected water to cross to the far shore. Having preserved his energy gliding along the breakwater, the gallant coolie now started to paddle frantically. He was very strong. The sampan sped along, throwing out a phosphorescent spray, and we covered the last stretch without any more rifle or machine gun bullets flying at us.

We approached the shore east of Lai Chi Kok village, an area I knew well, and it looked as if the boatman would land us opposite an exit across the Castle Peak Road leading up into the hills. I fully expected the road to be patrolled by the Japanese. Anyone escaping from the camp, by boat or by swimming, would make for this area, the shortest distance from the camp.

Inwardly I cursed the boatman and middleman. Their loud voices, particularly that of the coolie, had alerted the sentries, and our escape had been noticed; we had failed to make a clean break. The sentries would have seen where the sampan was heading, even in the dull moonlight. It was likely we would now be chased by patrols into the hills. Our absence would certainly be noticed by the Japanese at the 8 a.m. muster parade in four hours time. The sooner we were ashore and well inland the better. There was no chance in the boat to discuss these things, but Douglas and Eddy had probably come to the same conclusion: the danger had increased considerably.

The little sampan rode ashore on the stones and sand. I jumped over the side and ran as fast as I could up the beach, heading for a gap between two houses. Just as I was through the dark shadows formed by the houses and had reached the edge of the main road, a Chinaman came out of one of the houses, yelling blue murder, making a terrible, frightening noise.

I was meant to reconnoitre the road and, if clear, to signal the other two to follow me. If we ran into a patrol, we were to fade into the shadows, hide, and if attacked break away to meet at a pre-arranged rendezvous. All our careful plans fell apart with the violent disturbance caused by the Chinaman. Eddy yelled out, and in a flash, he and Douglas raced headlong past me, at full speed, straight across the road and up a white concrete lane, which stood out clearly in the moonlight. We ran flat out and were soon a hundred yards or so up the lane. Once clear of the houses, we stopped to collect ourselves, adjusting our small packs.

'Christ!' said Eddy, 'what was all that yelling about?'

'Thieves, he was calling "stop thieves, stop thieves!" ' Douglas explained. 'Everyone in that lot of houses seems to have joined in. Listen to it.' They were still shouting, barking dogs adding to the turmoil.

'Let's go,' I said. 'Watch out for the Jap patrol, Eddy, or

they'll be after you! The rendezvous is the bridge between two dams, the one I showed you on the map.'

They knew, for we had arranged all this in the camp. We shook out into formation. I led with the compass, the other two keeping me in sight from ten yards or so behind, the last one, invariably Eddy, looking back to give warning if we were being followed.

That idiotic Chinaman had given me a fright, but I was thrilled nevertheless at having got out of that dreadful camp. We set off up the concrete paved lane. I then branched to the right on a wide, earth-covered pathway, winding through sweet-smelling fir trees. I walked very slowly, trying not to step on twigs or fir cones or to start stones rolling down the hillside, making as much use as possible of the shadows in the very bright moonlight we now had with us.

It was very slow going. My instinct was to race ahead as far as possible, but I was afraid of losing the other two or of suddenly meeting a Japanese patrol. I crept up to each corner, peering into the shadows to make sure there was no one there, and then almost ran over the straight and moonlit stretches. Eddy, disliking his role at the back, kept pushing Douglas, telling him to move on and close up with me. Douglas, being the oldest and wisest, could see no sense in closing up on me, to be caught if I walked into a trap. It was exhausting work creeping up that pathway.

Still unnerved by the shouting earlier of the villagers, I was horrified to see round another bend the white figure of a man in the centre of the pathway, partly hidden in the shadows of the trees. I stopped dead, and stood perfectly still, petrified. I could hardly breathe. Douglas saw my rigid figure and stopped at once, as did Eddy. The white figure did not move. I stared harder at him. It was all so quiet, so calm; but very strangely I felt I was being given some message. Then a slight breeze disturbed the fir tree branches, a shaft of moonlight shone clearly on the man, and suddenly I saw a full-scale replica of Christ on the Cross, looking down on me with compassion and pity, as if blessing our venture. This was a signal of strength. I prayed, asking that we should get through. I prayed and prayed, sure that my prayers would be answered. I was no longer a fugitive, I was a free man.

'We're going too slowly. We'll have to press on. It's past four o'clock.'

'Good on you, Tony, go for your life!' said Eddy.

'Don't take any chances,' cried Douglas.

Eddy took this chance to pick on Douglas: 'Don't make so much noise. Those pantaloons you're wearing make a hell of a squeak as they rub together. They'll hear that in the camp!'

Douglas was dressed in ridiculous khaki-drill trousers that could be long trousers or could be turned and buttoned up to become long shorts. In the fullness of the cut of the cloth the trousers were indeed not unlike pantaloons. But before Douglas could reply rifle firing broke out in Lai Chi Kok village less than half a mile below us.

'Whatever is that for?'

'Probably shooting dogs. Hope the villagers haven't told the Japs about us.'

'Come on, let's get out of this!'

In the prison camp, those who had seen us go heard the firing in the village and thought we had been caught and shot. One of them went back to Jubilee Buildings and told them we had not made it.

The Crucifix stood at the entrance to a large Chinese Christian cemetery, at a junction of pathways. I decided to take the left hand path, because it would keep us further away from the Tai Po Road through the New Territories, which would have Japanese traffic on it and be guarded in places. As we progressed I found to my horror we were going westwards and downhill towards the Wu Tip Kok River. There was no turning back and despite grunts of disapproval from Douglas, I kept on at a good fast rate until eventually the path turned northwards and we started climbing steeply. As we crossed the skyline, voices broke out in a valley just below us, questioning our presence. They gave me a nasty fright, but helped to spur us on.

After passing some filter beds belonging to the Kowloon water system, I came to a number of pathway junctions, and each time took the path going nearest to the north, using the compass and occasionally the Pole Star. To avoid being seen on a skyline again, I later dropped down into a concrete water course which had run dry. It was about 10 feet wide with sides 12 feet high, and gave me an awful feeling of claustrophobia. Once in, we could not get out of it until we came across one of the steel step-ladders that were placed at varying intervals of about 100 yards. If a Japanese patrol found us we would be shot from above like rats in a ditch. The situation so alarmed me that at the next step-ladder I climbed out of the water course and took my party along a path that led to a bridge between two dams. This was the rendezvous I had selected, the place we were to make for individually if we had been attacked on the way. Without the compass and without my knowledge of the area I do not think we would ever have re-assembled if we had been forced to disperse.

There was a narrow tar-sealed road to cross before the bridge. I stopped and called up the other two. They were both very hot and out of breath. The camp training could not have been hard enough. We needed a rest. All was quiet and peaceful as we lay on the grassy bank overlooking the two large reservoirs, which looked beautiful in the moonlight. We did not talk: it was too dangerous. Sporadic firing was still taking place below us, about two miles away. I hoped the Japanese were not following the path up to the cemetery past the benign Crucifix. We just had to press on.

The dams were not guarded, so we crawled across the small bridge and set off quickly on a good path through a small forest of fir trees, the pine needles from which made our going quiet and easy. I knew the area well. I had often been here from Shamshuipo for walks or runs, occasionally with a girlfriend. Frequent army exercises were held up here, manning the line of defensive positions, the machine gun pillboxes, the concrete command shelters, earth trenches and barbed wire.

On our left was another reservoir, Shek Pui, lovely in the moonlight. Halfway along it we crossed the overflow from the reservoir and climbed down to fill our water bottles. Then we waded across the cold water and took another rest. It was safer to talk here than at the dams, which could well have been guarded.

'How are you going?' I asked.

'Fine!' both replied together. Eddy went on, excitedly, 'At least we're out of the camp, that's the greatest thing. How much further?'

'We'll go on as far as we can until it gets light,' I said. 'Let's go!'

Scaling the wall of the overflow, I kept close to the reservoir and well clear of a road on my right which had direct access to the main Tai Po road. As we reached the edge of the fir forest and were about to follow a path alongside an open water conduit a rifle shot rang out, from the direction of the two dams we had just crossed, followed by a second and third shot.

'Japs shooting at shadows,' I said. 'They just do it for fun.'

'They're too bloody close,' said Eddy. 'They must have followed us, or come up another way. They've been very quick.'

I thought the Japanese might have driven up the Tai Po road and then taken the small narrow tar-sealed road to the dams, but I did not say so. Instead, I set off at a rapid pace, climbing up the bare slopes of Golden Hill. We passed a group of concrete command shelters from which a nauseating stench of decaying bodies assailed us. Part of the battle had been fought here almost nine weeks ago. Soldiers had been left to rot where they were killed.

As we struggled to the crest of Golden Hill, just over 1,000 feet above the sea, first light, sparrow-fart, warned us the dawn was about to break. I hurried on, not wishing to be caught in daylight on the bare slopes. Very soon the omnipotent sun rose out of the China Sea south of Mirs Bay and over the lovely green and brown mountains of the New Territories, flooding the whole hill with its flaming brilliance. We ran fast downhill towards Smugglers Ridge and left the path, forcing our way through thick undergrowth and small fir trees. Quickly we cut down armfuls of the tough branches and small bushes with army clasp-knives and hid ourselves underneath.

There we lay, the three of us in a small nest on the southern slopes of Smugglers Ridge, from where we could still see a part of the famous Hong Kong harbour over Stonecutters Island and even the wonderful old Peak. We huddled together, scarcely moving, not daring to pull out even a white handkerchief or to talk too loudly, hoping desperately that we had not been observed while making the hide-out.

A palpable silence spread over the ground covered by fir and scrub and we began to feel safer, the feeling of freedom filling us with extraordinary exhilaration. Our satisfaction was supreme. Douglas, who had been very quiet on the march, suddenly exploded, as if just struck by the reality of the situation: 'It's marvellous, we've done it!' And, rather pompously, we shook hands with each other!

Then, as a shock, we heard a bugle call from Shamshuipo, the short reveille, 'Charley-Charley'. We were not very far away. I wondered when I would hear a British bugle call again.

4

Lost in the Wilderness

Unless we were discovered, we should have to remain in this hide-out until dark. There was nothing else for it but to lie here and wait. It was comfortable in the warm, rising sun. Eddy opened a tin of sardines with his clasp knife, and we shared out the contents, washing them down with Shek Pui reservoir water. It was a lot better than putrid rice! There was plenty of time for reflection. I wondered how the three of us, so very different from each other, had ever managed to undertake this mad venture together.

There was Eddy, the Kiwi, strong and tough, prepared to have a go at anything. He was dressed in his RNZAF uniform, blue tunic and blue trousers, because he had the idea that if he was re-captured in uniform the Japanese could not shoot him for being a spy. It was typically naïve. He would be executed just the same. I could not bear to think that they could execute this splendid young man, this cheerful buoyant extrovert companion, who was always encouraging me.

Douglas could not have been a more different character. Sometimes I felt sorry for Eddy, so recently out of New Zealand, travelling with us two Englishmen, though Douglas might better be described as an eccentric international 'pom'. I looked at him, lying there contentedly under the fir branches in those ridiculous pantaloons which had squeaked so loudly as he walked. He was wearing a serge khaki battledress, the monocle and, for some inane reason, a fore-and-aft cap with an IMS badge on it. He was the last person you might expect to have escaped from a Japanese prison camp. You would be very wrong. Douglas was a staunch and brave companion, full of enterprise.

I considered Eddy and Douglas were both mistaken to wear uniform, even if Douglas's get-up savoured more of fancy-dress. Uniforms would simply make our journey through China more difficult: European uniforms would make us so obvious in the middle of a few million Chinese. I wore an army jersey and long barathea trousers, with no badges of rank whatsoever. If re-captured, I hoped to be executed before being tortured, but uniform or my plain clothes made no difference to that issue. I had spent only nine years of my life in England, taken up by boarding school and Sandhurst. I was born and had a wonderfully happy childhood in India, which country I love dearly and where my father's family had served since the East India Company days. So I could also claim to be an international person, and perhaps more precisely a mad international 'pom'.

My musings were brought to a sudden end. Walking up the road, the road I had avoided in the night because it had direct access to the main Tai Po road, came a Japanese patrol of about fifteen men, led by a warrant officer carrying a large sword. They marched along very slowly, as if searching the ground, treading quietly in rubber soled shoes, hardly making a sound. Their approach simply horrified us. They were not more than 150 yards away, and the sight of them filled us with dread. Their forbidding yellow faces, the shabby uniforms, the floppy caps, loose fitting jackets, semi plus-fours, sloppy puttees, rubber boots, and the menacing bandy-legged walk, expressed all the brutality and bestiality we had come to fear. In a cold sweat, we kept perfectly still, watching their slow advance uphill towards Smugglers Ridge. We saw them go and still lay immobile, hardly daring to move a muscle. It seemed we waited hours, but it was probably only minutes. We had to be sure they had passed.

The heavy stillness was broken by a little bird, a wren, hopping from bough to bough. Eddy chirped up: 'Bloody bastards, aren't they? Are they after us?'

'Of course they are,' said Douglas. 'You should know,

you're tail-end-Charlie. Didn't you notice them on your tail last night?'

'We have got to assume that they are looking for us,' I said. 'They may come back again.'

We slumped into silence again, and went on lying there, sometimes sleeping. Occasionally a Chinese peasant would pass along a path only a few yards from our hidden position, taking a short cut to Gindrinkers Bay. At midday a number of Chinese coolies were led up the road by a small squad of Japanese soldiers. The party returned a few hours later carrying ammunition boxes and military material, which I assumed the Japanese were collecting from the machine-gun pillboxes in this area. However, this group did not worry us much; the soldiers were concerned only with the coolies, who made a lot of noise chattering to each other, thus warning us of their approach.

'Why was this called the Gindrinkers Line? Where does the line go?' Eddy asked.

'Down there below us, to the south-west,' I told him, 'is a bay called Gindrinkers. It was a favourite place to sail to, anchor, have picnics and drink gin. The so-called Gindrinkers Line was a defensive position which ran from the bay to north of Smugglers Ridge, where we are now, then to Tide Cove and through the hills to the east. The line is about eleven miles long, three miles north of Kowloon. Just the other side of the ridge is the Shingmun Redoubt. It's about 200 yards south of Jubilee Reservoir, that large reservoir we saw from Golden Hill this morning.'

I went droning on, as if I was giving a lecture, hoping not to bore Eddy, though he seemed anxious to learn what had happened on the ground on which we now lay.

'I think about 12 acres of defensive positions had been built here in 1938, concrete pillboxes, underground connecting tunnels, weapon pits, that sort of thing. My Regiment dug and wired a lot of it. You probably noticed the weapon pits and rusty barbed wire on the slopes of Golden Hill as we passed?'

'Who was defending this area?'

'The Royal Scots. That's the oldest Regiment of the Line, raised in 1633.' I was showing off my history. The Shingmun Redoubt was important tactically, dominating other defended localities and the slopes of Tai Mo Shan and Needle Hill. We could see the slopes of Needle Hill from our hideout, but not Tai Mo Shan, the Colony's highest mountain. I continued, 'The Redoubt was undermanned, garrisoned only by a platoon, about thirty men. They were overrun on the night of 10 December. Throughout the next day fierce fighting went on all round this part of Smugglers Ridge and Golden Hill. One of the Royal Scot companies held the position for many hours. Its company commander led bayonet charges to drive the Japs back, but they were outnumbered, out-mortared and out-gunned, and were ordered to withdraw.'

Eddy was silent, having had enough history. Douglas, monocle still in place, was asleep. A wood-cutter chopping down small trees came close to us and worried me a little, but turned away, and picking up his bundle trotted off down the valley. When Douglas woke we had our second meal of the day – this time the delicacy of a third of a tin of pilchards. Douglas said they were full of protein for the march. It was good to have a doctor with us, but the protein value of the pilchards would not do much to improve the physical condition of the doctor or the airman, about which I was not altogether happy. I had tried to train them to march long distances, but they ridiculed my insistence on fitness and passed it off as a lot of infantry nonsense, neither believing nor even daring to admit they would have to march very far.

By sitting up under the boughs of the camouflaged nest I could see Needle Hill, a sharp pinnacle, much higher than us, partly covered with scattered trees. Beyond it, higher still and much further away, was Grassy Hill, treeless but enveloped in grass and scrub, blue-green in the haze of the evening. On the map of the New Territories I pointed out these features, trying to explain the route I wished to follow. The idea was to descend into the valley of the Shingmun

River, about 1,000 yards north of us, to wade across and then follow pathways up to Needle Hill and along the saddleback to Grassy Hill. By keeping high we would avoid villages. I warned them that the first part, the descent to the river, would be difficult because we would be going against the natural run of paths, streams and valleys.

We stayed where we were until well after dark. The Japanese patrol did not return. It was difficult to remain inactive. I was keen to get on, and we finally made a move only two hours after darkness, far too early to ensure that there were no people about. We had not gone far before we had to jump for our lives off the path to avoid two men. It was not a good omen for a start.

'Let's hide up for a bit until we get some moonlight,' I said. 'We'll break our necks in the darkness. I remember a cave where we can hide.'

I led the way to the entrance of a lead mine, from which drifted the smell of wood-smoke and Chinese cooking. I kicked over a stone: immediately mutterings and noises came from within. A harsh voice yelled at us in Cantonese. We turned and fled down a path which we could only just see.

'Bloody hell!' swore Eddy.

Douglas said, 'Perhaps they could help us and guide us. They're Chinese.'

I would not agree. I was not prepared to trust them. We had no idea who might be in the cave. Eddy agreed with me.

We broke into the scrub and fir and sat down forlornly waiting for the moon. We were frightened and lost; the smothering darkness suffocated us, drained our vitality, depressed us. It depressed me most of all. We could be no more than three miles from the prison camp, surrounded by various dangers, and I was the one who was meant to be leading: here I was lost in the bushes, unsure of my bearings. Had I made a nonsense of it? Eddy, sensing my despair, tried to help: 'We're poor little lambs who've lost our way!'

As the moon rose so my vigour returned. I led the way, trying to follow a course with my compass to the north, to Needle Hill, which forced me to leave the pathways running eastwards towards the Tai Po Road. The cross-country journey over steep and rugged slopes, rocky crags and a maze of small hills made the going very rough. We kept slipping and falling, sending rocks and stones flying, making an infernal noise.

By midnight, we had still made no appreciable headway, nor reached the Shing Mun River. Three hot, tired, disgruntled escaped prisoners sat on a hilltop and argued, furiously.

'We will go downhill into the valley on the pathways going east and then follow the Tai Po Road,' I said shortly.

'We can't follow the road,' Douglas objected. 'It's sheer suicide. We might as well chuck the whole thing in and go back to Shamshuipo.'

'We can't go on like this,' Eddy interjected. 'We're making no progress. It's bloody hard going with all those hills and gulleys and ravines. We're wearing ourselves out. We *must* follow the road.'

Douglas was adamant. He refused to go down the main road. 'We'll be caught. We can't be far from Shatin, and there's bound to be a road block there.'

'We can walk in the ditches as Tony trained us, and fade into the undergrowth if anything comes,' Eddy said forcibly. 'We'll go carefully, but I'm going on the road.'

'Well, there you are,' I said, 'Eddy and I are going down the road, and you are coming too, Duggie, so stop arguing.'

We followed a path leading down the valley, keeping in our proper formation. When I reached the road I waited a while, listening; all was quiet. I led the way, using the verge and ditch and shadows, moving quietly and carefully. I knew that we were approaching a defended locality which had been held by the 2/14 Punjab Regiment as part of the so-called Gindrinkers Line. Ahead of us would be barbed wire and concrete pillboxes. I was almost certain one pillbox covered the road round the next bend, an 'L' shaped bend. I climbed up a spur above the bend as quietly as I could and looked over the crest. The pillbox was only a few yards in front of me, and standing by it was a Japanese sentry. His unsheathed bayonet on his rifle flashed in the moonlight. I stayed still and watched, my heart beating wildly.

He was looking directly towards me, attracted by the slight noise I had made climbing the spur. Only my head was above the crest. I hoped my glasses were not reflecting the moonlight. I stayed there, quite still, like a rat hypnotised by a snake. Eventually he turned away and stepped off in the opposite direction. I took a very deep breath, crept quietly off the spur and crawled back to Douglas and Eddy.

'There's a Jap sentry just over the hill,' I whispered. 'Come this way.'

We scrambled through the undergrowth, making a terrible noise, until we came to a double-apron wire entanglement, through which in panic Douglas and Eddy attempted to crawl, catching their packs in the wire and tearing their clothes. What with Eddy's Kiwi oaths and Douglas's puffing and panting, if that sentry was going to take any action he would have done so by now. In any case, I had no wish to struggle through the barbed wire. Only a few yards from where the other two were entangled I found a nicely cut gap, and walked through and round to the struggling pair.

'What *are* you doing? You should have taken your packs off.' They both cursed me roundly.

We were through the Gindrinkers Line. I knew exactly where I was, having once led a patrol on make-believe manoeuvres over this ground. Confidently I led forward my party, now looking like ruffians — Douglas with a great tear across the rear of his khaki-drill trousers, the pantaloons he had so proudly acquired in the prison camp from a Rajput, and Eddy, his uniform bedraggled, no longer the immaculate Fighter Pilot he once was. Descending onto dry rice fields, we waded across the wide shallow Shing Mun River and scaled a waterfall, filling our water bottles on the way. We then followed the course of the stream, which we left a little later to climb a large wooded hill.

We were a long way off the route I had chosen for that night. As the crow flies, we were still less than five miles from Shamshuipo, and had used up so much energy and were now so exhausted that we could go no further, even though it was only three-thirty in the morning.

I found a Chinese grave on the hillside, the concrete floor of which was flat and dry to lie on, the walls providing some protection against the icy-cold north wind. We huddled up in one corner for warmth with our one shared groundsheet spread over us, arguing about who should have the privilege of the warmest place in the middle until we fell asleep. We were too tired to post a sentry. It was only a few degrees above freezing, in one of the coldest winters in South China for many years. We did not carry much fat on us to keep out the cold. Douglas felt the cold very quickly and stayed in the middle. It was remarkable how he always managed throughout the journey to get into the middle place when we slept.

In daylight we woke with a terrible start.

'Christ,' I said, 'that's a Japanese bugle call.'

5

Yip pun Chye

'It's a Japanese bugle call!' I said again, incredulously.

'It's a Japanese bugle call all right,' confirmed Eddy, looking over the side of the grave, 'and there's a Jap army post on the road below us.'

I stared at the school building below. It was so close I could read the roman letters: FO TAN PUBLIC SCHOOL. Japanese soldiers were going busily in and out of it, obviously part of a garrison occupying the nearby village, the ancient walled village of Shatin. It was alarming to be so close to them. I picked up my pack and handed the groundsheet to Eddy to carry. Douglas put out a restraining hand.

'Don't panic. If we keep down they will not see us. Any movement will attract attention. Just lie down and keep quiet.'

Nervously we resumed our tenuous concealment. To distract us Douglas pointed out the magnificent view, so typical of the New Territories — the deep blue waters of Tide Cove, the green tree-covered mountains rising steeply on each side, and in the distance the great expanse of Tolo Harbour, littered with small emerald islands. Perhaps the grave had been sited here with a view to providing the family ancestors with such a beautiful tranquil scene in perpetuity. Douglas seemed to be enjoying the view as much as the spirits of those ancestors in which grave we now lay. He pointed out the Amah Rock, a pile of boulders on a hill resembling an amah; he told us the rock featured in many local legends. But we philistines were not interested in fine views or legends at this moment. Our concern was to get further away from the Japanese army post. We did not wish to wait. Hoping we had not been seen, we crawled away from the grave to a hollow on the far side of the hill and hid in the undergrowth. We could just see the slopes of Needle Hill, the peak of which disappeared into low cloud.

There was no sun that day. All the hilltops were shrouded in mist. We dared not move from our position, now camouflaged with fir branches. We lay there, very still and quiet, until about two o'clock in the afternoon when the mist from the mountains began to sweep into the valleys and onto our hill. We were so close to the Japanese, so likely to be discovered, that we took this chance to move under cover to a safer place. But no sooner had we begun to move than a light breeze cleared the mist and we were caught standing in the open in full view of a village below us. In an instant there were shouts from the villagers and barkings of dogs.

'They've seen us. We had better go down, or they'll come after us.'

Douglas agreed with me. 'Yes, let's go straight to them before they have a chance to tell the Japs. If they are hostile we'll beat it, fast. They may be friendly and help us. Come on!'

We descended the hill, through the fir and bamboo, looking for any sign of Japanese occupation before entering the village. With much commotion, shouting and yelling, the women and children ran out of the village, with all the young men. We walked quickly through the small cottages, sinister in their emptiness, into the centre of the village, where a huge tree stood in the middle of a courtyard. Waiting for us were three old men, stooping old men with deeply wrinkled faces, long scraggy beards, looking very frightened. They must be the village elders. No one else was to be seen. Even the dogs had left with the other inhabitants.

Douglas greeted them: '*Ni Hao! Ni Hao!*' They replied with a guttural acknowledgement, using a phrase which sounded like, '*Yip pun chye, yip pun chye.*'

With my limited knowledge of Cantonese, I thought they

were saying, 'Japanese people, Japanese people.' I asked Douglas in some agitation what the words meant.

'They are asking if *we* are Japanese people.'

I repeated it to Eddy, '*Yip pun chye, yip pun chye,*' saying, 'It's an expression that you should remember.' I was being patronisingly pompous.

Douglas assured the elders that we were English. They were clearly relieved. I think they had been dismayed by our sudden appearance and could think of nothing else to say except to ask if we were Japanese. The old men broke into a rapid flow of speech, rather like three old cockatoos all screeching at once, talking among themselves and at Douglas, who was able to understand only a little of what they were saying in their rough dialect. A few younger men, sallow-faced unpleasant-looking youths, returned to the village and proceeded to question us in pidgin.

'Where you from? Where you go? Why Japanese no take you? Any money?'

I thought of asking for food, but most of all I wanted to leave the village and get further away from the Japanese. We were not encouraged to ask for anything because of the unfriendly attitude of the younger men, whose insistent cry of 'any money, any money' was most disturbing.

Douglas told them we were in a hurry and must go. We moved off, climbing the pathway that wound up the valley following a stream. Three youths followed us. When we were out of sight of the village they ran in front, stopped us and led us into a clump of bamboo. They were skinny, small youths, dressed in singlets and shorts. They wanted to help us, they said, but if the village elders knew, they would be reported to the Japanese. In the next breath they asked how much money we had.

Douglas said they could help us by showing us the way. Again they demanded money. This was blackmail. If we did not give them money they would run off to the Japanese, less than a mile away, and collect a reward. Douglas offered them a few dollars. They asked for more, and more. The longer we spent here, the more time there was for anyone in the village who had seen us to inform the Japanese and receive his reward. We were caught every way. We just had to get away quickly. In desperation, Douglas took a wad of money from the left hand breast pocket of his battle dress blouse and handed them $50, a small fortune to a peasant. They watched hungrily as Douglas put the rest back into his pocket.

At last we were away. The three young men led, chattering and arguing incessantly, striding along in a running gait, turning every now and then to say something to us and then laughing hysterically. It was as much as we could do to keep up with the fast pace, but it was exactly what we wanted, to increase our distance from the Japanese in Shatin.

As we climbed higher the mist and clouds thickened and obscured visibility. The path seemed to be unfrequented, so we were alarmed when we ran into a group of Hakka coolie women, in wide-brimmed hats, rimmed with a hanging black veil, black trousers and tunics. Our guides shrieked with laughter at our fear.

'These girls,' they told us, 'have all been raped by the Japanese. When the soldiers left they told them to come back again.'

That these girls were friendly with the Japanese was not in the least to our liking. We had just joined the path on the saddle-back leading to Grassy Hill, the path I had planned to use on the previous night. It was a good opportunity to get rid of the youths, whom we did not trust at all. We told them to go. They rushed off with glee, wishing us a happy New Year, due in a few weeks, never having earned $50 so easily. It made us sick.

'Thank God we have got rid of them,' I said, then turning to Eddy I pointed at the map. 'Grassy Hill is 2,144 feet above sea level. The saddle we are now climbing along is the watershed between Jubilee Reservoir to the left and Tide Cove, over there.'

Eddy called me a pedantic ass. He was puffing and blowing in his thick uniform, struggling up the incline. As he was so irritable, I thought it was time to call a halt. It was dangerous, anyway, to continue on this path in daylight. We moved into a gully and hid in the undergrowth. Eddy lit a fire. He opened a tin of Quaker Oats and cooked porridge in his mess tin. It was very refreshing.

We felt safer off the path, hiding here in the undergrowth in thick mist. We were worried about the guides and the Hakka girls and the village people. None of them could be trusted not to inform the Japanese.

'Those blokes are not fair dinkum,' Eddy observed drily. 'They were too keen on the money. You were a mug, Duggie, to let them see that wad of notes. They'll either come after us for the rest of the money or dobb us in to the Japs. And how about the sheilas, they'll dobb us in as well.'

'Oh, I think they will be O.K.,' said Douglas. 'Those Hakka girls wouldn't tell the Japs. The Hakkas are tough, hard-working, peasant people, clannish and secretive and unpopular with the Cantonese. What those youths said about the girls being raped was a pack of lies. They dislike the Hakkas and they wanted to disparage them. No, the girls are all right. I don't care for those louts.'

Before dark we left our fire, scrambled through the undergrowth, followed a path running east of Grassy Hill summit and travelled some distance downhill towards Tolo Harbour. Suddenly a Chinese man came rushing down the hill from behind us at full speed and ran straight into Eddy, who grabbed him and held him by his arm. We looked at him in amazement.

'Who you?' he said in pidgin.

'English people,' replied Douglas.

'Come quick. Japanese come. Come quick!'

We chased after him, zigzagging down a steep, crooked path, until we came to a flat piece of ground overlooking paddy fields. We had descended 2,000 feet from Grassy Hill in a flash!

The Chinese man led us into a re-entrant, a salient in the hillside in deep undergrowth and sat at the cavernous entrance, listening. We were surprised and curious by these events and did not understand what was happening. After a while, he came back and said he had heard a Japanese patrol moving along the path just above us, but all was now safe. I had heard nothing, but the Japanese were trained to move very quietly. It was possible they had just gone past. Nevertheless, I asked this man from Mars, who had so suddenly appeared out of the blue, from where had he and the Japanese patrol come. He had been wood-cutting near Grassy Hill, he explained, and had seen the patrol turn off the path from the reservoir towards him. I looked for his wood-cutting axe. He said he had left all his kit and run. It seemed plausible.

He was a friendly little man, with an engaging smile, a rugged wrinkled face. He said his name was Wong. He spoke good pidgin and asked questions about us. Eddy asked him who he was. He said he belonged to the communist guerrillas. He pulled up his thin cotton trousers to show us scars on his legs. We were a good gullible audience. Wong was enjoying showing off.

'Where you go now?' he asked.

'Chungking,' replied Eddy.

'Aiyaa! Too far. How you go?'

'Walk.'

It was evident Eddy did not like our newly-found friend, perhaps due to his inbuilt fear and ignorance of Chinese people. Douglas and I thought Wong had just dropped out of heaven to help us. We loved him and his anxious, lined face dearly. Undisturbed by Eddy's pragmatic behaviour, Wong continued,

'Too far to walk. I can help. We be friends, soldiers who fight Japanese.'

'I'm a pilot, fly aeroplanes, not a soldier,' interrupted Eddy. I could have wrung his neck. I wanted to hear what help Wong could give us.

He said we could not walk through the land, that the Japanese were in every town and village, thieves and bandits were everywhere else. He repeated himself, 'You will never walk through the land.' He paused, long enough to make me wonder what did he mean? What was he going to offer?'

'I will help you,' Wong said in his high-pitched voice, wheezing through his yellow opium-stained teeth, now close enough for me to catch an unpleasant whiff of garlic-laden breath.

He promised to find a fisherman who would take us by junk to Mirs Bay, where communist guerrillas would lead us through China. He would come to Chungking with us.

It was wonderful, unbelievable! Here indeed was a friend who would get us a boat and lead us through the Japanese occupied territories, and even come all the way with us, the 1,000 miles to Chungking. I believed Wong implicitly; so did Douglas. My thoughts raced away. How easy it was going to be. I would send a telegram to my parents from Chungking to let them know I had survived the battle and escaped.

Disturbing my dreams, Wong spoke again, 'Yes, I will get junk. I want plenty money, for junkman, not for me. Can you give me money?'

He had laid the way too well for us to be careful; he had taken our confidence entirely. If he could get a junk, he must have money. This was no time to argue.

'Of course,' said Douglas, 'how much?'

'Perhaps one hundred dollars?'

'Of course, here you are.'

Again Douglas's hand went to his left hand breast pocket. He pulled out $100. As he handed it over Wong's face broke into a glorious grin, but his eyes followed every movement Douglas made, trying to see how much more money he had and where he kept it.

Wong chuckled away to himself and told us stories of guerrilla actions against the Japanese in which he had fought, lovely tales though highly improbable. He continued to build up our confidence in him. If he was a crook, surely he would have run off immediately he had extracted $100 from us. As it was he stayed on for a few hours after dark.

It began to rain and a bitter north-east wind swept down on us almost, it seemed, straight from Manchuria. Just as Wong was leaving, he said, 'I come back before long with food and clothes. Stay here. Don't move.' He faded away into the cold wet darkness.

We were excited. We thought it was marvellous luck. We would get through in no time. We talked about what we would do in Chungking, even Calcutta.

As the night passed, we huddled together for warmth, the groundsheet across our shoulders to keep out the drizzle, getting gradually colder and colder. Even so we were supremely happy, convinced our troubles were at an end, knowing we had a friend to help us.

At about eleven o'clock Wong appeared again, carrying a sack of food, three white cotton coats and three enormous Chinese straw hats. His approach took us by surprise. We did not challenge him for we had not posted a sentry. He beamed over us, the garlic breath stronger than ever; he must have had a good meal. He dumped the sack down, saying it was food for us, and telling us to put on the white coats and large brimmed hats, explaining that dressed like this the Japanese would think we were Chinese and leave us alone. He had found a junk, everything was arranged, only the boatman needed more money, say seventy dollars more.

'Okay,' Douglas said, taking out the money and counting out seven $10 notes.

'I want watch, must know time. Very dangerous if we go early,' pleaded Wong.

'Here you are,' said Douglas, and to my amazement handed over the watch he wore, a diamond-studded, ladies' watch, the property of his girl friend.

With many thanks Wong left, telling us to put on the white coats and big hats so that he would find us easily in the dark when he returned.

'No go move from here,' he said emphatically.

Off he went and we opened the sack.

'Good God! Whatever's this?' exploded Eddy. The sack contained only raw sweet potatoes. Ignoring our disappointment, we rubbed off the dirt and ate them. It was good food after the little we had eaten for so long, for months, and they tasted good, even raw. We were like cattle eating turnips and other raw things. Perhaps it was the raw food, or else the raw cold, that brought some sense into our heads.

'I'm not sure we should trust this bloke so much,' said Eddy. 'He's now got nearly all our money and your watch, Duggie. There is no reason why he should come back at all. I propose we move on. We're wasting a night here. It's bloody cold, and we're giving the Japs more time to catch up with us.'

'Move on? What fantastic nonsense,' retorted Douglas, 'I assure you Wong is genuine. We must wait here. You don't suppose I'm such a fool as to let him have my watch like that if I didn't think he was okay?'

'Well, you might well be,' I said, joining the fray. 'I must say I don't like the idea of him wanting more money and then the watch. We should have agreed to pay him when we were on the junk. I don't suppose Wong has ever owned a watch; he wouldn't be able to tell the time by it. He tells the time instinctively by the sun and moon.'

'Of course he can tell the time,' said Douglas, now quite angry, because even he was beginning to have misgivings, but was not prepared to admit them. 'You don't really think this man is going to go through all the danger of getting a junk for us without knowing if we could pay for it? Why should he trust three tramps like us?'

'Speak for yourself,' Eddy retorted, still quite smart in his good blue RNZAF uniform, except for a few tears. 'I'm sure I saw Wong in the crowd at the village this afternoon.'

'Don't be so silly. You can't tell one Chinese from another. What a suspicious nature you've got, Ed. Whatever you think, I reckon this is about our one and only chance of getting through.'

'Well, there's no sense in taking chances,' I put in, trying to stop the argument. 'If Wong is the crook Ed and I think he is, he won't come back. He knows he has most of the money. But he may go to the Japs for a reward.'

Eddy was for moving to another hideout, and throwing away the white coats and straw hats. Eventually we agreed to take up a new position on the brow of a small hill, sufficiently in the open to allow a quick escape downhill into the flat paddy fields in the valley below us.

It grew colder. While two of us huddled together for warmth and tried to sleep, one stood up on sentry duty. The aggressive Kiwi had acquired a good stout stick. As the night drew on and nothing happened I became convinced Eddy and I had been right: we had been double crossed. We should be marching, but we could not because the rain made it too dark to see the way clearly enough.

At about three on that cold damp morning, as I stood on sentry with Douglas and Eddy literally just at my feet, I heard a rustling noise in the undergrowth where Wong had left us. I kicked the other two and they jumped up beside me, disturbing the stones as they rose, making a clatter.

Suddenly, out of the darkness, with a terrifying shrill piercing yell, seven men stormed over the brow of the hill at us, waving choppers and bayonets, yelling in Cantonese.

'*Yip pun chye! Yip pun chye!* (Japanese people! Japanese people!')

Not only did I recognise the words, '*yip pun chye*', but with a strange subconscious instinct I knew immediately that I had experienced this same frightening scene many times before, in an oppressive and paralysing recurring dream. Each time the nightmare ended with a dreadful sudden drop, a ghastly helpless fall into a bottomless void. Each time I knew I had been killed.

In an instant, the men were upon us. The leader, threatening Douglas with a dagger, charged at him, snatching at the left hand pocket of his jacket, in which he kept the rolled up notes of money. Douglas stepped back to avoid the dagger and then, striking upwards with immense power, struck the attacker a crippling blow with his clenched fist, hard and full in the face, knocking the man backwards head over heels.

Eddy stood steadfast awaiting the onslaught, his stout stick raised above his head like a bludgeon. Another man, a bandit, as were they all, wielding a huge chopper, struck out at Eddy. Before the blow could land Eddy gave him a most terrible whack over his wretched skull, a tremendous blow, that made a crack like a rifle bullet. It must have been heard miles away. The man moaned and fell to the ground like a broken, crumpled doll.

A small man, shouting and swearing, took two running steps and leapt at me, aiming an axe at my head. Making a quick side-step to my right, I dodged the axe, which glanced off my left shoulder, tearing away the jersey but not cutting the flesh. As I turned I hit my attacker with my right fist on the side of his chin, a full right-hook, with all the weight of my body behind it, a terrific and dreadful blow, hard enough to break a jaw. He groaned and slumped to the ground, like an animal pole-axed, his falling axe just missing my feet. I jumped after him, driving both knees into his stomach as I landed. I clutched his thin throat with both hands, squeezed the air out of him, and beat his skull against a rock, lifting his head and smashing it down time and again, in uncontrolled ferocity. I was utterly desperate; I had enormous strength in me. It had all happened before, in that horrible nightmare. This present situation was an exact replica of the dream. My victim let out a hoarse, horrible scream and I felt I was killing him. As I did so some men began hitting my head with choppers or sharp bayonets. I knew this was going to happen also. In my dreams I had fallen into the void and died this way.

I protected my head with my right hand, warding off the blows, but I still continued to throttle the wretch with my left hand. In this moment of approaching death I became stronger, more vicious and violent, determined to kill this man first. My one hand clasped round his throat, I kept on squeezing and bashing his head against the rock. I had become a savage and ferocious wild animal; I would not let go. I had a manic determination not to be killed; nothing could stop me. But the blows on my head and right hand increased until I had to let go. I rolled over on to my side, drew up my knees and as another man charged at me, I kicked him, driving both feet into his stomach with all the violent animal strength I had developed. The tremendous force of the kick pushed me backwards off the slippery wet grass edge of the hill, so that I plunged headfirst down a steep cliff. I did not care how I fell. I knew I was alive, I had defeated the dream, the nightmare. There would be a bottom to this pit, I was not falling into a void. I had exorcised my evil spirit.

6

Pursued

As I lay bleeding at the bottom of the cliff, I could hear Eddy shouting oaths and the dreadful thud of his bludgeon cracking Chinese heads, followed by groans, more thuds, more groans and yells. The fearless Eddy had gone berserk. He was very strong, and was hitting the attackers with great force, driving them away. The Chinese bandits shouted to each other in desperation, picked up a body and their fallen weapons and fled up the mountain.

I crawled back up the cliff face and heard Douglas shout out: 'Don't hit me, you fool! It's me, Douglas!' And then, 'That you, Tony? Watch out, Eddy's gone mad. He'll clobber you with that stick.'

The resolute Kiwi was not going to be put down by anyone, least of all Chinese bandits, and had enjoyed delivering powerful blows with his stick. We began laughing hysterically, excited and thrilled at winning the battle with the bandits.

'Stuff that for a lark,' laughed Eddy. 'I really gave it to those bastards. They've got a lot of sore heads. They never got near me; they took nothing.'

'I dodged about in the bushes after I hit that first one,' Douglas said. 'They chased after me but didn't touch me. You all right, Tony?'

'Okay. Just bleeding a bit. Lost my glasses.'

We collected our pathetic belongings. I searched in vain for my glasses in the thick undergrowth, with the blood running into my eyes. It was essential that we moved quickly away from the scene of the fight and find somewhere else to hide. Going downhill towards the paddy I discovered a stream running through the centre of a bowl formed by encircling hills, well covered by small bushes and bulrushes. We crept into the rushes and hid ourselves.

'I'm bleeding quite a lot, Duggie. Can you fix me up?'

Douglas could not see well enough to do much, but he slapped a first-field-dressing on my hand and tied it up. He put another field-dressing on my head and told me to press it tightly with my left hand to stop the bleeding.

Later, when it became light and we were more settled in our new hide-out, Douglas dissolved some potassium permanganate crystals in my mess tin, washed my head with it, cut away the hair and stuck an Elastoplast dressing on two deep cuts. He washed all the cuts on my hand, saying that the tendon on my thumb had been severed. He made a splint for my thumb and wrapped the hand up again in a first-field-dressing, covering some of the small cuts with Elastoplast. He then made a sling for me out of the silk scarf he wore, to which he was most attached.

Eddy watched Douglas treating me with intense interest, gaping at the wounds and letting out cries of astonishment. Years later he wrote to me about the fight with the bandits, the 'Battle of Grassy Hill' as he called it, saying, 'I felt very ill when I saw the tendons in your arm wriggling about and those nasty gashes on your head. I didn't feel like my share of our staple diet! Raw porridge and bloaters, wasn't it?' Dear Eddy, he won the Battle of Grassy Hill, saved Douglas and me, but never claimed to have done so.

Our present position offered good cover in the bulrushes but the ground was so damp we could not lie down and rest. Eddy left us to make a reconnaissance and came back with news of a much better place, but told us that we could not move because he had seen three Chinese men beating about in the bushes where we had fought.

'Probably the same people looking for us or anything we might have dropped,' I guessed. 'Any movement may attract them. Did they have sore heads, Ed?'

'Not that I could see. I don't like this creepy-crawly business – always having someone searching for you – Japs and Chinks.'

'It could be worse,' said Douglas, 'but it does give you an uncanny sort of feeling, hiding in the daytime like a scared animal.'

To cheer ourselves up a tin of sardines was opened, not raw porridge and bloaters as Eddy thought in his letter. We filled our water bottles from the stream of muddy water and repacked our haversacks to be ready to move at once if we were discovered. Eddy found another stout stick.

'This really is quite a good spot, despite the damp. No one would expect us to be in the bed of a stream. I'm wet through, how about you, Tony?'

We were all pretty wet and cold, but it did not matter as long as we were hidden. Quietly, we discussed the reasons for the attack. It was obvious the attackers came from the village near Shatin, the men Eddy had so appropriately described as 'villainous bastards'. They were probably just local thieves, Wong included. He was no communist guerrilla, just a good con-man. His so-called bullet wounds could have been anything, burns probably. They wanted our money, watches and anything we had in our packs. Once they had robbed us of everything of value, they would hand us over to the Japanese. It was a pity we had been hood-winked so easily, although only Eddy, the one who was meant to be so ignorant of Chinese affairs, had been suspicious always. Typical of him that he never once blamed Douglas or me.

I was worried that my wounds might turn septic and I would be unable to keep up. It had been agreed that if anyone was sick and could not carry on, the fit must go on to freedom. There must be no question of staying back, trying to drag the sick person through. We had been very insistent on this point and promised each other there would be no mock heroics. I wanted to hear how they felt now, if the situation arose, so I put it to them. I was surprised at their violent reaction.

'That's a lot of nonsense,' said Douglas furiously, 'we won't leave you. We'll even carry you if we have to. We'll make it together or not at all.'

Eddy strongly agreed. 'My word, Tony, we would never leave you. We're all in this together, we'll stick together.' There was no more to be said. A strong bond of comradeship had been forged between us.

As the evening drew on we discussed our intentions for the journey that night, planning our route as well as we could huddled over the map like conspirators, rather as we used to do in the medical inspection room in the camp. First we had to traverse a valley to hills nearly a mile away, then find a path leading over the highlands for about three miles to a large and highly populated valley, and finally steal across the main road and railway and make for Birds Pass. It would be an arduous journey, ten or twelve miles, much more if we had the strength.

'When we cross the first valley, we will have to hide and wait for the moon to get up,' I said, rather as if I was giving out orders, 'we must avoid all villages, even if it means long detours round them. Put on your packs now and be ready to go. You, Duggie, climb out and have a look round.'

He was back again in no time. 'We're almost completely surrounded by Chinese. There are groups of them on the hills on both sides of this bowl. I think they saw me. Let's break for it now!'

We jumped up and raced downhill along the stream bed. There were shouts from all around us. We felt like hunted animals which had broken cover, rushing down in a mad wild race. In a few minutes we found a path running along the south side of the fields and accelerated our pace. Someone not far behind was chasing after us, shouting at us to stop. Douglas was leading. As we came to a small fir copse he jumped off the path to his left and slid down a ten-foot grassy bank. Eddy and I followed, landing in a heap at the bottom. As we lay there, panting for breath, a number of Chinese men rushed past running straight on down into the valley. It was terrifying.

Happily, night comes on very quickly in the tropics. Within a few minutes it was beginning to get dark, but I could still see the direction we should follow.

'We'll cross the paddy and make between those whitewashed walled villages.'

No one followed us across the paddy. We strode over a hump-backed bridge spanning a small river in the middle of the valley, but as we approached the gap between the villages the dogs began to bark. Soon children came out to look, saw us, and ran back into the village to tell their honourable parents. From the right hand village a party of young men, armed with long sticks, ran out towards us, shouting at us.

We stood still, wondering what to do, realising it was hopeless to run away. At last, Douglas took the initiative and called back in Cantonese.

'We are English people.'

They were on us then, friendly in their approach, asking us if we were hungry, if we had fed.

'These are Hakka people,' Douglas told us, 'They are more friendly than the Cantonese. They will help us, probably.'

One of the young men invited us into his village and we accepted, unsure whether we were walking into a trap. Our suspicions were reduced by their friendly attitude and especially by the little children, who were round us in large numbers, heavenly little creatures like big dolls, all exactly alike in long trousers and blue jackets, waving their arms about and shouting to each other to come quickly to see the comical foreigners. They shrieked with laughter at us and particularly at the curious monocle. They were so excited, so full of exclamations, so many 'Aiyaas, aiyaas', that they made us feel welcome.

We were led through a beautiful round gateway, built in the wall surrounding the village to protect it from bandits, past the awful stench of primitive sanitation and pigs, past ancient cottages into a charming paved courtyard with a fine fung shui tree growing in the centre.

The village headman, an imposing, tall, dark-skinned man dressed in a smart white cotton jacket and long trousers, invited us to sit down at a stone table. The village headwoman, weather-beaten, wrinkled, bent from hard work in the fields, dressed in traditional black trousers and tunic, with a blue apron in front, shuffled up to us and served tea, the common courtesy offered to travellers. We were welcome.

An oil lamp was brought so that they could examine us more closely. There were more cries of 'aiyaa, aiyaa', when they saw the blood of my head and hand. The wounds were bleeding freely again due to the exertion of the chase into the valley. A woman brought a bowl of hot water and a hot towel and washed and cleaned my face and hands. Another bowl was brought for Douglas and Eddy, who washed and smartened themselves up.

Our anxiety and worries were over for the time being. We felt very happy again, sitting round the table smoking the headman's cigarettes, sipping boiled water, talking in pidgin. A great contrast to the way we had spent the day, hiding in the bed of a stream, being hunted and chased like wild animals.

The headman told us his name was Chen. He had been overseas as a seaman in the Blue Funnel Line, which accounted for his smart westernised dress and good English. We were surrounded by all the people in the village, all those delightful children. I asked why they laughed at us so much. Chen said bluntly that Douglas spoke Cantonese in a humorous way, and that the eye-glass was very funny. 'The foreigner with three eyes, they call him; you are ugly with such big noses!' The headman translated the story of our adventures to the people, who made exclamations of surprise at every incident. The Hakka women made a fuss of me because of my wounds. They improved our morale a great deal.

Then Chen told us that the gang which had attacked us were Cantonese people, naming their village, and that they were 'very bad men'. The previous day they had played the same trick on two foreigners whom they robbed. One had hurt his leg and could not get away. Both were dragged off to the Japanese, who beheaded them in Tai Po Market square that day. A good reward was paid to the 'bad men'. We were very shocked. We were also lucky to get away. A patrol of sixty Japanese soldiers had been up this valley today, searching all the undergrowth on the way.

A woman brought rice bowls, chopsticks and a large plate of steaming rice, vegetables and fish. It was the first properly cooked meal we had eaten for months, and we devoured it like savages, much to the amusement of our hosts, especially the children. There were shrieks of joy when Douglas filled his rice bowl for the seventh time.

'Never before have I seen a seven bowl man!' an elder remarked.

Having eaten as much as our shrunken stomachs could stand, Chen insisted we take the remains of the meal with us. So we packed our mess tins with the rice and vegetables, those nutritious vegetables that the Chinese only can cook, cabbage, bean sprouts, mushrooms, bamboo shoots.

Headman Chen then gave us packets of Players and Camel cigarettes, which we took with delight, but also with dismay at being unable to return this generous hospitality. The youngest baby, in a lovely long red dress, red colour for good luck, was presented to us to be admired. We made a great fuss of the infant with such an enchanting little face. Douglas, with brilliant inspiration and obvious ceremony, slipped two ten dollar notes into the baby's tiny hand. Everyone in the crowded courtyard watched inquisitively and there arose an instant murmur of approval. Our friendship was accepted.

'Now is the time,' whispered Douglas, 'to ask for a guide.' The request was accepted immediately.

After many farewells and handshakes and good wishes for the forthcoming Chinese New Year we left the courtyard with a strong young Hakka guide. The children followed us to the big round gateway, some poking our legs with their fingers to find out if we were real, braver ones holding our hands. It was a grand farewell.

We blessed the villagers for their chivalrous and

courageous hospitality — courageous and audacious because a Japanese garrison of 600 men was quartered in Tai Po, only two miles away. If their friendly reception became known, they would all be killed, and the village sacked and burnt.

In the pitch darkness, the agile young guide led us quietly and slowly up a steep hill beyond the village, through a wood of thick bamboo and on to the crest of the hill. We could just see the outline of a path, which he said we must follow. He then took us back to the edge of the wood, urging us to hide until the moon rose. He stayed and talked with us a little, saying how terrified they were of the Japanese, imploring us to bring the British back quickly. Douglas said his village would be the first to be liberated if it lay within his power!

Below us we could see clearly the lights of Tai Po and hear Japanese bugle calls and shouts. The great moon began to rise in the far distance, beyond Tolo Harbour. It was an enchanting sight as it gradually lit up the vast expanse of water, throwing elegant shadows of the many different island groups, growing each minute in splendour and radiance. This moon was our lamplight to freedom, our passage to China. I rejoiced in its resplendent power, the great beauty it brought with it.

7

Battle of Cloudy Hill

My dreaming meditation was broken by Eddy. 'It's just like being on a moonlight picnic, sitting here feeling contented with a belly full of Chinese chow.'

Douglas added a few choice words, suggesting that Eddy might invite the Japanese to join us in the picnic.

'They'll be here without an invitation if you go on talking so loudly,' I interjected, softly. 'You're both too noisy, never speak quietly, tramp about like elephants. You ought to know how to creep about at night, Douglas!'

He was not amused, and argued about the futility of attempting to stalk surreptitiously across China. Fortunately the moon had now risen sufficiently to see the crooked way ahead. I borrowed Douglas's monocle, which happened to be the same strength as the glasses I had lost in the Battle of Grassy Hill, and led the way. Stepping and stumbling over stones, rocks and pebbles on the rough path, we made good progress. As we trekked over the highlands the magnificent scenery lay stretched out before us like a landscape painting – the gleaming waters of Tolo Harbour, vivid mountains, shaded obscure valleys. The beauty inspired us.

After about two hours we came to a mountain village on the pathway. The ground was too rough to make a detour. I decided to walk straight through making a noise as though we were Japanese, and strode into the village, close to the old houses. There was no need to ask Douglas and Eddy to make a noise; they stumbled and grunted and panted naturally. A dog barked, shouts came from within the houses. Douglas made a series of guttural noises clearing his throat, spat and in an imitation of Japanese-Cantonese mumbled something like '*yip pun chye.*' The shouts ceased, and soon we were out of the village, away from barking dogs. It was a hair-raising experience, especially for Eddy as 'tail-end-charlie'. We had taken a rather impetuous chance, a dangerous one, and Eddy was not pleased.

'Don't do that sort of lark again, Tony. I've only one pair of pants!'

We descended into the Lam Tseun valley, a large and beautiful fertile valley, well-watered, terraced in parts, much cultivated and, what concerned us mostly, highly populated. Everywhere there were villages or hamlets. Through the centre of the valley ran a wide dirt road, likely to be frequented even at night. It was very dangerous.

I crept along the edge of a stream, swollen from the previous night's rain, from which we filled our water bottles. We had a short halt and I pointed out the road and some of the villages. Douglas's monocle helped me to pick out these features easily. It was hell keeping the stupid thing in place, but I did not lose it because it was tied to me with a string.

To our surprise, we did not have much difficulty in crossing the valley. Perhaps it was because we were very careful. Leading the way over paddy fields, I waded the deep river some way downstream from a bridge, so that I could cross the dirt road and avoid the villages. I turned north-east on to the lower slopes of a mountain called Tai Tan Yang, to avoid more villages and then due east to the main road and railway line.

We crouched behind the gum trees that lined the road, breathing the sweet smell of eucalyptus, and listened for any sounds. The road stretched far into the distance to the left and bent round a hill to the right, not far from where we lay. In the moonlight I could see clearly up and down the road. There was no traffic, and it seemed safe to cross. Suddenly I heard a car approaching from Tai Po to the right. Except for the gum trees, there was no cover on this side of the road; on the other side a deep ditch lay between the road and railway.

'Come on,' I yelled. 'Quick, over the road now.'

We jumped up and bounded across, flinging ourselves into the ditch just as the headlights of a car swung round the corner. It passed by in a second.

'Good God, Tony, let's take it a bit easy. What with shooting through that village and now this road, that's the second risk you've taken in the last hour. Our third chance may not be so good,' complained Douglas.

I was annoyed and very tired. We were all in this thing together. Why should Douglas blame the close shaves on me? We seemed to be breaking into arguments too easily about the smallest things.

'All right, all right,' I replied, peevishly, 'I'm leading, and I have to make decisions instantaneously. There's no other way. Let's have a rest. I've almost had it.'

It was now three-thirty in the morning. We had been on the march for many hours, climbing up hills and stumbling down them on rocky rough pathways, wading streams and rivers, always searching the next few yards ahead for any signs of attack. It was a constant enervating struggle against nerves and vitality. No wonder we needed a rest. Stepping gently over loose stones and sleepers of the railway, I followed a creek to a clump of weeping willow trees. There we settled down on the bank under the willows, eating some of the rice and vegetables our kind Hakka friends had given us, smoking a cigarette from the gift packet of Players. It was a simply glorious moonlit morning, the stars glittering brilliantly. I slept a little, the other two keeping watch.

Feeling refreshed, we strapped on our packs and started again. Ahead lay a large flat plain of dry rice fields, through the centre of which ran the main road and railway. On the other side, to our right, a mountain called Cloudy Hill towered above us. To the north, the direction in which we wished to go, stood Birds Hill, a round wooded hill about 1,000 feet high, at the far end of the plain. The cleft between it and Cloudy Hill was called Birds Pass, our immediate objective. We soon found a path running up towards the pass, but astride it stood two villages.

'Let's climb the slopes round to the right of them, over Cloudy Hill,' I suggested.

The other two disagreed. 'No, let's go in between the villages. It'll be miles and miles going round them. It's quite a big gap. We can get through easily.'

We strode across the bare paddy towards the gap. There were few trees for cover and we felt very conspicuous as we plodded over the furrows. No alarm was raised and we were almost past the narrowest part of the gap when one of us fell on the hard uneven ground. That slight noise was enough, however, to rouse the dogs, which began barking furiously at us. We increased the pace, but within a few minutes people were shouting at us from both villages.

'They are shouting "stop thieves, stop thieves," ' Douglas warned us, 'We had better stop.'

'No don't, don't stop,' Eddy insisted. 'They will rob us like those others tried to. Keep going. We can get clean away. Come on, run!'

A man ran after us and fired a shotgun. We raced along, trying to get right through the gap without being caught, but large groups of men armed with sticks and hatchets were pouring out of both villages and converging upon us.

As they approached we jumped a wide brook in the hope of delaying them. Douglas shouted at us to split up, saying he would draw them away. He turned off to the right and most of the villagers from the village on that side chased after him, but those from the village to the left continued after Eddy and me. They were soon on us. I was no match for a fight because of my wounds, but Eddy stayed with me, and taking off his pack, pushed me against a tree and turned to face the howling mob of peasants, as a stag turns to fight in the last extremity of the chase. They rushed at him, beating him fearfully with long sticks, but they got almost as good as they gave from Eddy's pack, which he swung at their heads with immense force. He was a powerful man, splendid in defiance.

Surprised by Eddy's spirited defence, the peasants paused in their assault, stepping clear to avoid further blows. We could hear Douglas swearing in Cantonese in an impassioned yell, followed by much shouting from the people round him. The peasants then jumped at us and grabbed us, taking us into the right hand village, where Douglas was also held.

Douglas was white with rage. Shouting at his captors at the top of his voice, he harangued them in Cantonese, speaking clearly and slowly enough for me to understand most of it.

'We are escaping from the Japanese. How dare you stop us, you swine! How dare you beat us!'

Douglas stood before them, legs apart, hands on hips, defiant and belligerent.

'This land still belongs to the British. We will return, very soon! You will be punished for any harm you do us!'

He paused to see the effect of his words. The thugs looked very unpleasant. He needed to say something which would touch their immediate lives, customs, traditions, behaviour, ancestors, joss and face.

'What sort of people are you? Pigs that rob poor travellers within sight of your homes? Is this your customary hospitality?'

They were beginning to listen, some looking ashamed. Persevering, Douglas tried to be more aggressive: 'Such behaviour will bring nothing but bad luck on you, your children, your land. Think of your ancestors watching you from their graves — how would they regard your behaviour? They would be disgusted. You low down sons of pigs, you will pay dearly for molesting us!'

There was an awesome silence. Furious at Douglas's remarks, the young men moved towards us raising their sticks. A tall, dark, saturnine-featured man stepped between us, holding the youths back. In faultless English, he said, 'What is it that you want?'

'We want our haversacks returned. We want to be allowed to go on our way in peace,' Douglas replied.

They argued among themselves, angry and hostile. Douglas's speech had deterred them from opening our packs, but Eddy was not prepared to wait and suddenly snatched at his pack and retrieved it. Immediately he was set upon by the youths. He defended himself valiantly and was still in possession of his pack when the tall man (who was the headman) stopped the fight. The headman turned to Douglas and spoke.

'We respect you English people but you fight too much. For good face we will let you go. We do not rob travellers in our village. You may take your haversacks.' Pointing towards Cloudy Hill, he said, 'You must go up that path, otherwise you will meet the Japanese in Fanling.'

Douglas and I picked up our packs, slung them on our shoulders and set off along the path indicated, winding up the steep slopes of Cloudy Hill. I did not like it.

'We're going in quite the wrong direction. I'm sure there's a trap in this.'

We started running to leave the village further behind us, dropping into the usual marching formation.

Eddy shouted, 'We're being followed!'

We ran on, climbing the steep and rough track, going as fast as we could. Out of breath and exhausted, we stopped at last at a sharp bend and jumped into a ravine beside the track.

'They are going to do us over properly this time and steal everything,' cried Eddy. 'Let's fight for it. Get your clasp knives out!'

We opened the blades. I was unaccustomed to using my left hand and my knife felt rather ineffective, but, even so, it was a good weapon. We were angry with the peasants, determined not to be robbed, desperate, pugnacious, with no thought of the outcome, with just one simple aim, to stand and fight.

As the gang of Chinese youths approached we crouched low in the bushes, only two yards from the path, waiting for our victims. It was an intense yet stimulating feeling. We would surprise and terrify them with our ferocity. It was a supremely dramatic moment, almost too much so, for the tension was overbearing.

Stumbling, kicking stones, the youths made a noisy ascent. Eddy waited until the first man was in front of him, then with a tremendous yell, a Maori warrior's roar, he threw himself at the wretch, slashing at him with his knife and knocking him flying. Then he turned on the next one, driving him off the path. Douglas and I followed, imitating equally ear-piercing yells. Slashing and hitting, we burst straight into the mob of youths. Surprised and terrified, they jumped out of the way. We were through them in seconds and raced headlong down the hill to the level dry rice fields, running in glorious abandonment for our lives, thrilled with the excitement, overjoyed at our victory.

The moment of triumph was not to last long. Out of the villages came hordes of men after us. We split and ran separately in different directions. I kept falling over the paddy banks. Each time they leapt on me and beat me with long sticks. Many times I recovered, regained my feet, and drove them back with my knife. When I attacked they broke away. I was filled with contempt for them, and furious that I did not have two hands with which to fight. At last, a hard blow from a stick knocked the knife out of my hand. I was forced to the ground, kicked and beaten until I submitted. They took my pack, ripped off my watch, took the compass and searched my pockets for money.

I was dragged back to the village. Eddy soon joined me, almost berserk, struggling hard against four men who held him. Then Douglas was brought in. At once he started another speech, speaking slowly and with great determination: 'Let go, you swine! You'll pay for this! Your village will be burnt to the ground. The Army will be back in a month!'

The crowd began to listen, awed by this fearsome Englishman, amazed at his strange use of their language. Douglas continued: 'We fight the same enemy. The Japanese are your enemy. You will get nothing from the Japanese except rape, disease, brigandry, and ruin. They will eat your crops, burn your houses and kill you!'

The mention of Japanese behaviour, that they knew so well, the loss of crops and houses, really drew their attention. Douglas concluded: 'We are going to bring the British back. If you harm us you harm yourselves; you will be punished for any harm you do us. Let us go and leave us alone.'

An astonished silence was followed by everyone speaking at once, shrieking at each other in high pitched voices. Finally the headman, the same sinister, sadistic-looking man, pressed forward, speaking articulately in English.

'What do you want?'

'We want to go in peace. Give us back our possessions and let us go.'

'We shall keep those things we want. We are poor people. We have many debts to settle before the New Year. It is very unlucky if debts are not settled by the New Year. You must understand. You have brought us good joss. Your watches, money and clothing will help to pay our debts.'

'Keep them, they will bring you bad luck,' retorted Douglas. 'But give us back our packs and compass and mess tins and food.'

'And the clasp knives,' I said.

They handed back the almost empty packs, the compass, mess tins and some food. The headman said that was enough.

'The bastards have got my log book,' shouted Eddy, not realising the headman spoke English. 'Tell them to give it back, Douglas. I must have my log book!'

The headman, who might well have agreed with Eddy that these youths were a lot of bastards, found the log book and handed it over, and then refused point blank to return anything else, not even the groundsheet, which I demanded. That was enough. The crowd became hostile again, refused to hand back anything else, and started pushing and kicking us.

'Go! Get out! Go quickly!'

We moved away, reluctantly without most of our possessions, still being kicked and pushed across the paddy fields. At last, when we were free of them we crept into a haystack, sore, tired and hungry, and lay there shivering from the cold until dawn. Douglas re-bound the bandages on my hand, which had not fared well in the fighting. Eddy complained of a broken rib: he could not laugh. But he had his precious log book, which contained also the guide-book map of the New Territories, the trace of the map of China and my letters, papers and rough diary. Apart from a few cuts and lots of bruises, we were still in one piece, not badly hurt. We still had a mess tin half full of rice and vegetables and a few tins of food. We had lost clothing, except for a few socks, but we still had the compass and a little money which Douglas had hidden cleverly on himself. Moreover, we still had the determination and resolution to get through. We were not desolate. The words of Paul came to me, 'And now abideth faith, hope, charity, these three; but the greatest of these is charity.' We had an abundance of faith, we had never abandoned hope, and we had charity, or love, in the comradeship that now existed between us.

Nothing could stop us.

8

Into China

The eye-glass had survived the 'Battle of Cloudy Hill', as Eddy aptly put it. I plonked it in my left eye and limped off across the paddy towards Birds Pass, feeling bruised and sore. Douglas and Eddy struggled along behind, walking lamely, like a couple of old men. Even though we had lost most of our possessions, I felt pleased with our performance. We had fought hard, although severely outnumbered; we had left quite a few sore heads and knife wounds. Undaunted we travelled as fast as possible on the flat paddy fields, keeping as close as we could to Cloudy Hill, for we were in clear view from the railway and main road, only 500 yards away. Peasants of a small village at the foot of Birds Pass stopped and questioned us, offering us tea. They were Hakka people, friendly and polite. Douglas bought a clasp knife for $5, essential to open the last tin, but we did not stop to drink tea. We had to get under cover.

Two Chinese followed us into the pass and volunteered to take us right through to Chungking. We had heard this story before. They guided us into a secluded spot in a clump of fir trees, where we were told to stay until after dark, when they would return. They promised to take us to Plover Cove and sail us from there in a junk to Mirs Bay and then to Free China. It sounded like a gramophone record repeating itself. We would have told them to clear off, except for the fact that they impressed us with their politeness, their good pidgin English and their smart woollen jackets and trousers and European felt hats. Moreover, they did not ask for money and were concerned for our safety. Fanling, they said, was infested with Japanese; we would never get through that way.

When they had gone, I said, 'We really cannot trust anyone. They may well be guerrillas, but how can we be sure? We must just depend on ourselves.'

Douglas and Eddy voted to move on at once.

We plodded on cautiously up the pass, keeping to the side of Birds Hill and descending along the valley of a stream, called River Cheaab, a tributary of the Indus. I knew all this country like the back of my injured hand. Each year we had spent three months in camp at Sun Wai, playing soldiers all round these hills and valleys and so-called rivers. Every natural feature had been described topographically in Indian or English names by the map makers, hence Golden, Needle, Grassy, Cloudy, Birds hills, Cheaab, Indus, Ganges rivers, Laffans Plain, etc. It was ludicrous. Chinese names would have been much more attractive. Leaving the Cheaab, to avoid a village, I led downhill over some gardens to a ridge called Queens Hill.

'Named after the Queen's Royal Regiment, 2nd of Foot,' I informed Eddy, who was ignorant of these things. He did not seem to be very interested. 'Formed by Charles II for Catherine of Braganza in 1661, more than a hundred years before New Zealand was discovered!'

'Shut up, Tony,' said Douglas, fearing I might be suffering from brain damage caused by my head wounds. I was certainly a little light-headed. 'Come on, let's hide in this clump of bamboos. It's a good place.'

It was a shaded bamboo grove. We had not met anyone since the two Chinese had left us; no one saw us going into the bamboos. We felt safe. Looking round, I found a Chinese grave, shaped like a horseshoe, dug into the hillside so that the rounded end lay about five feet below the slope. A recess in the back wall held porcelain jars and urns, containing the remains of ancestors long since departed. I wondered if the spirits of the ancestors would resent our uninvited intrusion. I hoped they would approve because we were fighting the forces of evil, the Japanese, who had been so cruel to the Chinese. If anyone came to add to the strips of coloured paper with Chinese characters written on them, or to light joss-sticks, we would have to move out quickly. The fragrant incense from former sticks still hung soothingly over the grave. It had obviously been visited recently; it was unlikely therefore that anyone would come up today. We settled down to rest while Douglas administered first aid, patching up wounds and cuts, administering aspirin for broken ribs and brain damage — typical treatment dished out by all regimental medical officers, normally with a pill named 'Number Nine', which produced disastrous and highly explosive results. Fortunately Douglas had not included Number Nines in his medical stores, relying no doubt on the water from streams or rivers to be as effective.

'Good Lord, Duggie,' I exclaimed, 'that's Kwan Tei village down there! Do you remember we used to have amateur jockey races on the course on the other side of the road? I rode in the mule race, a bare-backed mule.'

'You fell off!' laughed Douglas.

'No, I didn't, I won.'

'You won't win now, unless you shut up and keep quiet. You're hyperactive, so quieten down.'

From the grave there was a good view through the thinly scattered bamboo, if you sat up. I searched for signs of danger and saw many. The immediate threat was a main road, just 800 yards to the north. It ran from an important crossroads at Fanling two miles west to the fishing village of Sha Tau Kok, on the eastern border between the Colony and China. The large walled village of Fanling itself, an ugly stone-grey place, lay near the crossroads and a railway station. It was the place I had been warned often to avoid, because it was infested with Japanese. Closer to us than Fanling village was an even greater threat, the Hunters' Arms. This was an old Chinese house set within a walled garden. It used to be the meeting place of the Fanling Drag Hunt, a club, a warm refuge for thirsty officers living under canvas close by. Now it was occupied by the Kempeitai, the

Japanese secret police. An officer in the prison camp had been taken there for interrogation and returned to the camp a mere shadow of his former self. The thought of it filled me with dread.

'Fanling and Hunters' Arms must be avoided at all costs,' I informed my two comrades. 'Pity,' said Douglas cynically. 'I was hoping we might pop in there for a chota-peg this evening.'

'I wish we could,' I said, with palpable memories of the many happy hours I had spent in the Hunters' Arms when I was stationed annually at Sun Wai camp. It brought back memories also of my horse, a beautiful Australian waler, a chestnut mare, provided for me by the army as the Adjutant's charger for ceremonial parades. I hoped the Japanese were caring for her; she was such a gentle handsome animal. I tried her in the local drag hunt, but she was not as good as the Manchurian ponies most people rode at crossing stone humped-back bridges or avoiding hidden Chinese graves; so I preferred to hack with her for miles and miles over the wide expanse of Laffans Plain to the border with China, and along the willow-covered banks of the Sham Chun River. The long rides gave me a detailed knowledge of the country. Little did I know how very useful this knowledge would prove to be.

A slight mist lay over the rice fields, stretching in every direction. Already farmers were moving out of their villages leading buffaloes to work, rounding up herds of ducks with enormous long poles. The peasants did not seem to notice trucks filled with Japanese soldiers driving back and forth on the main road. The women in a little village just below us went on happily with their household chores around their houses, never looking up at an approaching vehicle.

The sight of a truck sent me into panic. It was easy to imagine that the villagers with whom we clashed last night, the people who had robbed and beaten us, might have informed the Japanese. They knew we were going towards Birds Pass. All the Japanese needed to do was to drive round to where we were now at the foot of the pass and search it.

That was not the only cause for alarm. Just over 1,000 yards away a few Chinese coolies were repairing a bridge on the main road, supervised by two Japanese sentries. We had got ourselves into a very bad position, far too close to Japanese, to villages and peasants working in the fields, for we could not move without attracting their attention.

The small village named Kwan Tei below dismayed us also. It contained so many people — women, children, old men — and too much activity. On the sides of the main doorway of a house long strips of red paper were being hung, each with four large characters written on them, for good luck or to keep evil spirits away, I presumed. It was a pretty village, some houses whitewashed, others with brick walls verdigris with age. Roofs were covered in age-old blue tiles, the eaves upturned; and an enormous tree, its once-thick lower branches severed, spread over the houses with a profuse mass of branches and leaves. It was a place to avoid when we moved again.

Eddy was suffering from the blows he had received in last night's fight and was very quiet. I was suffering from the trauma of both fights, last night and the one before, but it was only now that the shock made itself felt. Douglas became quite fatherly, treating us as his patients. He thought I was slightly concussed. We were both becoming panicky at the dangers surrounding us. To relieve the tension, Douglas opened a tin of bully, our last tin, which we consumed gladly, sipping evil-tasting river water from our water bottles to wash it down. We felt better, happy to be cared for by the doctor, who now occupied our timid thoughts by talking about himself; about his childhood in France and England, his upbringing in an ancient society, conforming to a rigid style of education, a pattern which had no margins. You had to behave, you called the prefects and masters 'sir' at the beginning and end of each sentence, you were beaten with a cane for the slightest misdemeanour, you played rugby and cricket, irrespective of whether you wished to do so, you became the English public-school boy.

'Not much different to me,' interrupted Eddy, 'at that

Presbyterian school they sent me to. Only I loved rugby football. What happened to you after school?'

'Oh, I went off to the unbelievable freedom of a university, hardly believing that such a life could be true; and then the permissive yet self-contained society in a decrepit old hospital.'

He then told us how he had joined the Indian Medical Service and served in North West India. He spoke about the British Raj, the frontier, the glamour, Pathans and Gurkhas. He loved the Gurkhas, describing them as honest, natural, loyal and courageous, and with no servility. He told us of the Gurkha rifleman who complained of an infection in his right ear. In order to syringe it out Douglas asked the rifleman to hold a kidney-shaped enamel basin under his ear. The Gurkha immediately placed the basin under his left ear. 'They have hard heads,' laughed Douglas, 'but you can't see right through!'

A truck stopped at the bridge. In deep silence, we watched, anxiously. Two soldiers jumped off it and two soldiers climbed into it. The truck turned round and drove back to Fanling. We breathed again. The poor coolies working on the bridge were not relieved. They had to go on working, a little harder now with fresh sentries to point a fresh bayonet at them in encouragement. They were, of course, slaves, receiving no pay or reward for their work. This was how the Japanese treated people in the countries they overran.

Due north of us stretched the large expanse of undulating country called Laffans Plain, used as a military training range but also cultivated with vegetables, maize, rice and citrus orchards. The plain descended gradually into the valley of the Sham Chun River, which marked the border with China, about eight miles away. It was exciting to think that we were at last in sight of China, even if it was occupied by the Japanese.

'There are only a few villages on the plain,' I told them. 'We should cross the Sham Chun River tonight. We'll march across country on a compass bearing. I'll set the compass now.' Using the monocle I gazed into the far distance at a massive range of mountains. 'I'll set it on that one, the high one. It's called Wu Tung Shan Wei, and is well inside the Chinese frontier.'

It was a beautiful mountain, with wooded lower slopes but completely bare of trees at the summit. I told Eddy it was over 2,000 feet high.

'Good God,' he said. 'We are not going to climb it, are we?'

Douglas looked disturbed also. 'No, Ed, we are not. It's just a landmark, the highest and easiest to pick out.'

It was fortunate we had seen the mountain, because in the afternoon it began to rain. It also got quite dark. It was miserable sitting in the grave in the rain. It would be better to be marching.

'I should say it's about half-past five,' Douglas guessed. 'It will be dark about a quarter-past six. Let's get off this hill now and cross the main road while we can still see.'

Stumbling down the hillside, we followed a narrow path within 50 yards of a small hamlet. The rain had stopped. A small child playing in the yard of a house saw us in the sunlight and cried out in alarm. A very old Chinese lady with bound feet hobbled out to see what the fuss was about. She stared at us in surprise, then suddenly realising we were Europeans, squeaked in pidgin, 'Hallo, you English? You hungly? You likee chow chow?'

She was a dear old lady, typical of the old type of amah who looked after European children, sweet and kind, offering us hospitality at once. Of course we were hungry, we always were, but we dared not enter her house with the Japanese sentries so close to us.

'No thank you,' I replied. 'Thank you very much, we have fed. Please do not make noise.'

But already her voice had attracted a group of children from Kwan Tei village, who were running over the dry paddy fields to discover to whom the old grandmother was talking. We broke into a run, climbing a small hill to get under cover in the scrub and see more clearly the way to cross the road. The children, enchanting round-faced little devils, thinking we were running away from them, followed us and stood below the hill laughing and shouting and calling for mothers and honourable grandmothers to come and join in all the fun.

'Tell them to shut up, Duggie,' cried Eddy. 'Look, those Jap sentries on the bridge are looking this way already.' Not only the sentries, but the Chinese coolies on the bridge, who had stopped work, were now looking at us, attracted by the commotion.

Douglas yelled in Cantonese, 'Shut up, shut up, go away, run away!' He sounded very rude, but his words only produced hoots and shouts of laughter. The children thought Douglas was very comical.

'We haven't a chance in hell if we stay here. Look, a sentry is coming over,' warned Eddy.

That made us really move, over the crest of the hill, out of sight of the children, into the bed of a stream. Following the stream we came quickly to the road, at a place where the stream turned abruptly to the left, running parallel to the road and bringing us closer to the sentry at the bridge. We crawled carefully up the bank of the stream on to the edge of the road, beside a wooden hut, which protected us from the view of the sentries, and stood on the grass verge of the highway.

At that moment, we heard a vehicle approaching, from the right, from the direction of Shataukok. There was nothing we could do but shelter beside the hut and wait. Fully exposed to the road, we stood quite still, petrified.

A truck bore down towards us, its engine roaring. I went numb with fear. Then in an instant, it was going past. I looked up to see it was full of Japanese soldiers. Not one looked at us. We were left like three limp rag dolls, in the dust raised by the truck, as the sound of singing voices faded. The soldiers had been in full voice as they drove past. Most probably they were drunk; that was why they did not see us. It was an amazing piece of luck. Perhaps those spirits of the ancestors in whose grave we had spent the day had saved us. Someone was looking after us, certainly.

As soon as the truck was out of sight, we slipped our half-empty packs off our backs, to prevent a too obvious spectacle of being Europeans, and stepped out onto the road.

A party of Chinese women carrying great loads of bamboo poles across their shoulders were jogging down the road from our right, the way the truck had come. We must have been suffering from shock because we did not see or hear them until we were out on the highway, crossing immediately in front of them.

They stopped dead and stared at us in amazement. We walked on, across the verge of a road, over a ditch, and into a field. Oddly enough, the women did not make a sound, but just stared at us in dumb astonishment, stupefied by our sudden appearance.

I longed to break into a run, but it would have aroused their suspicions to do so; our only course was to walk as nonchalantly as possible, as if we had every right to be there, pursuing our normal duties. It felt as if their eyes were burning into my back. Every slow step I took was an agony, expecting them to shout after us to enquire who we were. Added to this was the thought that a rifle shot from a sentry would crack at any second. I did not dare look back.

Fifty yards from the road, the longest fifty yards I had ever walked, I came to another stream, named ridiculously River Indus, now just a dry nullah, running at a right angle to our course. We dropped into the gully and ran as fast as we could along its dry bed, well under cover from the road. After going round one or two bends the nullah turned south, back towards the road and the Japanese sentries.

'Hell,' I puffed, 'we'll have to get out of this and walk across the open fields again.'

It was an unpleasant thing to do. We were now closer to the Japanese sentries, and within easy range for a good rifle shot. My superiors had taught me that the Japanese were too myopic to be good rifle shots. I had plenty of experience to disprove such nonsense. I did not want to take any chances; I did not want a bullet in my back.

'Like hell we will,' Douglas objected, obviously thinking

of the rifleman and a bullet in his back. 'We'll wait here in the damned ditch until it gets dark. There's no cover out there. There are lots of people back on the road who might see us and raise an alarm.'

It seemed a sensible thing to do. Why not wait here until it became dark? But Eddy had given it more thought.

'We've already raised about five alarms, Duggie. I bet you the Jap sentry is now questioning the children. The other sentry will ask that party of coolie women why they stopped on the road, what were they looking at. By now both sentries will know that three Europeans are on the loose round here. If the sentries don't follow us, a patrol will. If they have dogs, they will sniff us out in this dirty little creek in no time. I'm going over the top!'

It was clear that Eddy had made a sound appreciation of the situation, and I supported him. I told them I knew this ground backwards and blindfolded, that just across the open paddocks lay an army field firing-range, where the ground was broken and where we would find plenty of cover.

'Good on you, Tony,' Eddy said. 'No one is going to catch me. Let's get as far away from that bleeding road as we can and as fast as possible.'

We scaled the side of the gully and walked across the parched paddocks. At last the broken ground was reached, and we ran some way through the scrub and coarse grass. Then I remembered a series of trenches had been dug in this area as part of army training. Soon I found a communication trench which I followed until we came to a large covered dug-out. By coincidence it had once been my company headquarters in some previous manoeuvre. Here we stopped to recover our breath and senses.

We seemed prone to difficult situations, from which, with extraordinary luck, we managed to retrieve ourselves. I wondered if my prayers were being answered.

After a brief rest, we left the security of the dug-out and began marching to the north. The light rain and clouds had cleared and stars illuminated the landscape sufficiently to find the way.

It was a joy to walk over the level yet undulating plain after stumbling and crashing through all those mountain pathways on previous nights. I felt safe in the starlit darkness. We forgot the soreness and the bruises from the beatings last night. It was very cold and invigorating, and we made good progress. Without any discussion or argument I avoided villages automatically, twice making long detours, stepping easily across the dry paddy whenever I had to leave a beaten path. We met no one. No dogs barked at us. I became convinced a Japanese patrol could not catch us up on the plain.

We stopped to dig up sweet potatoes with the clasp knife and pick peas in a vegetable garden. We ate the peas, pods and all, washed the potatoes in a dirty, muddy little stream, and took a few raw mouthfuls. Eddy refilled his water bottle from the stream. Douglas reprimanded him, in medical terminology — 'You'll get the shits!' We hurried on. In the cool starlit night, with the wide plain around us, I had the most glorious feeling of freedom, knowing I was well on my way to China.

In the early morning we came to the road which ran close to the Sham Chun River and the border with China. If an alarm had been raised it was likely the Japanese would be patrolling this road. If they were taking things seriously, they would post sentries on all crossing places over the river, on dams and fords. There were no bridges, to my knowledge.

The pathway from the plain led us conveniently between two well separated villages to a bend in the road opposite a hill called Pak Fu Shan. Creeping up to the dirt road, we stopped to listen, looking up and down it as far as we could see. It was very quiet. We crossed.

The slopes of Pak Fu Shan were well covered in fir. In the cover of the trees we stalked round the hill, getting happily further away from the road with each pace. Stepping over a well worn pathway, across paddy and then flat earth which may have been salt pans, we came to the Sham Chun River. At long last, after five nights and many fights and frights, we had reached it.

It was a tremendously exciting moment, a dangerous one also. I knew that here there was an old Chinese Customs Station not far away on the other side which had been occupied by Japanese for the last three years. The river was much wider than I had expected. It must have been dammed further downstream. Anticipating that dams or fords might be guarded, I was certain we could not find a better crossing place. We would have to swim. In trepidation we waited and listened. It was very quiet. The tropical moon was rising over the mountains to the east.

Packing our clothes into our army haversacks and strapping them high up on our shoulders, we slipped naked into the cold green water and swam noiselessly and slowly across. It was refreshing gliding naked through the calm chill water, but frightening also because I could not see what was on the other side, in the moon shadows formed by weeping willow trees. Perhaps the Japanese were waiting for us in those shadows. How foolish it would be if we were recaptured now!

There was nobody on the other side. We dressed quickly in the shadows. Eddy broke the silence as ecstatically we shook hands.

'We've made China! We've bloody well made it to China!'

9

A Willow Pattern Plate

We were not in the least tired, although we had eaten no food apart from a few peas and mouthfuls of raw sweet potatoes. So exhilarated were we by the crossing that we felt we could go on for ever.

Peering through the willow trees I could see in the clear moonlight miles of rice fields ahead, beyond which rose a prominent hill to the north, in the direction I wished to go. Strapping on our packs we strode off buoyantly over a well-used pathway and along the hard bunds of the paddy fields, which we traversed quickly. An earth road came up before us, recent vehicle tyre marks showing in the dust. We waited a little, but everything was still and quiet, so we pressed on, soon finding a good path leading up the hill.

A new phase of our odyssey had begun. So far I had known the ground, known where we were going, sometimes in great detail, all of which made the journey easier. Now we would have to find our way in country entirely strange to us. We knew nothing of the conditions in this part of Japanese-occupied China, but we had concluded in the prison camp that we could not expect much help from the local inhabitants, or much food. Although we had planned to be self-sufficient for this part of the journey, most of our food had been stolen. Douglas suggested we could live on what we dug up in the vegetable fields, not a very cheerful thought. We were already very hungry. However, I did possess the map of this territory, which I had copied on tracing paper, and that showed the rivers and roads, village and mountain names, and most important, the direction we must take to reach Free China.

Our aim now must be to attain freedom by travelling to the East River. We did not know if the large town of Waichow would be occupied by the Japanese. To be safe, therefore, we should attempt to strike the river east of Waichow. From our present position we should travel in a north-north-easterly direction for about 100 miles.

The first priority was to climb the hill and observe the country which we had to cross. I followed the path leading to the top as the sun began to rise. Foolishly, we walked straight on to the bare granite crest and stood there for a few minutes, silhouetted by the setting moon and the rising sun, admiring the view and planning the route for the next night's march. It was a beautiful view in the dawn light. To the west stretched the vast expanse of the Sham Chun valley, the famous rice valley of old, and beyond it, the muddy waters of Deep Bay. To my dismay we were very near to the railway bridge at Lo Wu, the only bridge across the Sham Chun River, now half demolished; and we were much too close for safety to large villages and a Japanese army base a short distance from the bridge.

I pointed out the danger to Eddy, who regarded as equally dangerous the valley of a wide winding river to the north through which ran the Kowloon to Canton railway and a good motor road. To the north-east stood the massive Wu Tung Shan Wei in splendid glory. I told Eddy it was the mountain on which I had taken the bearing, the one of over 2,000 feet he thought he might have to climb. Beyond, ranges of glorious mountains stretched east and north in illustrious majesty to Wu Tung Shan, a gigantic twin-peaked beauty higher than any mountain we had yet seen.

Going downhill, looking for a suitable place to hide in the undergrowth, I stepped unexpectedly on to a wide, well worn pathway. Suddenly four Chinese men, armed with knives and bayonets, jumped out at us. With rat-like instinct for preservation, I leapt into the bushes, Eddy and Douglas following me. But we were surrounded quickly, the bandits indicating that we should raise our arms above our heads. We refused; Eddy gave them a Churchillian gesture; Douglas shouted a few coarse words in Cantonese. We were too tired to fight or to run away, but each time they came near us we shouted at them and took a pace towards them, as if we were going to strike them. They were an evil-looking bunch of men, hatless, dark-featured, in dirty padded winter jackets and baggy trousers. They became aggressive at our resistance and pushed us roughly along the path until we reached a group of ruined burnt-out houses near a creek. Forcing us into the creek they made us sit down on the bank and stood over us, bayonets pointed. One man ran off down the valley, ominously in the direction of Lo Wu and the Japanese army base. The rest gibbered at us in a local dialect. Douglas did not understand a word. We did not seem to care, though I was furious that we had allowed ourselves to be caught through standing in full view on the summit of the hill above them. Eddy expressed our thoughts for us.

'I'm completely browned off with all these bloody bandits. We've got nothing to lose, nothing for them to take from us. Let's just ignore them.'

We sat there disregarding our smelly and ugly guards, resting after the long night's march, still pleased with our achievement at crossing the river into occupied China. I was almost too tired to worry that their companion might have gone to the Japanese, although that nasty little thought kept recurring.

I looked around to see if there was any way of escape. I could see a pathway running through large orchards to a river. It seemed to be a well-used track, probably a link with the New Territories and Hong Kong. Watching the path I became intensely interested in the approach of an extremely tall Chinese man, followed by a woman. The bandit guards, pointing sharp bayonets at us, had their backs to the approaching couple and did not hear or notice anything until the man stopped in front of us, staring down in amazement.

He was exceptionally tall for a Chinese man, with strong wide shoulders and features more negroid than asian; his hair black and curly. His face was quite unusual for a Chinese, so unusual that I was sure I had seen him somewhere before. When he recovered from his astonishment he spoke clearly in English.

'What is happening here? Whatever are you doing here?'

I was almost as surprised as he was, and suspicious too, because I had made so many mistakes and had learnt not to trust anyone. I replied as nonchalantly as possible.

'Oh, we're on our way to unoccupied China!'

Obviously baffled by my facetious reply, he said, 'But I know you. Were you in the army in Hong Kong? Who are you two?'

'Doctor,' said Douglas flatly.

Eddy replied offensively, 'Fly-fly man,' implying that he was speaking to an illiterate coolie, and then, 'Who the hell are you?'

The tall man took no offence. 'I am Percy Davis. I used to own the World Radio Company in Kowloon.' Looking at me he said, 'I am sure I know you.'

I told him I remembered him, that we had escaped from Shamshuipo prison camp. Our bandit guards were looking very perplexed, not understanding a word of this talk, not quite sure what to do with us. The bayonets were withdrawn.

'But what are you doing here? What are these men doing to you?'

'Oh, they're just another bunch of bandits,' Eddy told him, 'we meet them at every corner!'

'They're not bandits — just simple robbers. Everyone is a robber since the Japs came here. Take no notice of them.'

He turned to the woman with him, speaking rapidly in Cantonese. She turned about and went back the way she had come at a jog-trot, the usual method by which Chinese country people cover great distances. Facing us again, Percy told us the robbers lived nearby; they would not dare to rob us in his presence, or to harm us, but they would expect some 'tea money', some commission.

Eddy exploded, aggressive as ever. 'What for? No bloody

fear! They'll get nothing. Tell them to push off!'

Percy suggested that these men, being armed, could become violent if they did not get some money, but noticing our very determined looks, said he would try and frighten them.

'Be ready to take the chance to jump up and run.'

Frowning, hostile and fierce, Percy harangued the three robbers. He went on for ages. At first the men answered back angrily and argued furiously, shouting and waving their arms and weapons at Percy. At least the bayonets were no longer pointed at us. Now very angry, his dark face puce with indignation, Percy vented his fury on them, raging in a deep loud voice. The guards' attention was fixed on Percy, they seemed frightened at what he was saying, ignoring us completely.

'Now,' shouted Percy. 'Follow me, run!'

We shot out of the creek like a flash of lightning, straight past the three robbers, almost knocking them over in our haste. They were taken entirely by surprise; we were racing well down the pathway before they recovered, running full tilt, Percy striding out with great leaps, Douglas close behind him. Eddy and I, trying hard to keep up with the mad cavalcade, rapidly increased our distance from the robbers, who started to shout and follow us. Soon we caught up with the woman, who stood aside to let us pass, looking astonished at what must have been a very strange sight: a huge Chinese-Negro being chased at full speed by Caucasian ruffians! If anyone else had seen this amazing performance, they might well have stopped and attacked us to save Percy's life.

In a citrus orchard we turned off the path into thick bamboo woods. Breaking into a walk, we followed Percy to a Chinese grave, hidden in the slope of the hill. He told us to hide in the grave while he sat on the edge regaining his breath, smoothing down his smart European suit, pushing his felt hat to the back of his head. He told us he was a Jamaican–Chinese, half-Negro, born in the West Indies. He spoke English with a slight Jamaican accent, and with a delightfully deep voice. He had been on his way to Hong Kong to collect his wife and to discover what had happened to his shop. The woman with him was his wife's amah; she would now go back to her village on the other side of the valley. There was no sign of our pursuers.

'Well,' Percy said, 'you're OK now, for a bit anyway, but they will come back to search the woods for you.'

He asked us many questions about the fall of Hong Kong, the surrender on Christmas Day, conditions in the prison camp at Shamshuipo and our escape. He seemed a genuine person, but we did not know much about him, and so were guarded in our answers about the escape and did not explain how we got out. We did, however, tell him about the people who had beaten us up, to which he murmured, 'We'll see to that.' I wondered what he meant. He impressed me with his knowledge, saying that he remembered Douglas riding about in a little yellow motor car. He probably remembered him mostly because of the monocle. He mentioned also the names of army officers I knew who had bought things in his radio shop. It helped to make me trust him.

Percy continued: 'In the next village I have a brother; he is a robber, like many people these days. But he will help you. I will go now to find him. You must stay here. Do not move.'

The last few words were very familiar. It gave me an odd feeling of despair. Could I really trust Percy? There was no alternative.

'There are Japanese soldiers everywhere; you could not possibly travel unaided through this country without being caught. You would not stand a chance. We know the unfrequented pathways and places to hide. Be sure you stay here.'

Despite a few misgivings, I was very grateful to Percy for getting us away from the bandits. It was unbelievable luck he had arrived at that particular time. The gods really were on our side; so much good fortune had come our way – the clouds that screened us from Japanese bullets, the sentry who did not hear us near Shatin, the kind people who fed and guided us, the truck load of Japanese soldiers who failed to notice us, Japanese patrols that never caught up with us, and now the remarkable arrival of Percy. Nevertheless, I was still apprehensive about Percy's robber brother and prayed Percy would return before we were caught again by some other rogues.

Eventually fatigue overcame us and we all went soundly to sleep for several hours. We were disturbed by rustling in the bushes. Eddy saw him first and got an awful fright.

'I thought it was all up then,' he wrote to me years later. A brown Chinese face, an ugly and villainous face, peeped at us through the undergrowth. Before we could rise, the man was with us, followed by another murderous-looking cut-throat. Oh, God, I thought, we've had it this time. And then a third person arrived, Percy himself.

'Hope I did not give you a fright,' he said, noticing our white and terror-stricken faces.

'My bloody oath, you did,' cried Eddy, fully awake now and his normal aggressive self.

Percy introduced his companions. 'This is my brother, Lee, and this man here is a thief.'

The second man looked the part, armed to the teeth as he was with two pistols and a knife in his belt. Lee, a tall, thin and strongly-built man with a vicious-looking face, was quite unlike his supposed brother Percy. He sported a particularly wicked-looking Mauser pistol.

We all shook hands, rather formally. Lee was greatly amused by Douglas's monocle and his type of Cantonese. He was also impressed by Eddy's RNZAF uniform, especially the wings over his left breast pocket. The expression 'Fly-fly man', used by Eddy again, did not seem out of place with Lee, nor did it deflect his gaze from Eddy's last remaining possession, a fountain pen, which he took, calmly inspected, and returned. It was not good enough!

Lee informed Douglas that he was a communist guerrilla, showing off his Mauser with pride. He invited us to become guerrillas. Douglas declined politely on our behalf.

Percy now spoke. 'My brother will lead you through to the Kuomintang army. However, in the village nearby there is another gang of robbers — not the same group that attacked you earlier. There are seventeen of them, all armed. They will take charge.'

It was all very disappointing. We did not relish the prospect of being handed over to a gang of bandits, or robbers as Percy preferred to call them, if in fact there was any difference. There was nothing for it, however, and we felt better about accepting our fate rather than running away from it. The fugitive, the hunted man, suffers from a humiliation and despair that becomes all-devouring. It was so much better not to be hunted or chased again.

'The robbers are waiting for us down by the river,' Percy said, 'only about a mile from here, from this wooded hill which is called Chin-Chi-Ti.'

What a lovely name! You could almost dance to it. Eddy wrote it down in the record he was keeping for me, for my diary.

'We must move carefully. The Japanese are very close. I will show you.'

He led us to the edge of the wood.

'There' — he pointed — 'is the road that the Japanese have built from Lo Wu to Canton. They use the road by day only. Along it, on the hills flanking it, they put groups of soldiers to guard their convoys using the road.'

Douglas and I knew very well what Percy meant. The Japanese were placing picquets on each tactical feature overlooking the road, just as the British did on the North-West Frontier of India when they wanted to move a column into the Khyber Pass. We looked at each other, understanding, but thinking that there must be a great deal of opposition around if the Japanese had to resort to picqueting. Percy explained for us without being asked.

'There are plenty of communist guerrilla troops here. They ambush the trucks unless the Japs post guards. These guards are very dangerous. They will shoot and kill you if they see you.'

He went on, enjoying what he was telling us and the look of concern on our faces. 'At night the Japs go back to their garrison posts, mostly in the towns. They never come out at night in parties of less than sixty. If there are fewer the guerrillas kill them. The communist guerrillas kill very many Japanese.'

We were impressed. Percy enjoyed showing off his local knowledge. I wondered, however, who Percy was. What was his real name? What was he doing here? Why was he so enthusiastic about the communist guerrillas?

'And look,' he pointed excitedly at the road, 'there you are, the picquets are going out now.'

We saw a halted convoy of trucks and thin lines of soldiers climbing up hills where the road went through a saddle, about a mile and a half away. Percy said the saddle was named Ku-Tui Ling. Not quite so onomatopoeic as Chin-Chi-Ti. Again Eddy wrote the names down for my diary.

'Hell,' said Eddy, 'I don't like the look of that. We're too bloody close to those nips.'

'You see,' Percy continued, 'we must be very careful now. They use very strong binoculars and pick up any unusual movement quickly and then send out a party of soldiers to find out what is happening. We must go before they start studying this hill with their glasses.'

We needed no encouragement to get under cover in the wood. Percy led us due east through the wood, downhill into a ravine, a deep narrow gorge, and then turned along its bed, until we reached the river.

Suddenly, we had arrived at a most beautiful place. The river, which rises in the high Wu Tung mountains that we had seen at dawn, must have been dammed a little further downstream, so that a small lake had been formed. Entirely enclosed by green-clad mountains whose steep slopes ran down to its banks, the lake was encircled by willow trees. Higher up-stream the river was narrow enough to be spanned by a very old stone bridge. Beyond the bridge, on a bend of the river, stood a graceful and old white pagoda, five storeys high, half ruined, guarding the river and its travellers from water devils. Lower downstream the weeping willows hung over the slowly flowing water as if beckoning a sampan drifting idly on the waves.

'The beauty of this place reminds me of a willow pattern plate,' I said. 'Do you remember the nursery rhyme?'

'Yes, I do,' said Douglas. 'It goes like this:

> Two pigeons flying high,
> Chinese vessels sailing by,
> Weeping willows hanging o'er,
> Bridge with three men, if not four,
> Chinese temples, there they stand
> Seem to take up all the land:
> Apple trees with apples on,
> A pretty fence to end my song.'

'Well, perhaps it's not exactly like the willow pattern plate,' I said, 'but there's the bridge, and we're the three men, if not four with Percy.'

Nice thoughts, a nice interlude. Douglas told us his version of the unhappy fate of the Lady Koong-se, and of her lover, Chang; and laughed happily. Percy laughed too, and then brought us back to life.

'Over there across the water are the seventeen bandits waiting for you. Captain Hewitt, lead the way over the humped-back bridge.'

10

A Marxist

On the other side of the lake, sitting in the shade of the willow trees, the bandits waited for us. As soon as we stepped down from the humped-back bridge they surrounded us, took our packs away and searched us. Finding nothing that interested them, they returned our packs and we sat in a circle answering questions. The bandits were concerned about the fights in which we had been involved, making exclamations of surprise as the story became more horrific. Great interest was taken in my wounded hand, from which Douglas was made to remove the bandages. It was now a grisly sight, and Douglas hastily covered it up again.

We examined our new acquaintances, a happy band of brigands, tough but friendly. All of them were well dressed, in new homburg hats and new clothes. Each carried two pistols, Smith and Wesson four-fives or Mauser automatic machine pistols. Everyone seemed to have three or four watches and a number of Parker fountain pens. Many had gold teeth. Banditry was obviously a profitable profession.

We stayed in the shade of the willows with Percy, a man for whom the bandits had great respect, while our robber friends left in groups to scout out the lie of the land. It was calm and peaceful resting there on the grass bank, lulled by the softly lapping waters of the lake. A minute tailor bird disturbed us with its insistent '*tch tch*' call. Despite Percy's warnings about the proximity of the Japanese, for the first time since we left Shamshuipo I began to feel secure.

Eventually the leader of the robber band returned with

others. They were reluctant to tell us their names for fear that we might incriminate them if we were caught, but the leader seemed to be called Ah Fong. He gave out his orders, Percy translating into his excellent English.

'Fong says we must go to a safer place. Fong's men will travel in front and behind us, that is, you three, myself, Fong and Lee. Guards will travel on the flanks, so we should get plenty of warning of any Japs. The Japs are inclined to send patrols out here to collect labourers to repair the roads. They were here yesterday. It's unlikely that they will be here today, two days in succession.'

'What do we do if we meet the Japs?' I asked.

Percy replied for Fong. 'The advanced, flank or rear guards, whichever make contact with the enemy, will hold off the Japs as long as possible. We will make a detour and run away very fast. Just follow Fong.'

Fong was very deliberate and sounded more like a trained soldier than a bandit. Later, we discovered that they were all communists, combining a bit of banditry with offensive guerrilla warfare; but they were not strictly recognised as part of the communist guerrilla army.

We got ready.

'Be quiet, do not talk,' ordered Percy.

Retracing our steps over the humped-back bridge, now symbolic to us as a bridge to freedom, we marched away, passing the half-ruined pagoda, many hundreds of years old, but still beautiful, retaining its graceful look of sanctity, even 'taking up all the land'. I wondered which gods it edified. I hoped it might be Kwun Yam, the Buddhist Goddess of Mercy.

Our journey took us along the course of the river, 'the willow pattern river', as Eddy (who had a habit of naming things) called it. Perhaps Hung Shing, the God of the South Seas, might be looking after us today, since we were going to follow the river to its source between the high mountains Hsiao-Wu-Tung and Wu-Tung-Shan Wei. Whichever it was, Goddess or God, I asked for protection.

In the lower reaches of the river we passed acres of

cultivated fields, some now growing winter wheat. In this open ground we could see how our friends had placed themselves. Little groups of three or four men were spread well out in front and on each side, the largest group staying behind us. They were splendid scouts. Any people they met, travellers or workers in the fields, were forced at pistol point to lie down with their faces on the ground, their big round straw hats forced comically on to the back of their heads, a guerrilla standing fiercely over them until we had gone past. Percy told us that they were only too pleased not to know who was passing, so that they would know nothing if questioned, or even tortured, by the Japanese.

As we advanced the flank guards moved quickly from one fir-covered hill to another, signalling back to us that all was well. They were well trained; their work as scouts, their use of ground for observation and cover and the way in which they moved quickly was highly efficient and professional. As a career infantry soldier, I was impressed by their superb fieldcraft.

Our band of merry warriors avoided all villages. We were led through plains of market gardens, where the stench told us that all those delicious Chinese vegetables were being grown with the aid of human manure, then through citrus orchards, scrub and scattered woods and beautiful mountain valleys. It was marvellous to walk along so easily and quickly in the daylight, especially through such interesting landscape, flanked by graceful green hills.

As evening approached, we turned sharply south-east and into the high mountains. Fong led us into a deep over-grown gully, where we sat down on the edge of a creek. The robbers, brigands, bandits or guerrillas – whatever you would care to call them and whatever they were actually – climbed the hills on either side and set up sentry posts. One party set off for food to the nearest village, Wu-Tung-Hsien-Tung. I loved these names. They had a romantic ring to them. Eddy wrote them all down.

Percy, Lee and Fong stayed with us, Fong playing idly with his Smith and Wesson four-five six-shooter, which was fully loaded, twirling it round on his finger by the trigger guard. The safety catch was on, but having spent years with pistols and small arms, trying to convince stupid soldiers of the necessity to take safety precautions, I knew how easily the safety catch could move, so that each time the muzzle flashed at me I winced. At last, to get away from the pistol, we got up and washed in the icy cold mountain creek, one of the tributaries of the lovely 'willow pattern river'.

The whole situation seemed a little unreal. On the one hand, it was very dramatic, with sentries posted on the hills to guard us, Fong ready with his pistol to defend us instantly, and Lee, Percy's brother, who had adopted the role of personal bodyguard, a walking arsenal of guns, knives and grenades; and yet on the other, here we were washing in the stream, waiting for food to be delivered, as if all was at peace, enjoying ourselves immensely.

'Like a bloody picnic,' declared Eddy, repeating the expression he had used way back at Tai Po.

A sentry cried out, a challenge followed quickly, then a response and another order from the sentry. Fong and Lee adopted positions of readiness, weapons poised for action. We clutched our clothes hurriedly, Duggie caught '*avec les pantalon en bas*', and faded into the undergrowth. Fong let out a sharp bark — obviously the Chinese for 'Who goes there?' — to which he received a quick response, the password no doubt. Two men stepped into the gully with food in wicker baskets, steaming hot rice, mixed with vegetables and fried pork. It was delicious, Chinese country village food, such marvellous vegetables, so superbly cooked. I have never enjoyed a meal so much, the first I had eaten for forty-eight hours. The wooden chopsticks worked away like mad as we ate all we could, sweet cakes as well. Percy, Fong and Lee took their share, but not much. They were highly amused at our ravenous hunger and how frequently we refilled the bowls. The remains of the meal were placed in our mess tins, which also caused more laughter.

As it grew dark, we set off again, climbing steeply up to a spur of the mountain on a good path and over a saddle between Wu-Tung-Shan-Wei and Hsiao-Wu-Tung. We understood now why they had waited for dark, for this last two miles took us over the bare, treeless face of the mountains. In the brief twilight and the starlit night we travelled easily, the excitement and our determination literally carrying us effortlessly up these mountains of over 2,000 feet, a trek we might have found difficult under earlier conditions. However, in youth the limbs have a marvellous, supple resilience, with immense power of recovery from fatigue. Moreover, Percy, Fong, Lee and Co. did not march slowly: they raced along, jogging in that rhythmical Chinese way.

Eventually we descended steeply wooded slopes, finding it difficult to see in the dark and sliding most of the way down on our bottoms. It was not much fun for Douglas in his thin and torn pantaloons.

We came to a halt just above a white-walled village, under an old lychee tree, sadly not in fruit at this time of year. A wedding ceremony was taking place and the air was filled with sounds of merriment, the beating of gongs, the explosion of crackers, the fragrant smell of incense. I could imagine the beautiful young bride, dressed conventionally in traditional red clothes, wonderfully embroidered in fantastic colours, with an extravagant ornamental head-dress, delivering her pathetic dowry for the marriage. And there would be the bridegroom, probably proudly dressed in a European suit (sadly not a graceful long gown of olden times), a young, anxious and expectant young man, now impoverished with the cost of all the food for the wedding banquet. It was difficult to believe we were still in Japanese-occupied China, only a few miles from a big base, or that we were still those three men struggling to cross the bridge to freedom, the euphemistic willow pattern bridge. It was to be a long bridge, but we did not know that. We were supremely happy.

Out of the darkness a young man loomed up carrying a lamp. In excellent English, he said, 'I am Ah Ting!'

It was too much for the hilarious Eddy. 'Or ting-a-ling by

1. Anthony Hewitt in 1944. *(right)*

2. Douglas Scriven in 1945. *(below)*

3. Eddy Crossley in 1946. *(below right)*

4. Colour Party, Shamshuipo Barracks, 1938, Anthony Hewitt on the right. Before the surrender to the Japanese, these Colours were buried at Flagstaff House.

5. Hong Kong, 1941, Causeway Bay to Murray Barracks, where the battle was fought.

6. 7. and 8. Peninsula Hotel on Nathan Road, along which prisoners were marched to Shamshuipo Barracks (*shown in the centre picture*), the Japanese prisoner-of-war camp. Officers were housed in Jubilee Buildings.

9. and 10. (*above*) Bamboo Pier, from which Tony, Douglas and Eddy escaped. After the war, Tony retraced his steps on the pathway encircling the cemetery.

11. and 12. The pathway to Golden Hill (*left*) and the village at Birds Hill (*right*) where they hid all day.

13. The Sham Chun River, which the escapers crossed to reach the Chinese mainland.

14. Chinese Communist guerrillas in training.

15. 'Heavenly little creatures like big dolls'.

16. Typical wayside stall in South China.

17. Sampan similar to the craft on which the three escapers
    journeyed up the East River.

18. Limestone mountains beyond the River Li at Kweilin.

19. Methodist Mission Hospital, Kukong, with Constance on the footbridge.

20. Nanda Devi, the Western Heaven (25,645 ft) in the Himalaya.

any other name, a wedding bell!' he cried flippantly.

Ah Ting made no comment. He sat down beside us and said, very seriously, 'Do you read Karl Marx?'

We all had, but only Douglas in any depth.

'Reading him,' Eddy said, 'does not mean that we agree with his theories.'

'Then you are no friends of ours,' Ting went on. 'We are all communists here: you belong to a capitalist nation and society, not unlike Japan; there is really no reason why we should help you. Our struggle is against the forces of capitalism. We fight the Japanese because they are capitalists and invade our nation, not because they are enemies of the Kuomintang, who are our enemies also.'

This was surprising talk after all the friendship we had received, after Percy had virtually saved our lives, for without him we would almost certainly have walked into the Japanese. What was this fellow getting at? Were we going to be ditched now? Our high spirits began a rapid decline.

'Who the hell is this man?' asked Eddy.

Ting continued to ignore Eddy, making matters worse. 'If we lead you through the Japanese occupied territories to the Kuomintang, you will join those who are our despised enemies. Your country, England, has made an alliance with Chiang Kai-shek, whose avowed intention is to crush the communists, led by Chairman Mao Tse-tung. Why therefore should we help you?'

There was a deathly silence, broken only by the beating of gongs in the walled village. We tried in turn to argue, but Ting could accept no argument. He turned everything we said into passages and phrases from Marx, sentences he knew by heart, using words such as proletariat, intelligentsia, bourgeoisie, class origins, and so on. Even Engels was brought into the oration, until we were thoroughly confused. He had an amazing knowledge of communist jargon in English and was having the time of his life lecturing us, telling us (the foreigners) thoughts which had built up inside him and which now exploded like a flood from a burst dam. He wanted to talk: he did not want to listen to us. In

particular he wanted to impress upon us the significance of
the Long March.

'Only seven years ago,' he said. 'Do you know what a
great feat it was?'

I said I had read about it — that it was a tremendous event,
militarily, sociologically, politically. Ting agreed: the March
had established communism in China *for ever*! From the
communist strongholds now in Shensi would emerge the
defeat of Japan and the Kuomintang, a far greater revolution
even than the Russian Revolution.

Douglas broke in: 'Comrade, tell me comrade Ting, is
everyone a communist in these parts?'

'Oh, sure, comrade, ever since Sun Yat Sen communists
have been very strong in this part of Guangdong or
Kwangtung province, whichever way you may call it.
Especially at the time of the civil war, Chiang versus Mao.
Before the Long March, large numbers of communist cadres
were ordered to stay behind here and spread the doctrine.
That is how the 'truth' stayed here.'

'What else are you, comrade, apart from being a communist?' comrade Duggie asked. 'Peasant farmer, anarchist,
teacher?'

'I was school teacher in Kowloon. High school teacher,
went to catholic school in Kowloon. I'm a good catholic-
taught communist!'

We laughed — and so did Ting, for the first time.

'Tell me, comrade, is Percy Davis a communist?' continued our comrade Duggie. But Ting did not seem to know
anyone of that name until we described the half-negro.

'Oh, yes, of course he is,' said comrade Ting, 'but that's
not his name. Nothing like Percy Davis. That's not a Chinese
name. He's the leader, the chairman here, the big man. Better
that you do not know his real name or that he is the big boss.
Forget it. It might bring trouble to you. This is Japanese
territory; it is dangerous to be a communist, or friends of
one.'

It was very illuminating about Percy. We had noticed all
along his undoubted authority. How lucky we were to have

met him, but in the circumstances, we understood that we were not supposed to know about Percy. Poor bespectacled comrade Ting, whom I had now come to like, despite his precociousness, was dismayed at having let the cat out of the bag. Fortunately this incongruous discussion and Ting's embarrassment were terminated abruptly. Percy returned from the village and told Ting to clear off.

Lee and Fong now arrived out of the dark, carrying an oil lamp, accompanied by the village headman, a dear old man dressed in black skull cap and a long blue gown, a kind smile showing above his long scraggy beard. He looked a wise old patriarch. Percy introduced us and said that the headman wished to congratulate us on our escape from the Japanese and that he knew it was our '*fungshui*' to get through to safety. He apologised for not inviting us into his village for traditional hospitality, but with the Japanese so close our appearance might compromise the inhabitants not only of this village but many others from which the bride and guests had come. Douglas thanked him in Cantonese for his politeness and courtesy, which Percy had to repeat for the old man to understand. Then through Percy the headman said that because he could not treat us as travellers should be treated he wished us to accept a gift. The venerable old man stepped forward and handed Douglas a roll of bank notes. We were dumbfounded. Then we all spoke at once, thanking him. It was a fantastic, wonderful thing. Lee led him back to the village.

We had been given $60, a huge sum. I asked Percy what '*fungshui*' meant. He was not sure, but thought 'destiny' would be the closest translation. The old headman had said it was our destiny to get through to safety. Was this a prophecy? It was not uncommon for old patriarchs to be prophets, especially with the Chinese. Much depended on the meaning and translation of the word '*fungshui*'. However, on that cold dark night, shivering under the lychee tree, I accepted the old man's words as an inspiration for the future.

So did Eddy. 'It's not the $60, it's his sincerity, his politeness, treating us as guests because we travel through his land, that's what really matters. He seemed to feel that he was responsible for looking after us, as if we were refugees — which of course we are. Isn't it odd, our first contact with the Chinese finished with an attack, next time we were fed and given gifts, then attacked again, now given gifts. The Chinese say even numbers are lucky. What will happen to us next time?'

Percy joined us. We told him how indebted we were to the headman and how we had been discussing Karl Marx with Ting. Percy seemed annoyed with Ting, possibly because he might have talked too much, told us things we should not know.

'Don't worry about him,' Percy said. 'He learnt all this communist language in Canton, from communists left there after Chiang Kai-shek had driven out the communists. He's a good school teacher. Today he has been reading his English books so that he could speak to you, but he does not understand what he says.'

He paused for a while, thinking. 'We will help you and send you through to the Kuomintang, and perhaps one day you will come back to help China. You must remember that China, with its crippling poverty, is a happy hunting ground for communism; and also that in this part of China Chinese communism was first born. Despite Chiang Kai-shek's policy of forcing the communists into the Long March there are still many communists here. But those men are not true communists: they pride themselves that they are Robin Hood robbers and rob the rich only. They say Robin Hood was a communist, but in truth they rob the rich only because they are the only people worth robbing in this land of almost universal poverty.'

He never told us if he himself was or was not a communist. He went on, 'They have done very well recently robbing all the refugees from Hong Kong, people that are being thrown out by the Japs.'

Ah Fong interrupted to tell us his plans for the night. Percy translated. 'He says we shall leave shortly. It is a long march ahead of us. The Japs guard the Canton road closely because the country on the west side of the road is controlled by the communist army.'

Fong paused and asked Percy if we understood that we had to cross the road in order to go northwards towards the Chinese national army. We did understand, very clearly. Fong continued: 'To protect their occupied territory the Japs have set up a line of block houses interspersed with picquets. The only way to get through these lines is to use a very steep ravine, which no one has been up for years and from which direction the Japs are less likely to expect us. It is difficult and very dangerous.'

Fong then became involved in a very animated discussion with Percy. Clearly, he was concerned about our chances of breaking through the Japanese lines.

Eventually Percy explained: 'Fong says the Japs will know that three escaped prisoners are in this country. They will be searching for you. It is essential that we get through tonight, in the dark, before the moon rises, however hard or difficult or dangerous it may be. The longer you stay in this country the more likely you are to be caught. Do you understand?'

Douglas replied, 'We understand, we appreciate what you are doing for us and the danger you are putting yourselves in. We thank you for your great courage. We are ready to do this march, we will do it, however difficult it may be. We will not fail you.'

With this burst of rhetoric, Fong seemed happy, and indicated that we should make ready to go at once.

11

Through Japanese Lines

The valiant brigands assembled for the march. Some of the original stalwarts who had escorted us from the willow pattern bridge had stepped down, but even so, with Fong, Percy, our personal bodyguard Lee, we three and eleven others, there were still seventeen men formed up, ready for the journey. Ah Ting, the bespectacled communist teacher, did not wish to come. He appeared out of the dark to wish us a safe journey.

'Goodbye foreign comrades, goodbye, good luck to you on your Long March! Go right through to Shensi, go to Yenan and meet our Chairman Mao Tse-tung!'

He had more humour than I had credited him. Percy told him to shut up.

Fong was giving orders, and there was much activity, men going back and forth, forming up into correct places for the line of march. Eventually, with a word of command and a cheer, reminding me of King Harry at Agincourt — 'Workers of all countries unite!' repeated down the line — we marched off.

Almost immediately we were passing the white-walled wedding ceremony village into which sadly we could not be invited. It was understandable. The sudden entry of three total strangers could have been very disturbing to everyone at the ceremony, particularly the children. The state we were in, unshaven with a week-old beard, torn and filthy clothing, mine covered in blood, patches on my head, bandages on my hand, might have brought disaster if we had joined them.

Down the steep, winding mountain track, sometimes with vast drops beside us dissolving into deep black voids, we stumbled continually, hitting our toes against stones and rocks. The main group of robbers went on ahead, moving quickly, to scout out the land and give us early warning of danger. Fong led our group, which in army terms resembled a mobile tactical headquarters, the centre from which orders were issued. Percy walked behind Fong, Douglas keeping within touching distance of Percy, followed closely by Eddy and me. Lee came behind us, so at last Eddy was no longer tail-end-charlie. Three stalwart warriors defended us in the rear.

The twisting crooked path descended for about two miles until we reached the paddy fields. We followed the narrow bunds between the fields, falling off with persistent regularity, failing to restrict our language as we fell, and breaking the silence so strictly observed by the disciplined professional brigands. At times we were hysterical with laughter at the sounds of thumps, groans and often very vulgar words as in turn we fell off into a muddy ditch. Like most Asian people, we laughed at each others' misfortunes. Percy kept imploring us to keep quiet. Our Chinese gentleman-robbers sped along quickly, seeing far better in the dark than we could. It was extremely difficult to keep up with them, but we simply had to maintain the jog trot almost all the time. We were clearly much fitter and stronger than I expected, using unknown sources of strength and energy. The urgent need to get to the ravine before the moon rose forced us on. To avoid the few inhabited villages, Fong left the main pathways, which made the going across country even more difficult. Some villages had been burnt and destroyed by the Japanese invaders, and we could save time by walking straight through the ruins.

After three miles or so of traversing paddy fields, our group waded a deep river and then began to climb uphill again on a stony broken track, bruising every wet toe as we went. Fong crossed a stone bridge spanning a fast-flowing stream and then called a halt. Percy explained we were at the entrance to the ravine; that the scouts would go ahead to clear the way, to break or cut back the thick undergrowth. It was a comfort to have got this far.

Fong did not let us rest long. He began the climb, quietly pushing back the undergrowth, trying to find a foothold, mounting step by step up the almost perpendicular pathless incline. It was so dark that the guides were forced to light matches to find the way, despite the extreme danger of showing a light. The cliff side of the gorge fell away in a sheer drop into the blackness, as if into a bottomless pit. It would be all too easy to stumble and fall. Douglas missed a step and plunged into the abyss, falling headlong into the branches of a fir tree. He was unhurt, but made a lot of noise. Struggling, sometimes on hands and knees as the incline became even steeper, we finally reached the head of the gorge. The brigands were waiting for us below the shelter and cover of a steep escarpment. A long whispered conversation took place between Fong and Percy and Douglas, who then reported to us.

'There's a Jap post on the hill above us. They're sending a chap up to see.'

We waited silently while a gallant young man scaled the rock face of the escarpment and disappeared into the fearful blackness of the night. After he had gone, there was not a sound to be heard, except for the fir trees rustling in the slight breeze. It was an eerie, frightening silence.

'I hope he doesn't stir them up,' whispered Eddy, breaking the suspense. 'We'll never get down that gorge in the darkness.'

Then we heard the man running along the hilltop and sliding down the cliff face. Automatically, all of us started retracing our steps down the gorge, but the man began shouting. When he reached us the man was laughing, almost hysterically.

Percy explained: 'All is well! He says he walked straight into the barbed wire of a Japanese post; a fire is burning but the Japanese have gone!'

A little in panic, Percy told us that we must climb the cliff as quickly as possible, because the Japanese might return at any moment. It would be a mobile patrol that stopped to light a fire to cook a meal at one of their defensive positions, and then proceed, but they might easily retrace their steps — might even have suspected that the head of the gorge was a likely passage through their lines. With a rush and scurry everyone made for the cliff and scaled it with the help of the first light of the moon, a moon sparrow-fart. As a bunch of rather disorganised individuals, we scrambled over the final edge of the cliff and ran along the hilltop. We found a gap in the barbed wire fence, and all seventeen of us squeezed through. We leaped over the dying embers of the fire left burning by the Japanese mobile patrol and jumped again over a series of slit trenches, almost fox holes, all part of the Japanese defended position so recently evacuated. There was a frantic search for another opening in the encircling ring of barbed wire and then we were through, through the post and running hard along an open knife-edged ridge, chasing along like a mad, undisciplined horde. We had achieved our objective, and each man knew instinctively that we had to get far away from that sinister Japanese post as quickly as possible.

Fong called the halt, drawing us up, rather like quelling the stampede of a mob of brumbies, panting and frothing wild horses. Quickly we reassembled.

Percy whispered, 'We are through the Japanese lines!'

Douglas began shaking hands vigorously with Eddy and me, saying, 'We're through, we're through the Jap lines. How bloody marvellous!' — and then shaking hands with Fong and Percy, even with our stalwart bodyguard Lee. They probably thought Douglas was crazy, but they laughed and embraced us, saying we had done well on the difficult march, but that it had been necessary to go so fast to get through that ravine before the moon rose.

As the moon came up, we were walking along an easy but ill-defined track, seldom used, on the crest of bare treeless hills. We still had to cross the main road, but we could see now the lie of the land. The main road ran along to our left, to the west, following the valley of a river, mostly in shadow from our hill, not easily discernible. On the other side of the crest there appeared to be an enormous lake. It was beautiful, glistening in the gentle moonlight, but it was a mirage; it turned out that the lake was mist and fog covering rice fields and vegetable gardens.

After a few miles we came to another ravine and halted. Percy said the road was about half a mile away. The scouts had gone down first to make sure all was clear. He warned us it was a difficult ravine to descend, asking us again not to make too much noise. It was cold and clear, and very quiet. There were no villages within miles of us. All the strain of the previous night marches, alone with Eddy and Douglas, had gone. There was no more looking nervously always at the next few yards ahead, searching for any signs of immediate unforeseen attack; now we had these gallant brigands to protect us. Or was it the pagoda at the willow pattern bridge that protected us?

At last Fong decided to advance. There was a small thin path running down the side of the ravine, crossing and recrossing a stream. It was desperately hard to avoid slipping and sending stones cascading down. It was almost as hard to contain oneself from letting forth the most horrific vulgar European oaths; oaths that somehow seemed sacrilegious in the presence of our polite and dignified Asian friends.

The scouts were waiting at the road and led us underneath it through a culvert near a hill called She-Hsia-Shan. Making a detour round a village, we traversed cultivated fields and orange and tangerine orchards, moving at a fast pace. There was no time now for self-congratulation and hand-shaking at having crossed the main road.

As dawn broke we were many miles north of the romantic little wedding village we had left at dusk. We were guided over scrubland into a wood and told to wait with Percy.

'They are going into a village to get food, after which we will go on again.'

'In daylight?' queried Douglas. 'Surely it's a bit dangerous?'

'No, not now, we are through the Japanese positions. This

country is controlled by the communist guerrillas. If we keep going we should be almost half way to the Chinese National Army by this evening.'

'That will be almost forty-eight hours non-stop on our feet,' complained Eddy, who preferred to travel in aeroplanes. 'Any more precipitous gorges to climb?'

It was bitterly cold waiting for the food, which took some time to arrive. As before, it came in wicker baskets, with chopsticks and small rice bowls. We thanked our kind hosts profusely for the marvellous hot rice and vegetables. Our voices disturbed a crow pheasant, a cuckoo with dark brown plumage and light brown wings, which fluttered away into the shrubby and wooded hillside.

Immediately we had finished we set off on the march again over the rolling countryside. We noticed that all the streams were now flowing northwards — towards the East River, we hoped. It meant we had crossed over the watershed between the Sham Chun valley and the northern waters. It was a great encouragement. There were plenty of signs of devastation caused by the Japanese. As we passed a ruined village, Percy told us that the Imperial Japanese Army had been here.

'This is how they lay down their New Order in East Asia. This is how they civilise us!'

There was scarcely a soul about. Our guides led us by the regular pathways, routes that had been used for centuries, often paved with great big wide paving stones of granite; no attempt was made to avoid people, some still inhabiting the blackened skeletons of their villages.

At about midday, we ascended a small hill overlooking sugar-cane fields, through the centre of which ran a large stream. To our left, the west, the Kowloon to Canton railway showed up, running round a prolonged bend, the point of the bend being as close as half a mile away.

'We're not going near the railway, are we?' asked Douglas, worried at the nearness of the line. .

'No, of course not,' replied Percy, 'our way is straight on, going north. This is the closest we come to the railway at that big bend you can see, just before it goes into that cutting.

Don't worry, the Japs do not use the railway, the Lo Wu bridge is destroyed and communist guerrillas blow up other bridges.'

'Look!' interrupted Eddy. 'Look at all those people on the railway, hundreds of them. Whatever is happening?'

Long lines of people were walking along the railway, most of them carrying their possessions in great bundles on sticks over their shoulders, men, women and children, plodding along the rough track of loose stones and wooden sleepers.

'They are refugees from Hong Kong,' Percy answered, 'making their way to Free China. The Japanese are driving them out. There is little food in Hong Kong.'

As we watched this sombre spectacle, we noticed that a little further up the railway, at the cutting Percy had pointed out, the thin black line of refugees had been brought to a stop. It appeared they must be held up by some sort of control. Our guides, chattering quickly together like a bunch of cockatoos, were obviously very apprehensive of the control post. Fong shouted some sharp orders and he and Lee and the rest of the brigands ran off down the pathway towards the large stream, gaining shelter in the sugar-cane.

'Come on quickly,' shouted Percy at us. 'The refugees are being stopped and examined. It could be bandits or guerrillas. We can't take chances, quick, down the hill and into the sugar-cane.'

It was too late. We had been seen. They shouted at us, and when we tried to move on opened fire with Mauser pistols and rifles. The three of us with Percy, dived into a ditch and lay there. The rest of our gallant brigand band ran through the cane and away over a hill. Regrettably that was the last we ever saw of them. We should have liked to thank them, especially Fong, the leader, and Lee, who had acted always as a bodyguard. They had risked their lives by helping us; if caught by the Japanese they faced torture, a horrible painful death and probably the destruction of their homes and families. Their courage had been magnificent.

Waiting in the ditch, we wondered what would happen next. We hoped our assailants were communist guerrillas and not bandits. The firing stopped, but we could hear them crashing through the sugar-cane towards us. The crops waved in front of us and suddenly a Chinese man, pointing a Mauser pistol at us, pushed his head through the bushes and literally leered at us. His sudden appearance frightened the life out of us.

'Jesus!' cried Eddy, 'we've had our chips this time!'

He did not move, our visitor; he just stayed there covering us silently with his vicious gun, staring at us. Three other men worked up on the flanks while the first one watched us, and then the four of them rushed at us, yelling something in Chinese, pointing long bayonets fixed to rifles. Percy jumped up quickly, raising his hands above his head, a huge man in comparison to his ugly captors. We stood up also, reluctant to raise our hands, but we complied after a few proddings from the sharp bayonets.

The four men wore uniform, a khaki-drill type of jacket buttoned up to the neck, khaki riding breeches, long fawn puttees, brown leather slipper-like shoes, and floppy peaked caps with a red star above the peak. Immediately, they searched us for arms, while Percy, who did not seem to be greatly concerned, explained who we were and what we were doing.

'They are the Yau Kik Toi, the Communist Red Army, the guerrilla army,' he told us. 'They say this is their territory, controlled by them. No one can pass without permission. Don't worry.'

The four dirty and scruffy communist soldiers marched us off to the railway line, still insisting we keep our hands raised, pointing their big Chinese or Russian rifles and very long bayonets at us. On arrival at the control post we were allowed to lower our hands and sit down, a villainous soldier standing over us. It was a similar situation to the one when we met Percy first, only this time Percy was involved in a long discussion with our captors. I assumed by their behaviour, the exclamations and more friendly facial expressions, that they knew who Percy was. He told us what was going on.

'There is nothing to worry about. These men are communists and they will look after you.' We sighed with relief. 'They have sent for their officer, Captain Lee. He will come shortly. I will stay until he comes. I know him.'

We were relieved, but asked what had happened to our friends, the brave band of brigands who had looked after us so courageously, and Fong and brother Lee.

'They have run away because they fear the communist army, who will either enlist them into their ranks or shoot them for being robbers. I have told them how the robbers helped to keep you away from the Japanese, led you through the Japanese lines last night and therefore virtually saved your lives. I don't think the communists will go after our friends. They understand that they did not rob you and that they did a very brave thing.'

We lay on a bank beside the railway line and watched the refugees streaming past. They were a pathetic sight, carrying in their loads all their earthly possessions. Some carried small children in baskets hanging from their shoulder poles. All appeared terrified by the communist soldiers, who were extracting a toll from each person. There seemed to be no fixed sum or article for the toll: the soldiers searched each person, opened the bundles and parcels and took whatever appealed to them. Some refugees paid money, others gave up jewellery and watches, or even wretched articles of clothing. A man spoke to Percy, thinking he was a member of the communist control post.

'We have already been robbed of everything of value by the Japanese and by robbers we met on the way. Surely you are not going to rob us again?' He was stopped short by a soldier, pushing him with his rifle butt.

'Poor people,' Percy said to us. 'The awful thing is that this business of taking a toll from the refugees is really just a way for the soldiers to enrich themselves. Very little of what they are collecting will ever get to the leader of the communist guerrillas.'

It was not a pleasant sight to watch the refugees searched, robbed and bullied. We were desperately sorry for them, but there was nothing we could do. I was also concerned that some of these refugees could be followers of Wang Ching-wei, Japan's puppet leader in conquered China, who might easily pass information to the Japanese that they had seen three Europeans, ugly, scruffy, tired and unshaven, but nevertheless Europeans. I asked to move out of sight of the railway, to which the communists agreed, detailing a soldier to guard us in our new position.

When Captain Lee arrived, we were surprised by his very unsoldierly, unathletic, unmilitary appearance. He wore the normal dull grey felt hat and civilian Chinese clothes. Although he was armed, he seemed to be a singularly inoffensive little man, much more a scholar than a soldier. He was also extremely polite, a change from the soldiers we had met. Speaking excellent colloquial English, he apologised for having kept us waiting so long; he apologised that his soldiers fired at us. He offered to take us at once to his group headquarters, where he promised Percy we would be well cared for. He was very pleasant to Percy, for whom he seemed to have a high regard.

After more conversation Percy stood up. He said he would have to leave us now and resume his journey to Hong Kong where he had been going when he rescued us from the robbers. He said he felt we were now in safe hands with the communist army and that his responsibility was over. It was the moment I had dreaded; but he had to go. We shook hands and thanked him — such a little compensation for what he had done, but I think he understood how grateful we were for he smiled warmly, his big dark face expressing both joy and sadness. Just as he was leaving he handed Douglas some bank notes.

'To help you on your way, to help you find your "*fungshui*".' He seemed fond of us; we had great affection for him and were genuinely upset to see him go.

He walked away, waving goodbye, his huge tall frame sloping along, not in the rhythmic trot of the Chinese, but in the supple walk of a West Indian. We stood watching him fade away across the sugar-cane fields into the evening landscape, towards the beautiful Wu Tung mountains, the wedding ceremony village, the prophetic village patriarch, the willow pattern river and bridge, the place where he had snatched us away from bayonet-pointing bandits. Memories of him would never fade.

12

Communist Camp

'Follow me,' squeaked the gallant Captain Lee, so thin and so small, with hands almost effeminately delicate, so unlike a soldier. We found at once that he was an interesting substitute for our friend Percy, as we marched along into undulating hills of decomposed granite, accompanied by two soldiers. Captain Lee talked proudly of the exploits of the guerrillas, boasting about their successful operations against the Japanese. He told us the Kuomintang were the enemies of the people and that the Chinese nation would turn to communism when the war was over.

I was more interested in our immediate future. It was natural that I should want to know where we were going, but I liked to know where we were, so that if we were attacked suddenly by the Japanese and lost contact with our guides, we would not be altogether lost. After all, apart from Percy, our brigand guides had abandoned us at the very first shot fired at us. For this reason, I used the compass or the sun constantly to see the direction in which we were going, and to have some idea of our whereabouts. It was quite possible for a strong Japanese patrol to enter this country, despite its being 'controlled' by the communist army.

'We go to the guerrilla headquarters,' said Lee. 'About six miles. From this headquarters we control guerrilla operations between the Kuomintang and the Japanese, from the Pearl River to Bias Bay.'

We were marching due westwards along the valley of a river flowing towards us. The country was composed of hundreds of little red hills, mostly bare of trees, interspersed with valleys, defiles and gullies. One hill and one valley looked like all the others. The place was, in fact, a huge maze. Lee overheard me mentioning my bewilderment to Douglas.

'That is why we have chosen this area for our headquarters. It is difficult to find us, especially as we move our site frequently. In more than three years of war the Japanese have never found us.'

'Let's hope your good fortune continues,' Eddy piped up.

It gave us a feeling of security, marching along so openly with these armed companions in this queer labyrinth, with no distinguishable character or shape in any of the features of the land. Douglas was excited and happy.

'We've got nothing else to worry about. From now let's treat things as a holiday; a Cook's tour of China!'

At the first village, hardly a village really, just a few old stone houses and shacks, Douglas bought some sugared sweets and three sticks of sugar-cane. At the next village, a larger one called Shui-Ku, set in a grove of bamboo, Douglas decided to have a shave and haircut from the local barber. We were quickly surrounded by the inhabitants, full of curiosity, comments and advice to the barber, sharing our fun.

Captain Lee was not happy at the delay or the attention we had drawn upon ourselves. The barber was ordered to finish and we set off again, this time at a furious pace. That was the last village we saw. After many twistings and turnings − north-east, south-west, south for a long way, and finally north-west − moving now into far more difficult and desolate country, we eventually arrived just before dark at the headquarters, very much further than the six miles Lee had told us.

A few sentries were scattered on the surrounding hills, guarding all approaches to the headquarters, sited in a narrow valley. Small camouflaged atap huts had been erected on the hillsides. We stopped at a larger hut, the command hut, guarded by a sloppy-looking boy sentry, his rifle and bayonet larger than he was.

Lee said, 'You will have to wait in this camp until Comrade Wong, the commander, returns. He is away at present fighting Japanese near Waichow. He will decide what is to be done with you. I will get a man who speaks good English to look after you.'

He sent the boy soldier off to collect the man. Soon a small, plump, bespectacled Chinese man arrived, dressed surprisingly in grey flannel trousers and a dark blue blazer. He was astonished by the unexpected appearance of Europeans in the guerrilla camp and startled at the dirty, blood-stained sight of us. Quickly overcoming his surprise and embarrassment, he stepped forward, offering a chubby little hand to Douglas.

'How do you do?' His English was faultless. 'I am Lim Koon Teck.'

We all shook hands, rather seriously and formally.

'I am Duggie, this is Ed and this is Tony. He has hurt his hand.'

'Whatever are you doing here? Are you English? Have you come from Hong Kong?' Lim was full of curiosity, and could not contain himself.

Lee stopped him and told him to take us to a hut. We were thankful, for we were too tired to answer questions, and could hardly follow him up the slope to a hut.

A Straits-born Malayan Chinese, Chan Peng Leong, joined us and helped to put clean straw into the small hut. Both Lim and Chan wanted to talk to us, to ask questions and tell us about themselves but we were too tired to listen or even understand. We had been marching with very little rest and not much food for two whole nights and two whole days; in fact we had been going hard for more than a week. Impolite as it was, we were just too exhausted to keep awake for our kind hosts. Lying down on the straw, Douglas in the middle, we went out like a light.

We slept late into the morning, until the Malayan Chinese, Chan, arrived with a tray of rice and vegetables and fried

ducks' eggs, which we consumed ravenously. I thanked him
for his kindness. He replied in Malay, '*Ta'usah-lah, Tuan.*'
(There's no need.)

It was nice to hear Malay spoken again, nice to be called
Tuan, although it seemed out of place here, to a dirty and
scruffy man like me. I had been stationed in Singapore and
knew a little Malay. To show off my knowledge and thinking that a communist camp must be an egalitarian society, I
said '*Terema kaseh, makan yang baik sa-kali, Comrade Tuan.*'
(Thank you, the food is the best.) He was taken aback, either
at the bad Malay or by being addressed as '*Comrade Tuan*', but
then his warm brown eyes flashed at me. He burst into peals
of laughter, and then into a torrent of Malay. I had made a
friend. He was delighted to talk Malay to someone in this
strange camp of many different types of people and society, as
we were to discover later. From then onwards, Chan took
charge of us and all our needs.

I asked if the '*Tuan besar*', the Captain Wong, had returned.
He said he would not be back until tomorrow, but as we
were now awake Comrade Lee wanted to speak to us. He
brought us a bucket of water, and we washed and cleaned up.
Lee arrived, a little breathless from the climb up the slope to
our straw shelter, accompanied by Lim.

'Have you eaten? I am sorry, Comrade Wong will not
come back for a few days. You must stay until he returns.
There is much for you to do. We fight the same enemy. You
can help to train our men. Perhaps you would like to remain
with us and fight the Japanese?'

We ignored his question, but agreed to do whatever we
could to help train his soldiers. Everything was organised
quickly and each of us was given a small squad of soldiers to
instruct. Douglas delivered his instruction himself in Cantonese, without the help of an interpreter. He gave them a
very useful lecture and demonstration in first aid. Lim, who
turned out to be a Cambridge graduate, interpreted for
Eddy, who shot a tremendous line about the aircraft he had
flown and those he might have shot down with a little bit of
luck. He told them also, to their advantage, what a pilot

could observe from an aircraft, and took them round the
camp pointing out the deficiencies in camouflage.

My squad consisted of about twenty, including a few girls,
ranging in age from twelve to eighteen. Each was dressed in a
made-up uniform of bits and pieces taken from the Japanese
and Kuomintang. Each young recruit carried a rolled up
blanket across his shoulder, a small bag of rice, a water
bottle, a rifle, bayonet and ammunition. I was impressed that
each was equipped ready to move at a moment's notice, and
also by the determination and courage in their youthful faces.
The recruits were burning with curiosity about me, the
monstrous foreigner, asking many questions, the younger
ones quite unable to stop laughing outright at the strange
sight. I should have liked to learn something about them, but
I decided I had better get on with the instruction that Captain
Lee was so keen about.

The Malayan, Chan, was my interpreter. I spoke in bazaar
Malay: he interpreted in Cantonese. I wished to inspect the
squad.

'Line them up in two ranks,' I told Chan, 'and tell them to
unload their rifles and take out the bolts.'

As they unloaded, green and rusty cartridges fell from
their rifles. Some had to struggle to remove the bolts; they
were obviously unaccustomed to doing so. The rifles, British
Lee Enfields or Japanese, were all filthy and corroded. I sat
them down in a circle with a moderately clean rag, oil and a
pull through. Chan showed them how to clean a rifle,
translating my instructions. Then I made them clean their
own rifles and ammunition.

I repeated the rifle-cleaning lessons with more squads.
There seemed to be an air of bewilderment at my meticulous
insistence on cleanliness. Surely it was quite unnecessary; just
a foreigner's dementia. Logically, a bullet when fired would
drive out the dirt and mud in the barrel, without all these
ridiculous antics. A shot fired was surely the easiest way to
clean a barrel. I never succeeded in dissolving the bewilderment, but it was through these lessons that I came to know
the boy and girl recruits. They came from the peasantry,

with a tough and hard background, able to accept extreme
hardship. Many had been born in territory now in Japanese
hands. Driven out, their new homes were now mostly in
Free China. Some had fathers in the Red Army, some were
orphans, parents killed by the Japanese. Most had suffered
from losses in families or in land, due to the Japanese. All had
a deadly, fanatical hatred for the Japanese. Few mentioned
communisn, but they enjoyed shouting communist slogans
and singing communist songs. The songs meant a lot to
them, as they walked about the camp pathways hand in
hand, fully armed and singing. Every little hut rang with
sounds of singing, laughter and humour. They were a happy
bunch of boys and girls, all of whom believed they were
fighting for their homes, their land, their country.

In the days that followed my instructions progressed to
lessons in loading and aiming rifles, and to fieldcraft for the
young recruits. I taught some of the older soldiers how to
load and fire a mortar, an anti-tank rifle and a bren-gun, all of
which had been smuggled out from the battlefields in the
New Territories of Hong Kong. Chan handled the weapons
for me, my wounded hand preventing me from actual
demonstrations. These older soldiers were not so bewildered
as the recruits and were anxious to learn, seeming to accept
the presence of the foreign soldier without much concern.
They were even more virulent in their hatred of the Japanese.
We three Europeans were popular with them because we had
escaped, making the Japanese look foolish.

Douglas continued with first aid lessons and improved the
hygiene and sanitation in the camp. Everywhere parties of
men, women and children were to be seen filling in
fly-ridden latrines and digging new ones. The three-eyed
small barbarian chased the workers with a savage tongue,
using strangely pronounced Cantonese words and odd
expressions, but everyone worked hard. Captain Lee was
delighted. Douglas also spent long hours looking after the
sick and wounded. His small fore-and-aft cap, so different
from the floppy Red Army peaked cap, was greatly admired
and gave him authority. With few medicines and stores he

improvised cleverly and worked wonders, especially with the women and children. He was gentle and kind and sympathetic towards them, and they came to love him, especially the children, who followed him round the camp, hanging on to his pantaloons. They laughed at him, for he was a great joy to them; his presence gave the sick confidence and the will to overcome their afflictions.

'You are a good doctor,' Captain Lee said. 'The longer you stay with us the better' — which, of course, was not what we wanted at all. We wished to move on to unoccupied China.

Eddy grew tired of shooting a line to an audience which did not appear to appreciate his great qualities, and instead devoted his time to lying on the hilltops with the sentries, looking for Japanese and learning some of the communist songs.

On the first day Chan had produced blankets and clothing for us, had taken us to the camp shop to eat cakes and to meet many friendly and polite people. We discovered that the camp had been designed to train recruits to be guerrillas, and to help refugees from Hong Kong cross over into Free China. The refugees came from all walks of life. Lim, the Cambridge man, who had worked in a shipping firm in Hong Kong, was one of the refugees. He was not a communist, had no wish to be a soldier or a guerrilla, and was terrified by the whole place. Chan, the Malayan, was an ardent communist and had been sent from Malaya to work with the guerrillas.

Occasionally our instructional duties were disturbed by alarms that a Japanese column was approaching the camp. Each time everyone packed up their kits and moved away to hide in the labyrinth of small valleys and gullies, to return a few hours later.

We asked again to see Comrade Wong but were told the Kuomintang army had repulsed a Japanese attack on Waichow and that Wong's guerrillas were very busy joining in the fight and harassing a retreating enemy. We were asked again to fight with the guerrillas. Douglas used my wounds as an excuse, saying that he must get me into a hospital.

Later, to try and get some urgency into the guerrillas, he added that if they could get us through to the Kuomintang we would try to get material assistance for the guerrillas — arms, munitions and medical supplies. This excuse was very well received by Comrade Lee.

The days passed quickly. We worked hard at our instructions. The food, though very rough and plain, was good, and we built up our strength. It turned very cold and we froze on the straw with only one blanket at night, but we did not mind. We were so fortunate to be here. In any case, the cold drove the flies away and retarded the activity of the fleas, with which the straw abounded.

In the evening we used to join the guerrillas in their sing-song round a log fire. Eddy was our star piece. He sang with quite a good voice 'The Road to the Isles', 'Honeymoon Yodel', and 'The Maori Farewell'. The communist soldiers tried to join with us in the 'British Grenadiers' and 'Alexander's Rag-time Band', but without much success. I really enjoyed the patriotic fervour of the communist songs, the rhythm and enthusiasm with which they were sung, especially 'We follow our Chairman', and 'We are all experts with the gun'. These camp fire evenings were happy events, we three capitalists in complete harmony with all our communist friends.

One evening comrade Captain Wong returned. His arrival caused a great stir in the camp, people running about announcing that the commander had arrived. Captain Lee brought him to us. He was entirely different from Lee. He was thickset, short and strongly built, with a strong full face. He looked the part of a soldier and was well dressed, with a prominent red star above the peak on his cap. He wore a jacket with large pockets, riding breeches, leggings and boots, and was armed with a Mauser automatic pistol. He strode up to me with a friendly smile, almost breaking my left wrist in a ferocious handshake. He was vivacious, animated, a leader. He spoke good English,

'Welcome to the Red Army. Very good you escape from Japanese. I will help you.'

A banquet was arranged to celebrate Wong's return and the victory the guerrillas had gained over the Japanese. We were invited to attend. The old cook, who had once been in the Royal Navy, and who had become a friend, prepared a special European-style meal with great care. A long trestle table had been laid with knives and forks; chopsticks were also set out in case the foreign implements were too difficult to handle. Oil hurricane lamps lit the festive scene under the one large open straw hut that the camp owned, used normally as a dining hall for the guerrilla soldiers. We were invited to sit on wooden benches opposite Wong and Lee and other officials and officers. Large jugs of rice wine were placed on the table and glasses were filled. Wong stood up and gave a toast.

'Our dear international friends!'

We stood and swallowed the glassful of wine.

Douglas replied, 'To our brave *yau kik toi!*'

We all stood again and swallowed another glassful.

The food was served, a former Hong Kong steward-boy moving round the table as if he was at Government House. It was not strictly European, similar to sweet and sour pork with lovely Chinese vegetables, the fried rice being served in separate bowls. It was the sort of food which would have tasted better if eaten with chopsticks, but I did not wish to offend the cook, so I used the knife and fork. So did Wong and the others, all looking decidedly uncomfortable. Douglas asked if it was permitted to use chopsticks, and with instant applause everyone grabbed their chopsticks.

Afterwards Wong made a long speech about guerrilla warfare, the destruction of the Japanese, and the future of China as a communist country. He ended with a toast, 'To English people!' Another glass of wine rushed down everyone's throat in indecent haste. I stood up to reply, making a short speech, stuttering a little, saying that we would get supplies for them from Free China, ending with a toast to the communist people of China. Another cupful of wine chased after the last one, in a desperate hurry.

Wong in another speech explained that the Chinese

communist army and the guerrillas here were not recognised by Chiang Kai-shek's central government but we could at least try to get some help, even if it was only medical supplies.

Douglas then gave a toast to Chairman Mao, confirming we would do all in our power to help. He emphasised the need to get us through quickly.

All the speeches and toasts had been accompanied by frequent '*um-sing*', '*kan-pei*', requiring the emptying of the glass in one gulp. Lee, now a little drunk, explained to Eddy that you must drink in one gulp, otherwise you get headache. We got headache all right, but also Wong's agreement for us to move on.

It was Friday, 13 February 1942, very cold and wet. Eddy had dysentery. We were told to be ready to leave at 1 p.m. There was plenty of time to walk round the camp, in and out of the gullies where the little atap-covered huts had been hidden in the hillsides, all better camouflaged now after Eddy's persuasion, to say farewell to numerous friends. One group of two men and a girl, bankers from Shanghai, told us that they would be travelling with us. We called on the old Royal Navy cook, to thank him for his excellent European meal. He was delighted to talk in pidgin. He spoke of the naval shore base, HMS *Tamar*, of the destroyer, HMS *Thracian*, and many other ships in which he had sailed. We were pleased to listen to him, because it gave him so much joy. We owed him much, the many good Chinese meals he had cooked us during our stay and the great trouble he had taken over the dinner. With the assistance of the ex-Hong Kong steward-boy, he had set out the table in the primitive thatched hut in a splendid way, using rice paper as table cloths, obtaining from somewhere in the camp those knives and forks.

I noticed in the corner of his little cookhouse Tin Hau, the Goddess of Heaven and protectress of seafarers, ensconced in a safe place. It interested me because all through the camp there were signs of Buddhism and other Chinese beliefs. Kwun Yam, the Buddhist Goddess of Mercy, was enshrined in various places, and Kwan Tai, the God of War and source of righteousness, occupied a place of honour near Comrade Captain Wong and Comrade Captain Lee. It made me realise that although this was a communist camp, there was a complete freedom of religious practice.

Chan, the Malayan, came running up to say that Comrade Wong wanted to see us before he left the camp to continue fighting the Japanese. We thanked Wong for all that had been done for us in the camp. Smiling, he gave each of us $100 to help us on our way. He said an escort of guerrillas would take us through to the Chinese National Army. To our joy, Comrade Tuan Chan Peng Leong was to be the leader.

We said goodbye to everyone. I appreciated most of all the very close contact we had with all types of people in the camp, cultured citizens, guerrilla soldiers, peasant farmers. They were so polite, so friendly. I learnt a little about China, a timeless land with an ageless culture that penetrated to these people and somehow engulfed all invaders. Even, here, locally in this district, you could see how the resurgence and resilience of the peasants was absorbing the Japanese invaders, how you found peasants still living in the burnt-out shells of their houses, still cultivating the land.

13

New Year of the Horse

Comrade Chan, the Malayan communist guerrilla fighter, was waiting for us at the command hut. Dressed in full marching order, rolled blanket, pack, Mauser pistol, he looked impressive, a real soldier. Smiling under his red star cap, set at a jaunty angle, he greeted me, '*Salamat, Tuan, apa khabar?*' I replied, '*Salamat, Tuan̈ Comrade, khabar baik!*' I was well and ready to march.

Chan introduced the escort, four young guerrillas, all in full kit, each with a rifle and bayonet. We knew them by their short names: Wang, Chu, Peng, Tan. They knew us, of course, and smiled and laughed at us; Chu jocularly throwing up his rifle into the port position, opening the bolt, and pointing out that it was immaculately clean. It was evident that we were going to have a cheerful happy escort.

The Shanghai bankers joined us, two rather drab small men wearing European suits, felt hats, thin leather shoes, inappropriate for cross-country marching, carrying small suitcases containing the remains of their entire possessions. The tall slim girl with them wore peasant clothing, dark blue blouse and black trousers, suitable for the journey, much less likely to draw attention. She carried a bundle, also the pathetic remains of her possessions. They had lost everything on a long journey from Shanghai.

By the time we were all assembled it must have been past three o'clock. Chan did not worry about the late start: he preferred to march under cover of darkness. Waving goodbye to all our friends and to the boy sentry with his large rifle and bayonet at the command hut, we went down the main valley at a fast trot, scarcely pausing for about seven miles. We stopped at a village close to the railway for a rest and food. This was the same village shop in which Douglas had bought cakes and sugar-cane on the way in. If the shopkeeper noticed anything at all, he would have seen that we three were much fatter; the food and cakes in the camp had had their effect. We bought more cakes to take with us.

As it became dark, Chan formed us up for the order of march: two guerrillas leading, Chan, we three, the bankers and the girl, two guerrillas at the end. Thus we advanced into a cold north-east wind and driving rain. It was so dark it was difficult to see more than a yard or so ahead. Each of us had to hold on to the pack of the person in front to prevent getting lost. Travelling in a north-easterly direction, we were crossing the natural run of streams, rivers and pathways, all of which seemed to go from south to north. As we floundered along ribbon-like footways made of walls of mud between rice paddy fields, we slipped and fell every few yards. We fell into rivers, streams and deep ditches. Soon we were wet through, cold and covered with mud. We were three strong and very fit young men and could take it, but the Shanghai bankers and the girl, city people, were having a dreadful time; moreover, they were making a terrible noise, often dropping suitcases into the water, getting far wetter than we were.

'That poor sheila is having a rough go,' said Eddy.

So was Eddy, who had to ask us to wait for him at frequent intervals while he squatted down in the mud.

'Duggie warned you,' I said, kindly.

Chan persisted with the march, trying to get us along. By about midnight, after hours of this desperate struggle, he decided we had suffered enough.

'You sound like a regiment on the march. You are too slow. We must go back and find shelter.'

We retraced our steps, falling into the same treacherous places until we came to a three-storeyed square tower, known as a fighting tower. Built many centuries ago, it was designed to provide protection for travellers who would climb to the third floor, pull up the ladder and remain up there in safety. We did the same, but any guarantee of safety was very dubious. Anyone could shoot bullets through the old wooden floor or light a fire underneath the floor and burn the occupants out. If the Japanese came they would catch us like rats in a trap. Nevertheless, the tower offered shelter from the freezing cold wind and the very wet rain. There was no means of drying our clothes and I do not think any of us had ever been so cold, but it did not dampen our spirits. We laughed and talked with the guerrillas, recalling funny incidents in the march — Douglas fell into a deep hole beside a bund and virtually disappeared: we could not see him, but at last there he was, just a little round, fair-haired head sticking out above the water, a head with an eye-glass still in it! Even the girl, who was very cold and wet, and Eddy, suffering badly from dysentery, joined in the merriment.

At dawn we climbed down the ladder, made a fire outside the tower and dried ourselves. It was still cold but the rain had stopped; the distant mountain peaks were snow-capped. Chan posted two guerrillas as sentries, one up the tower, the other on a hill not far away. The other two, Chu and Tan, opening the ration bags they carried, cooked a rice porridge, '*y-t'iao*', for us over the fire.

The girl and the bankers soon warmed up and dried themselves. I asked how they had come to be in the communist guerrilla camp after their journey from Shanghai. Supposing I was suggesting they had come all the way straight from Shanghai, they laughed and said, 'Oh, no, we left Shanghai more than three years ago, when the Japanese came.' They told me how their house in Shanghai had been destroyed by bombs in the fighting and how they had got away as refugees by sea to Hong Kong, in a small coastal steamer. In Hong Kong they thought they were safe, worked again as bankers, but when the Japanese captured Hong Kong they were driven out, once more refugees. They had lost their possessions in Shanghai, then again in Hong Kong, and finally, from the little that was left, I gathered they were robbed in the New Territories of Hong Kong. The communist guerrillas, the '*yau kik toi'*, had befriended them and taken them to the camp for shelter. Their story was typical of the plight of people whose lives had been ruined by the Japanese.

Chan arranged the order of march for the daylight journey. He sent three guerrillas ahead to act as scouts; Chan led us and the Shanghai people. Chu formed the rearguard. Chan told me that bandits might be a greater danger than Japanese, and that there were large numbers of bandits roving this country-side, on the lookout for refugees. This was why Comrade Wong, the commander, had appointed such a strong escort of five men — 'four,' he said, laughing, 'with nice clean rifles!'

We were away at a jog-trot in the sunshine, making far better progress than last night across carefully cultivated fields. It was now possible to avoid the holes and ditches into which we had fallen in the night.

Before long we had passed the low-lying cultivated country and ascended a pass between rolling hills. Wang, one of the young guerrillas, scaled the higher hill on the left, to guard and watch our progress through the pass. Running down the hill like a mountain goat, he rejoined our column, telling us the hill he had just left was named after him, Wang k'nei ling. Chan told him to stop making silly remarks and ordered him to run up the next hill, this one on the right, the name of which Chan told us was She-tzu-k'eng.

Leaving the pass Chan led us on to an attractive plain, wide open country, almost treeless and uncultivated, stopping eventually about midday at a burnt-out village. A very old man, bent double with arthritis, came to welcome us; this dear old man, his village ruined by the Japanese, the country full of bandits, came out to meet us because it was customary to offer hospitality to travellers. He greeted Chan and the guerrilla soldiers most warmly, straining to look up at them from his perpetually bent position. We were invited to enter the ruins and sit down on the fallen walls in the courtyard. A very old lady, perhaps truthfully not quite as old as she appeared to us young men but nevertheless bent and worn by the terrible hardship of her life, came out of her house with boiled water for us to drink. It was most refreshing. Chan and the guerrillas had brought food and cakes for them. Chan told us their village had been destroyed by the Japanese because these people had befriended the communist guerrillas. Many people had been killed, those who had survived had gone away, except these two old people, who were too old to leave. The old man had been born here: he must be buried here. The guerrillas looked after these two, bringing them food as today. Some of the younger men of the village were also guerrillas.

The old lady returned with more boiling water and filled our cups, adding a green leaf to make delicious tea. We all sat round happily eating cakes which we had bought at the stall near the railway the previous evening. Chan kept two of his men on sentry duty outside the village ruins, interchanging them at times. These young men were remarkable, so well disciplined, so polite. All four were about eighteen or nineteen years of age, all so cheerful, loving their role of escorting the foreigners, showing off a little as they ran up hills to scout out the lie of the land, happy as they sat with us in the courtyard laughing and singing patriotic songs.

We had a long rest with the lovely old couple, partly because they were enjoying our company so much. At last Chan rose, called in the sentries, wished the old couple a happy New Year and set us off on the march again. In the evening we came to a large river and a long lake flooding from it. Delayed a little by Eddy, the bankers and the girl, we marched on into the dark, beyond the black waters of the lake under a clear sky. We came to a village, its great walls looming up against the stars. Voices inside challenged us. Chan gave the password, not too loud, lest someone hiding close by might hear it. There was much talk. Then the guards threw open the huge gates, and we were met with shouts of welcome and '*Goong-hay fat-choy!*'

It was Chinese New Year! The Year of the Horse!

The village had been attacked by Japanese not long ago. Much had been destroyed, including the livestock. Makeshift structures had been erected to keep out the cold and rain. Nevertheless it was warm. An old lady fed the fire with green sticks, clouds of smoke whirling through the place.

The local guerrillas were overjoyed at meeting Comrade

Chan and his gallant men. They were filled with curiosity about us, including us in the shouting and backslapping.

With so few resources, the New Year was still celebrated, though there could be none of the traditional ceremonies – no barrage of fire-crackers to dispel evil spirits and usher in a happy New Year, none of the customary exchanges of gifts, no feasting, no new clothes, and no visits to relatives and friends. All of us, including the guerrillas and the peasants, were victims of Japanese oppression. We had nothing to offer, nor did the inhabitants. The Shanghai girl produced a few sticks of incense, which she lit before a hastily written strip of calligraphy.

Douglas, sensing the poverty and the desire to uphold conventional customs, was curious about the small white bags held by the children. The Shanghai girl explained that they contained flour which the children had probably saved for months to make dumplings for New Year's Day. After eating a dumpling you could make a wish, and everyone must have at least one dumpling, so the dumplings had to be small.

Our attention was taken away from this happy, innocent scene by the raucous demands of the guerrillas, who were now well laced with rice wine, 'sham shui', and were singing patriotic communist songs. With great fervour they sang, 'Arise, who do not wish to be slaves' and, 'We follow our Chairman', the noise of their lustrous voices filling the walls of the ancient stone village. Eddy, joining the fun, was in great form and let his hair down with a succession of remarkably well sung songs, and then the three of us sang very slowly and solemnly, 'The Eton Boating Song'. The Chinese loved it, I never knew why; perhaps it was the tune that got to them. We had encores, they hummed and copied the tune with us, 'Swing, swing to-ge-ther; swing, swing to-ge-ther; we'll still swing to-ge-ther!' It was a tremendous success.

And with all this going on the old lady, weather-beaten, wrinkled and bent with hard work, suddenly produced food, a goose, the only goose left in the village, and rice and vegetables, all beautifully cooked. That meal was miraculous, produced in that ill-lit, half destroyed house. How sad to eat the only remaining goose, their last bit of food. How wonderful for them to provide this hospitality to strangers and travellers, to all the guerrillas as well as us. There was not much to eat, but it was delicious, and Chan added small sweet cakes that his guerrillas had brought with them.

The guerrillas drank more rice wine and went on singing. Perhaps before dawn we would have to gather our few things and flee once more before the Japanese, but for the moment it was sleep. We grabbed blankets from drunken guerrillas and lay together, Douglas in the middle to keep warmer, on a wooden bed with wooden pillows. The incense was still burning. Perhaps this New Year would end the suffering in China, and in the world.

Ironically, Sunday, 15 February 1942, was the very day on which Singapore surrendered, although of course we were not to know of this until much later. This New Year, instead of bringing an end to the suffering, as I had wished, brought unbelievable suffering to the prisoners of war, to those I had left in Hong Kong, and now to the many thousands in Singapore, where the Japanese committed terrible atrocities.

14

Marching to Freedom

It began to get light. The wooden bed was hard and cold. Eddy sat up.

'The fleas and bed bugs have had a feast on good New Zealand blood, imported from Midlothian and Yorkshire. I'm getting up.'

'They've had more of their proper share of Indian, originally good British blood.'

Douglas would not be outdone. 'And far too much of vintage French and English!'

Scratching like a bunch of baboons, we threw the offending blankets onto the guerrillas and hurried through the open gateway to the cold fresh air outside. The village was dirty and smelly, but the fleas were indigenous to the blankets.

Douglas pointed out a shrine at the foot of a large old banyan tree, alight in the first rays of the tropical sun. 'Animism,' he said.

'What is animism, Duggie?'

'I suppose, Ed, it's a primitive belief that natural living or dead things possess an innate soul. The inhabitants are probably Hakka, rather different from those who looked after us in the New Territories, but they hadn't had their village demolished. The people set up these animistic shrines at the foot of certain rocks and trees where spirits are believed to dwell. If you look about you will see these shrines all over the place.'

Chan and Chu came round the corner of the old wall. Chan greeted me in Malay and asked if I had a headache. I had a wonderful understanding with Chan, a '*lai wong*' as it is called, so that we spoke naturally to each other as equals. He used pidgin English whenever his rajah malay became too difficult for me. He was always polite and respectful, called me '*Tuan*', but was never servile. In many ways he resembled the Gurkha, he was honest, natural, loyal and courageous. There was no colour between us, we were two men of almost the same age, two soldiers in fact, only of slightly different pigmentation.

I replied that I did not have a headache. Did he? He said, 'No, nor has Chu, but those other men drink too much and are careless. Chu and I are on guard. The early morning is always the time Japanese or bandits make an attack. This is no place to be drunk and stupid.'

He was a good soldier. I had been wondering if any sentries had been posted. They had all been so happy, so excited about the New Year, so pleased to have the foreigners singing with them, but forgetful of their security, except Chan and Chu.

Wang, Peng and Tan emerged from the battered gateway with their rifles and equipment and blankets in place. They greeted us warmly, Tan trying to hum the smooth waltzing tune of the boating song. They were cheerful and alive. Chan, as a joke, lined them up and inspected their rifles; imitating me looking displeased. They dropped a weighted pull-through down the barrels to clean the rifles, all except Wang, the comic, who pretended to fire a round. He was quickly put in place by Chan.

All this simple humour, this making a joke of me, the meticulous foreigner, reminded me also of the Gurkha soldier; these animated young men had much of the same qualities. For his sins, Wang was sent off to fetch water for the three foreigners to clean up.

The children came out, tiny little creatures in padded clothing, round arms and round legs looking exactly the same length, to offer us each a dumpling. We thanked them, giving the donor a hug to help get over the terror of being so close to a strange foreigner, and ate the dumplings carefully, making our wishes.

'What did you wish?'

'Don't tell him, Tony, it's bad luck,' shouted Douglas.

The children thought it was very funny and laughed because everyone else laughed. These foreigners were most comical. The honourable grandmothers and mothers and first or second aunts and elder brothers and sisters came out to see the cause of the laughter. This gave us the opportunity to thank them for their wonderful hospitality.

Four of the guerrillas whom we met last night emerged to announce they would be marching with us to our first stop, which would be a guerrilla base, a headquarters. They were an untidy, dirty-looking lot. They did not wear red star caps or uniform like our five men, but carried rifles and bands of cartridges across their shoulders. They were older than our four, and tougher. Chan, noticing that I did not welcome them very warmly, said they would be very useful, that there had been trouble with bandits near here yesterday.

Chan was still in command and sent the newly joined men out in front as a screen to act as scouts. The rest of us marched together in a composite bunch, including the Shanghai men and the girl, whom Eddy persisted in calling a 'sheila'.

Douglas said, 'Her name is not Sheila, nothing like that you stupid colonial, you know nothing of Chinese names.'

'I know her name is not Sheila, you pompous pom. "Sheila" is a term for a girl, used by ugly Aussies, not normally by well mannered Kiwis. I shouldn't have used it. I won't again.'

With that short sharp exchange we marched off, waving goodbye to our hosts, the soldiers shouting slogans and singing patriotic songs. As usual we sped along at a trot, over open country and wide ancient pathways, covering the distance very quickly.

After about an hour we came to slightly hilly country. A shot rang out, followed almost immediately by four shots, then four more. Our scouts were firing. Chan told us to get down and take cover and ran forward to find out what was happening. He was soon back. He told us a group of bandits had fired one shot at the scouts, one shot only and then retired.

'That was to make us look to the front,' he said. 'They or some others will come round the back to try and get you.'

He was quite right; behind us another group of bandits

was approaching. The four young men with us had already placed themselves in a good firing position, and Chan joined them to give fire orders. They fired together, all four together, and although the range was rather long the bandits stopped. Chan repeated the volleys twice and then ordered us to continue the march. Oddly, the bandits never returned the fire.

With Chu and the others keeping a watch to, our rear, we hurried on towards a village on the sky line, which turned out to be the guerrilla base. Passing sentries posted well out from the village, we walked into the centre and were welcomed by an elderly guerrilla soldier. Word about us had gone ahead. Immediately he asked for the doctor. A guerrilla had been badly injured by bandits. Douglas went straight to their small improvised hospital. He was with the man for about two hours, and came out looking white and drawn, smelling of chloroform, saying the man had been shot in the stomach. He had done all he could but there was not much hope. Douglas offered to stay with the man, but Chan was opposed to this, and the elderly soldier said the Red Army girl nurses could look after him. We had been given a meal while Douglas was operating, but he did not want anything to eat now.

'It's a pity that we fight among ourselves,' said Chan. 'We have to look out for hostile bandits as well as Japanese.'

We passed through the large market village of Pingshan, where every house had been destroyed. The Japanese had left the place only a few days before. Charred houses were still smouldering. Guerrillas were clearing Japanese earthworks, bunkers, trenches and fox holes — quite why I could not understand. They would have been useful to withstand another Japanese attack.

We marched on, how many miles I had no idea, but we covered about four miles an hour and seldom stopped. I had always liked marching in the army and I was enjoying these marches. Douglas and Eddy kept up well, never complaining of the pace or the lack of halts. The Shanghai people struggled along.

In the evening we arrived at Ki-keuk, a small unwalled and

impoverished village of stone houses with picturesque roofs. Strips of calligraphy hung in doorways, and there was the smell of incense burning. After a basic meal of rice and vegetables, we were given a bed of hard wooden boards with rough porcelain pillows, but to our joy, '*meintois*', Chinese eiderdowns, to keep us really warm.

In the morning there seemed to be some hitch about continuing the march. We did not mind. We could do with a rest. We were enjoying ourselves. We lazed about all day, sitting in the warm winter sun. Walking to a tea shack, we bought delicious fly-covered cakes and drank tea and hot water and ate more sweetmeats; not that we were hungry, rather that it was an opportunity to talk to people who were curious and friendly, yet astonished that one spoke Cantonese like a girl, the other addressed all his conversation in Malay through his Malayan-Chinese friend, while the third man, dressed in blue uniform, unshaven but not as ugly as the other two foreigners, spoke in English and was easily understood by those who spoke pidgin.

It was fun talking to them all, mainly old men and women and children. They had suffered so much in the last three and a half years of Japanese occupation, but their spirits were high because at last there had been a military success. The Japanese had advanced and attacked and occupied Waichow, but had been driven out by the Chinese National Army, unfortunately not before the Japanese had committed vile atrocities and destroyed many buildings. Attacked on all sides by communist guerrillas, the Japanese had withdrawn from places like Pingshan. This was interesting news. If we had arrived earlier we might have been caught up in the fighting, or we might have been forced to make a long detour eastwards to reach the East River.

Next day, starting early, we marched through safe open country, long stretches of moorland, with only a few villages, generally white-walled and scattered over the countryside. There were no bandits. The houses began to look slightly different, the roofs with a more pronounced turn-up at each end, the tiles a beautiful deep blue. We stopped once at an old

Buddhist temple. A monk in saffron gown, disagreeable in appearance and with a sour face, was reluctant to let us enter. Chan wished to proceed, not wanting our presence known too widely. We never learnt the name of the temple or the god it enshrined.

Later, we climbed over a huge humped-back bridge, many centuries old, spanning a wide river, the headwaters of which arose in those beautiful Wu Tung mountains. Again there were cries of, 'Bridge with three men, if not four' — Chan being the fourth this time.

In the late evening we stopped at a school to shelter from the extreme cold. Chan seemed worried about something and not inclined to enter the town of Tamsui, or to get any food. We were too close to the Chinese National Army for his liking. If taken by them he would be shot. So we stayed in the school for the night without food. To keep warm we broke up a school desk and lit a fire with it.

Chan told us he would leave us in the morning; he must return to the camp, but Chu and Tan would guide us until we made contact with the Chinese National Army. They would lead us round Tamsui, not into it, because the town gates were guarded by police who might be unfriendly and delay us. However, the Shanghai bankers and the girl wished to enter the town, so we parted. They had survived the journey well, unsuited as they were for such a passage. The girl said she hoped the dumplings would bring good luck.

I asked Chan what he would do now. He had intended to return to Malaya, but this was impossible now that Hong Kong had fallen. He would stay with the communists in China. In Malaya, he said his group would be working with the British forces. None of us knew, of course, that Singapore had fallen.

Early the next morning, as we were getting ready to leave the school house, an angry man, the schoolmaster, abused us for using a school desk as firewood. Douglas and I pretended we could not understand and left him to Eddy, who got into great difficulties, and eventually gave him $20 Chinese to pay for the damage. That settled the schoolmaster, but Eddy, very annoyed at being left to face the music, grumbled and sulked. It made me realise how tired we were.

We set off, sad to part from Comrade Tuan Chan, who had led us so courageously and who had been our companion for so long; sad also to know that the gallant Comrades Tan and Chu would not travel much further with us. This meant, in fact, that our association with the Red Army, and all those remarkable and brave people we had been so fortunate to be with since meeting Percy, had now come to an end.

Tan and Chu pointed out a pass in the hills into which our road ran, saying that they could come no further; beyond the pass we would find the Chinese National Army. We said goodbye with emotion, and watched the pair turn and trot away, two figures gradually diminishing into the vastness of China, two rifles, two rolled up blankets on their backs, the last I remember of them.

We were alone again, the three of us stepping along the winding dirt road, striving to cross that mythical bridge to freedom, wondering what would be in store for us when we met the Chinese Nationalists, the Kuomintang Army.

15

Celebrations

The pass, a cleft in two rounded hills covered in brushwood and stunted forest growth, was an insignificant feature on the skyline, apparent only because of the vivid blue backdrop of the tropical sky. It was surprising that this diminutive pass should be the boundary between communist guerrillas and the national army, a frontier dividing ideologies, separating the Chinese people. It was pernicious that this old civilisation, once the Celestial Kingdom, should again be torn apart by a political catalyst.

However, to me the rugged pass intensified a sublime sensation of relaxation and pure happiness. Inside me my spirit sang; it was the inspiration caused by being free, free not only from the Japanese but from inhibitions that had confined my life, shackled by stringent rules. I was liberated, emancipated, now rushing to cross the pass to real freedom.

Almost as soon as we reached the summit of the pass and gazed upon the luxurious green valley below us, we saw in the distance two men, one descending from a telegraph pole. They came to meet us, armed with rifles, dressed in khaki-drill jacket and long trousers, with caps not dissimilar to those of our Red Army friends. They halted in front of us and, surprisingly, saluted. It may have been Eddy's blue airforce uniform that induced the salute, or perhaps it was just natural Chinese politeness.

Douglas, acknowledging their salute, explained who we were, from where we had come. The two soldiers, who wore private, first class, badges of rank and signallers' flashes, expressed no surprise at all. They seemed at first to accept the situation as if meeting escaped European prisoners-of-war was an everyday occurrence. Perhaps it was a Chinese custom not to show emotion, to accept surprises stoically. Perhaps they did not understand Douglas's Cantonese, or, more likely, were too shy to respond.

At last, after a long pause, they burst out, speaking to each other, both at the same time. They were deciding what to do with us and what to say.

'We are the National Army. Welcome!' they said eventually in Cantonese. 'Come, we take you to our headquarters, many li from here.'

It was an occasion of great moment for us. At last we had made contact with the Chinese National Army, our major aim from the start. This time we refrained from handshaking. The closeness of the two unemotional soldiers, as yet unfriendly, restrained us, which was very odd, since we were now really in Free China, even protected by an armed escort.

However, as we walked along, this time at our own pace, not at a guerrilla's jog-trot, the two young men overcame their shyness and asked innumerable questions, began to laugh and enjoy themselves thoroughly. For them, this meeting with the strange, bearded, dishevelled foreigners was probably one of the most amusing experiences of their lives as down-trodden conscripts in the army. The incident would be sure to gain them much face. They would dine out on it over their chopsticks and army chow for many a day. We now had a happy, friendly escort.

Douglas discovered that 'many li' meant about fifteen miles; not much after all the long distances we were now so used to covering in a single day, although the route was not so easy here. The main road having been destroyed, we wandered along crooked pathways through paddy and vegetable fields, so delaying our progress. One of the soldiers decided to leave us and run on ahead to give warning of our arrival. We continued our relaxed journey through the beautiful fertile and rich valley, sometimes following the course of a wide sparkling river. A few arctic warblers, migrating from

Northern Norway, sheltered in the rushes, and pelicans fished in the marshes. Suddenly we arrived at the army base.

The army headquarters was established in a delightful, Mandarin's house, surrounded by well kept walled gardens, with lychee and orange trees and groves of larger ornamental trees. The sentries at the main gates gave us a rifle butt salute as we were led into the inner courtyard. Standing on whitewashed steps, between two magnificent deep blue pillars, stood the splendid figure of what could only be the Commanding Officer, tall, good-looking, very smart in a beautifully tailored grey uniform, highly polished belt, automatic pistol in a holster, and wearing white kid-gloves.

He shouted at us in French, abrasively in a harsh voice, saying he was Major Goh Guan Ho, the Commanding Officer. Douglas, who had spent much time on the south coast of France, replied immediately in French.

'How are you, Monsieur le Commandant. We are officers of Britain, escaped from the Japanese in Hong Kong. We place ourselves in your hands!'

The Major was astonished, amazed to be addressed in faultless French. Almost at once his surprise turned to delight. He rushed forward to greet us most warmly, saying, 'Welcome, welcome to the Chinese National Army,' speaking in an educated Parisian accent. He was obviously very pleased to meet someone who spoke French so well.

With great charm, treating us as if he was proud to care for us as guests of his nation, he ushered us into a comfortable waiting-room, congratulating us on having escaped from the Japanese, and asking immediately numerous questions about the actual escape from the prison camp and the subsequent journey. We were careful to say little about the guerrillas and communists, except that they helped us, fed us and led us courageously through the Japanese-occupied territory. All the questions were asked by Major Goh. He was in complete charge. Two other officers were also present with us in the waiting-room, dressed in clean but drab field uniforms; they seemed terrified of the Major. In turn they were ignored, not even introduced to us.

Hot tea and cakes were brought in by an orderly and Goh changed the subject to talk about France with Douglas. He was a graduate of the École Militaire, he informed us, but his real love seemed to be Paris. Fortunately Douglas knew Paris well, so the two got on like wildfire.

It was an unreal situation, sitting here in this lovely house, listening to Goh and Douglas talking French, close to the battle lines of war-torn China, so soon after the primitive existence we had been experiencing recently. It was an amazing situation and lucky that Douglas was such a good linguist. Goh might have been difficult to get on with. As it was he addressed us only in French, never in English. He ridiculed, in a jovial convivial manner, Douglas's Cantonese, saying it was 'brothel Cantonese'.

Eventually our unwashed odour must have been too much for the Major, who called for barbers to cut our hair and shave us and orderlies to prepare hot water baths. The shaving with cut-throat razor was painful and terrifying, the razor wielded by a vicious-looking feudal serf; the scissors were blunt, but it was a great relief to be clean-shaven and to have short hair again.

We took it in turns to have the hot bath, Douglas first because he was four years older than I, I went next, being three years older than Eddy. A stupid idea, but precedence was only a joke with us. The bath was a great big porcelain Soochow tub, into which the orderlies poured piping hot water. I felt like the Mandarin, the obviously First Class Mandarin who had owned this house in better times and who bathed in this beautiful bath. I wallowed in sheer luxury, so wonderful to be in hot water, and with soap, a funny kind of Chinese soap, but still soap, and finally clean towels with which to dry. I felt terrific. It was wonderful to be clean, even if I had to put on my dirty old blood-stained clothes again.

The Major was obviously pleased with our improved appearance, Eddy looking handsome and Douglas debonair, monocle shining in place. However, he was concerned with my bound-up wounded hand and with Eddy, whose delicate condition had been explained to Goh by Douglas. An officer was ordered to take us to the medical section. Here Eddy was given pills and a medical orderly cleaned up my cuts, put black-coloured ointment on them and re-bound the hand. During all the journey from Hong Kong, at least from Tai Po, near where I was wounded, Douglas had looked after me with great care, washing the wounds with potassium permanganate and keeping them clean. I was therefore reluctant to have a Chinese Army medical orderly dress the wounds, but it was a kind gesture and I could not refuse.

When Eddy and I got back to the Major and Douglas, we noticed that they had already got stuck into the rice wine; both were flushed in the face, both enjoying themselves immensely, telling each other some very funny jokes. It seemed so utterly incongruous that we should now be drinking wine with a Chinese officer, enjoying French jokes, that we laughed the more. Our laughter was so infectious that Goh laughed throughout the whole evening. He ordered a very special dinner, wonderfully cooked, superb rice, vegetables, pork, frogs' legs and other dishes. We drank to the New Year, to the Year of the Horse, to good luck. Douglas, the intellectual, was also able to impress the Major in slightly more sober moments with his wide knowledge of French artists and writers, so much so that Goh asked us to stay another day; fortunately we declined. Goh had treated us handsomely, but despite his charm and education, he was conceited, and showed a distinct streak of brutality in his dealings with his officers and staff. I would not have liked to stay with him too long.

It was a remarkable evening, a celebration at having escaped from the prison camp and got through the Japanese lines. We retired to warm wooden beds with thick *meintois* to cover us. It was such a luxury to have a bed each.

We were invited to stay on for the morning meal, noodles and dumplings and other things. In daylight, we watched the staff at their work in the headquarters. It was clear to see that everyone was terrified of Major Goh. He was the only one dressed in especially smart uniform, with a well-cut jacket buttoned right up to the neck, and wearing white kid-gloves and a smart peaked cap.

The headquarters was not a happy place, though it was interesting to see a man so completely in command; everyone jumped to his orders instantly, and the discipline was severe. Although he had obviously enjoyed himself last night the Major regarded it as his duty to provide hospitality for us; we would be a nuisance if we stayed longer. Thanking him profusely for his lavish hospitality, we said goodbye. He seemed a little hungover and quite pleased to see us go. An escort of two armed soldiers had been ordered already. The guard turned out at the main gate and gave us a full salute, accompanied by a bugle call. We acknowledged the salute and set off.

We walked very slowly, stiff from all the marching of the last week, suffering also from headaches. As we walked we talked about Goh.

'Oh! He was a dangerous character, wasn't he?' said Eddy. 'Those white kid-gloves terrified me. They reminded me of the senior Japanese officers. Do you remember, the commandant in the prison camp, Colonel Tokunaga, wore white gloves like Goh?'

'Yes, it's a custom in the Chinese Army, for senior officers,' I said, 'Chiang Kai-shek went to a military school in Japan. He probably introduced white gloves into his officer corps.'

'That's right,' said Douglas, 'Goh was one of Chiang's élite corps of graduates from Whangpoo Military Academy. They are said to be ruthless. They run the Chinese Army.'

It seemed strange that such a talented officer should be at this outpost. I assumed this was because the Japanese had been driven out of Waichow so recently. Goh would be there for a few days only. We all agreed that the headquarters was vastly different from the communist guerrilla camp; Goh's soldiers did not sing. Perhaps it was as well that they did not try. 'Arise, who do not wish to be slaves', would hardly have gone down well in that place.

However, we were now at last on our way to Waichow, well fed, shaved, hair cut, bathed. Our two scruffy-looking soldiers were delighted to be out of the headquarters and to go along with us, if only because their charges gave them considerable stature. They would shout out to all the passers-by, informing them who we were. Douglas interpreted their comments about us as being rude and obscene, but we did not care.

Despite the fresh cold winter air, and the beauty of the gums and willows lining the road, it was not an easy march. The highway was paved with enormous blocks of limestone, a road along which you could imagine chariots of officials of former dynasties, the Sung or Ming dynasties, and elaborately uniformed cavalrymen making their way to the Imperial Courts in Peking. This was, in fact, a very important highway in Imperial days, leading from the great city of Canton all the way up the east coast of China through large cities such as Amoy, Foochow, and northwards to Peking. Now the road was in a very poor state, destroyed in many parts, and bridges demolished, so that we kept wandering about in digressions, crossing temporary bridges spanning tributary torrents from the hills, or crossing rivers by ferry.

After all the walking in the last weeks, frequently at a trot, trying to keep up with our guerrilla guides and their eternal rhythmic step, my calf muscles had bound up into painful knots. The same had happened to Eddy and Douglas. Nevertheless, as an infantryman, I was determined to enter Waichow walking on my two feet, as was Eddy, to exhibit the superiority of the Royal New Zealand Air Force. Douglas, however, complained of a torn cartilage in his knee. As a doctor, he should know. Eventually he succumbed to the temptation of a bicycle, riding on the back, legs sticking out sideways, looking ridiculous. He paid the driver handsomely.

The so-called highway was fairly well frequented by travellers, so that stalls had been set up at frequent intervals to sell cakes and tea and hot water. Our passage was considerably delayed by these stalls, where we fed ourselves and shouted refreshments to the two soldier escorts and the bicycle driver.

Late in the afternoon we arrived at the gates of Waichow.

16

Giant Pagoda

Our two youthful soldiers led us proudly through the massive gates of the city, shouting out that their charges were foreign military officers. They drew the attention of groups of soldiers lounging about smoking and expectorating. Many took intense interest in us, following us and asking questions. Even with these army conscripts from all parts of China, most of whom must have seen many foreigners, it was impossible to escape from the innate inquisitiveness of the Chinese people. Except for soldiers and old men there were only a few women and children about, and those there were seemed to be mainly refugees. As with the conscripts, our arrival caused a stir among the refugees, pathetic homeless groups of people, giving rise to more banter from our two escorts, so that we proceeded through the streets of rubble of this badly damaged city like a procession of conquering heroes, followed by a considerable mob.

We came to the Office of the Military Governor, a dilapidated grey stone building, its top storeys destroyed by bombing. The escort led us into a waiting room crowded with refugees with their innumerable small bundles of possessions. With an awesome show of authority our two privates, first class, requested the people to make way for the auspicious foreigners. A soldier clerk came through the mob and was handed a letter from Major Goh. We were asked to wait a few minutes, long enough for our two young men to explain in detail the reason for our presence to an attentive audience, many of whom made frequent exclamations of surprise. I never knew what was told of us; it must have been a good story. Our escorts were determined to make the very best of the last few minutes with us, but then the clerk soldier returned and invited us to enter the Governor's office. Our escort saluted, said goodbye very reluctantly, their day of great importance ended.

The Governor, a small and fat gentleman in an ill-fitting loose khaki field uniform, quite different in every possible way from the appearance of our Major Goh, received us most affably. He was courteous and pleasant, and asked no questions. Looking down at the letter from Major Goh, he congratulated us most warmly for escaping from the Japanese. This praise had now become almost universal with everyone we met. It seemed that the Chinese took great pleasure in the fact that by escaping we had brought derision upon the Japanese, the enemy they hated so much. It was evident that the Governor was very pleased to receive us and was enjoying the meeting. Like the other Chinese people who had cared for us, he treated us as special guests. He said he would arrange for us to continue our journey by travelling in a boat up the East River. He gave Douglas a bundle of Chinese money, told us to report the next day, and sent for a guide to take us to the Italian Catholic Mission, where we would be given a bed.

At the Mission we were taken to a Chinese priest, Father Ma, dressed in long brown gown and leather sandals. He had a lovely round fat, smooth face full of humour, kindness and compassion. He welcomed us with great warmth, smiling all over his pleasant face, his bald head bobbing up and down with pleasure. He was an immediate friend. We all loved him. We explained briefly how we happened to be here. He seemed to know already for in this land a thousand eyes are always watching and news spreads quickly.

Father Ma took us to the St Joseph's Hospital and introduced us to a Chinese nun, a sister in charge of a ward. The hospital was full of sick and wounded people, and there were no real beds with mattresses for us, but she found us a flat wooden bed, big enough for the three of us, normally used for outpatients on a verandah of the hospital, well away from the sick patients. The sister, dressed in long white dress and the conventional head-dress that nuns wear, found us a spare blanket. Her little Chinese face was particularly beautiful under her head covering. She had a very sweet smile, but was smiling at us in shyness and embarrassment because she could not find us proper beds and only one blanket. She was very polite, treating us again as if it was her special duty and responsibility to look after us. Douglas tried to explain that we were used to any kind of primitive existence and could not say how grateful we were for a wooden bed and one blanket. His kind of Cantonese did not go down at all well in a Catholic hospital. The sister forgot her shyness and embarrassment at once and shrieked and shrieked with laughter, filling the ward with her shouts. Immediately, other nun nurses ran in to find out what was happening, and joined the sister in the hilarity, tears running down her face as she told each nun what Douglas had said, or tried to say.

The situation was getting out of hand. Father Ma, hearing the joyous laughter in a very sad hospital, came to see what was going on and joined in the laughter also. He suggested that we might like to celebrate our arrival in Waichow by going out to dinner in a restaurant. The charming old rogue had arranged a marvellous feast for us in the best restaurant in the city; only a few existed, in fact, but this one had survived the Japanese attacks. We sat at a superb round table, the delicious food placed in the centre for each person to take what he wanted. There also appeared a huge jar of rice wine. My diary says, 'We had an excellent meal — it cost $93.' A strange item to record. The money, of course, came from the wad given us by the Governor, who probably suggested that Ma should arrange the banquet.

We must have been very merry for me to start hitting Ma on his priestly head with my chopsticks. I do remember how much the reverend Father had laughed at funny stories about our journey, at Douglas's Cantonese, at the encounter in the hospital with the pretty nun.

The Father explained in a serious moment that early in the Sino-Japanese war the mouth of the Pearl River had been blocked by the Japanese navy, cutting Canton off from all shipping. Waichow, then a grand old city of more than 100,000 people, became an important river port, importing goods overland from Hong Kong, and one of the major sources for the supply of war materials into China. Later, the city suffered much damage from bombing. Following an amphibious assault at Bias Bay, Waichow was occupied by the Japanese for nearly three years, during which they committed vile atrocities and destruction. The troops were withdrawn for the invasion of Hong Kong, but after its fall, troops on the loose, with nothing else to do, advanced towards Waichow, plundering and sacking the countryside on the way, eventually re-occupying the city. During their disorderly advance they were ambushed and attacked frequently by communist guerrillas, so that their numbers were much depleted when they reached Waichow, making it easy for the National Army to repulse them and for the guerrillas to inflict further casualties.

Our dinner party was interrupted by the intrusion of a small fellow wearing thick spectacles, who was introduced as the communist party representative, and a strong thick-set man, who was said to be a guerrilla leader. I was surprised that communists were free to enter Waichow; I thought they would not come beyond the pass where we had met the two soldiers in the National Army. Seeing our astonishment they explained that as a result of a truce between the communists and the Kuomintang, communists were now represented in the central government in Chungking. In small places, bordering on communist controlled territories, limited representation was permitted. They were the only communists officially recognised and permitted in Waichow.

The communist party representative was a scholarly individual, rather like our old friend Comrade Captain Lee in appearance, who said he had received many messages about us and had followed our progress with interest. Douglas told him how much we appreciated all the help we had been given by the guerrillas, which was well received. The guerrilla leader then told us that our encounter with the guerrillas had caused much amusement.

'Who was it that made them clean their rifles so much? Who is the singer? Who is the doctor?' We owned up to our various crimes. He then said, 'You are much respected for the help you gave our comrades, I congratulate you.'

Father Ma, who was translating all this, beamed all over his jovial round face, and clapped. We were embarrassed. Then the guerrilla leader asked us to sing a song, 'The song Comrade Chan liked.' It must have been the boating song. We hummed the tune, but we did not feel like singing it. There was too much tragedy and suffering in this city to sing; there was even a palpable smell of death about the place.

Almost as suddenly as our visitors had appeared, they disappeared again into the night – a night blacked-out against air-raids. It was astonishing what these two men knew about us. All the messages had travelled by word of mouth, for there was no other means of communication. It was dangerous that so much information had been spread around about us. A traitor or a spy could well have picked it up.

Dear Father Ma brought us back to our previous discussion, continuing with the recent events in Waichow. Because of the casualties and disgrace the Japanese had suffered by being repulsed in Waichow, a very strong column had re-entered the city, and in an act of revenge and rage had committed the most dreadful atrocities on the people and destroyed much of the beautiful city. Most of the women and children and young men had evacuated the city ahead of the Japanese, but those who had remained had been slaughtered, tortured or maimed. A few of the survivors were now in St Joseph's Hospital. Some of the dead were still in demolished buildings.

The Father's expressive face showed deep signs of anxiety and sadness as he told us these things, but he became more cheerful when he explained that again the Chinese National Army had driven the enemy out of the city and once more they had been attacked constantly during the withdrawal by the communist guerrillas; in fact by our gallant Comrade Captain Wong and his troops. This was the fighting that had been taking place while we were resting in the communist guerrilla camp.

It was time for bed. After a final '*um-sing*', a sort of night-cap, we scrambled in the dark over the rubble and broken street surfaces back to the hospital, to the comfort and safety of our wooden bed, and one thin blanket, for both of which we were very grateful.

I woke at first light. It was cold on the open verandah. The one thin blanket had got itself wrapped firmly round Douglas, who was asleep, as was Eddy on the other side. I did not know the time, for the robbers had taken my watch, but I knew it was a Friday. I got up and washed and walked about the hospital grounds.

I met the sister, walking elegantly towards me. In the dawn light her handsome face under her hood was strikingly beautiful. She asked if I were coming to Mass. I followed her through the gardens to the Mission Chapel, a graceful building, the interior of resplendent beauty. Father Ma was there.

'I am not a Catholic,' I said. 'I pretend to be a Christian. May I come to Mass?'

He replied, 'Of course, Anthony, we welcome you.'

I knelt in the tiny wooden pew made for Chinese people, too small for me, and thanked God for my deliverance from the Japanese and other dangers. The little nuns sang and chanted beautifully to an old organ played by an elderly nun. I returned refreshed to my sinful companions.

Later we looked round the city. It must once have been a beautiful place, with many lakes, and pagodas placed on tree-covered islands, especially a giant pagoda, to protect us from evil. A humped-back bridge, slightly damaged, spanned the water between the island and the main shore. Douglas could not resist drawing attention to it: 'A willow pattern bridge with three men, if not four.' This time the fourth was the genial brown-gowned Father Ma, who was showing us round. There always seemed to be a fourth when the willow pattern bridge came to mind — brave Percy Davis, gallant Comrade Chan, and now jovial Ma.

Having stood Ma a morning meal at a stall, we reported to the Governor. This benevolent gentleman explained that the boat journey would take a few days and that we would have to feed ourselves. He gave us a chit to draw a sack of rice from the Government food store, more money to buy food on the way and finally tickets for the boat. He was concerned for our safety as well as our welfare.

'Look out for youself all the time. Plenty pirates on river, plenty robbers in village.'

'Any Japanese?' I asked.

'Not very likely, but maybe.'

Well, we were warned. Father Ma had told us that the Japanese were in residence at the large town of Sheklung, only 40 miles west of us, and of course they had a large garrison in Canton, 100 miles westward; so they could at any time make a thrust into the East River valley, foraging and pillaging, there being few reliable Chinese National Army troops in this area. As for robbers, we were already well acquainted with them, but pirates would be a new experience.

Douglas went back to St Joseph's Hospital to help with the sick and spent the day there, telling us later of the horror of the wounds inflicted by the Japanese on the people, especially on the women and children. He said that even though the Japanese had not looted the Italian mission, only because Italy was in the war on the side of Germany, the hospital was dreadfully short of medical supplies and that they had to improvise in every possible way. He said he had done the job of many different specialities, even as an orthopaedic at times. He had worked and talked in Italian to the Italian missionary doctor. Care of the sick transcended national antagonism.

Meanwhile, Eddy and I had been getting the Governor's chit for rice honoured, and extracting the sack from a feudal Mandarin type of official; 'petty bourgeois' the communists would have called him. Bystanders collected, filled with curiosity, ever-ready with advice and questions. Having discovered we were going to sail up the river in a boat, many of the by-standers accompanied us to the floating pontoon, alongside which was our boat, or rather, a barge, a long flat-bottomed river barge. I greeted the coxswain in my best Chinese.

'*Ni hao? Ni hao?* How do you do?'

He answered very politely in pidgin, inviting us aboard, enquiring if we had tickets. He said the boat was full already, mostly Hong Kong refugees, but that he would squeeze us in. We could not sail today, he told us, because the motor boat that towed us needed engine repairs, but we would leave at dawn tomorrow and must come aboard this evening to claim our space on the deck.

The motor boat was tied up alongside the barge. Its engine, a Ford V8 car engine, had been completely stripped down by two mechanics, who were being advised by a small crowd of onlookers. It was obvious that we would not sail today, which suited us perfectly.

The coxswain gave us three rattan mats on which to sleep and allowed us to hire three *meintois* to keep us warm, which I accepted and paid for at once. The boat seemed to have about forty people on it already, but a fat girl we had met at the Government food store, who was also a passenger on the boat, showed us a space big enough to sit down, where we left our mats and *meintois*. She and her three companions, a girl and two young men, university students, said they would look after our things for us. Eddy and I then went off to collect Douglas and Father Ma for another evening meal, this time not quite so lavish in quantity or liquidity.

Back on board, we stepped over the legs of sleeping passengers, shown up by the light of an acetylene lamp, and squatted down in our reserved spaces for the night. There was not enough room to lie flat and the *meintois* were flea and bug ridden, but we had a little supply of rice wine surreptitiously imported by Douglas; we were warm, a little drunk, very happy and looking forward to the next episode of our adventure.

17

Swing, Swing Together

All night the mechanics worked on the engine of the motor boat under an acetylene lamp. By dawn, they had it chugging away on charcoal gas and cast off with a good deal of shouting, towing the barge against the fast-running current of the East River. The giant pagoda in Waichow, shining in the morning sun, diminished into the distance. So began the eleven-day journey up this great river, with its many junks and sampans, some sailing, some pulled along by men from the towpath.

Without exception our fellow passengers were refugees from Hong Kong, intelligent and cultured people, probably once wealthy and established, now with their only remaining possessions stacked in bundles beside them. They were travelling in war-torn China to get away from the Japanese, in the hope of finding refuge with relatives, fearful of the terrible poverty and the austere wartime conditions they would have to face. They talked freely to us about the trades and professions they followed, and about their children, beautiful children with little round faces, deep brown eyes and black straight hair, now a little bewildered and frightened at all the strange happenings they had been through recently.

Food was cooked by the crew on a charcoal fire in the stern of the vessel. As the engine in the motor boat broke down frequently, we spent a good deal of time tied up alongside villages or small hamlets, from which we bought oranges and tangerines and fly-covered cakes. Because of the Japanese blockade of supply routes, imported engine parts were unobtainable, and these had to be improvised out of junk iron to keep us going. So slow was our progress that some passengers left to walk along the main road which followed the course of the river, making more space for those left on board. We did not mind how slowly we travelled for we had no special need to get anywhere quickly. Besides, regular sorties ashore became a necessity for Eddy, who still suffered from dysentery. Without these stops he would be forced to attend the public latrine at the stern, which consisted of two separated planks overhanging the water. I was never game enough to have a go, or to watch how it was done. There was nothing to hold on to, nothing to stop you doing a back roll into the water from a very insecure squatting position. I much preferred the fields, a habit I learnt in India as a child. In towns the Chinese public lavatories were indescribable, but I discovered that the 'ladies' were a little better than the 'gents', so I always used the ladies, regardless of the scathing ridicule hurled at me.

The river turned from east to north-east in direction at a distinctive bend where stood the Temple of the Goddess of Mercy, Kwun Yam. It was here that the boat's crew, who acted also as armed guards, were put on the alert because this very wide stretch of river was notoriously infested by pirates. Even after payment of protection money, we were safe only from river pirates. If we happened to become stranded through engine failure we would be easy prey for local robbers.

As evening approached, we sailed into the small town of Kwaisin and tied up for the night. The coxswain paid protection money to the town chief and also to the pirates, and we went ashore. Our appearance caused a great stir, as did our smell and our large feet. The whole town was filled with cries of 'Come and see, come and see the ugly foreign devils.' It was an unpleasant town, so we retired to the boat to spend the evening playing bridge with the university students, the small well-rounded girl having taken a fancy to our handsome Eddy. Later the students joined Eddy in a number of songs, and finally, as a nightcap, Douglas, Eddy and I sang slowly and solemnly 'The Eton Boating Song'. Again, it went down with acclamation; we taught the words to the students, and henceforth we were all swinging together up the East River. A warm south wind had started to blow, unlike the icy north-easters we had encountered so often on the march. There was little shelter from the wind on board, though a hood of rattan on a bamboo frame kept some of the rain off.

The fourth day on the river was very pleasant, warm and sunny. We tied up at many pretty villages, where houses many centuries old remained intact, beyond the main threat of Japanese invasion. We went ashore, causing intense curiosity among the peasant people. We bought more cakes and oranges and sugar-cane. Often we met in these villages the Hoklo people, traditionally boat-dwellers, an ancient race that had been in this area from earliest times, possibly before the Cantonese and the Hakka people came into the region. The crew on our boat were Hoklos − lean, haggard, grim and desolate-looking, the men immensely muscular. They spoke their own distinctive dialect of Cantonese: Douglas was incapable of understanding them.

At this stage of the journey the river became narrower and sandbanks were frequent. On the bends small pagodas stood, as sentinels against the evil spirits, and to warn the voyagers of the presence of sandbanks. In the evening, as the motor boat towed us towards one of these pagodas, skilfully avoiding sandbanks, a number of small craft set out from the east bank of the river, following us and closing in. The passengers became agitated, their shrill Cantonese voices rising to a crescendo, like a shrieking bunch of galahs. The rugged Hoklo crew grabbed their old and rusty rifles, loaded them with a round up the spout, and took up position on the running-boards amidships. With the Ford V8 engine at full throttle, we turned and drove towards the shore, straight at a small village. The pirates in the small craft began shouting at us and firing rifle shots into the air, but the gallant engine increased the gap between us and them. Villagers were now lining the bank, cheering and waving, some firing off guns, just to increase the clamour and turbulence. The excitement was so intense that at first I was not perturbed, but the passengers, particularly the women and small children, were utterly terrified. Douglas, seeing their anxiety, scrambled along the deck, quietening hysterical mothers, gathering small creatures into his arms. They rushed to him and clung to him.

Suddenly the barge ran aground, and the motor-boat engine spluttered and chugged ever harder, the propeller splashing the water into foam, leaving us immobile and stranded. As the pirates closed in, our guards opened fire with rifles and Mauser pistols. There was shouting and yelling and more screams from the passengers. I prayed earnestly to a graceful pagoda standing on a hill nearby. I saw sampans from the village approaching us, full of armed men. In a moment, they had boarded the barge, crossed the crowded deck and opened fire on the pirates, now at very close range. The increased fire was altogether too much for the pirates, who turned about and fled downstream.

We were saved! Or, had the barge now been captured by the village ruffians? Whichever was the case, there was a great sigh of relief from the beleaguered passengers. Amidst much talking, shouting and noise, the punt-poles were taken up and the crew, helped by the villagers, started to pole the barge off the sandbank and into the village, to be tied up to the bank.

The coxswain and the master in the motor boat went ashore with the armed village men. We three and the four university students followed to see what was happening. They were led to the entrance of an opium den, where the village chief met them and took them in. From the look of the chief, the glazed yellow skin, the bleary hooded eyes and the set of his gaunt body, he was clearly an opium smoker.

We crossed the paved courtyard to a tea house opposite the opium den, where we drank hot sour tea and ate fly-infested cakes. The students said the village chief would claim that they had salvaged the motor boat and barge; if the pirates had got us, all the passengers would have been robbed. Double protection money would now have to be paid. We would not know the outcome until the opium den conference finished. The students thought all passengers would be called on to pay a levy. They believed also that the whole thing was a big swindle, that the pirates and villagers were probably in league with each other, that the crew might even be in it also, that those people were all Hoklos, boat dwellers, all related. They emphasised that although there was a lot of shooting, no one seemed to have been hit.

We sat on benches at a dirty wooden table, talking. We had got to know the fat girl, May-may, the two men students, and Peh-gek, the other girl, quite well. Despite the peasant-type clothing she wore, Peh-gek was very attractive, slim and tall for a Chinese girl, with sensuous curves and delicate hands, a lovely oval face with creamy satin-like skin and deep brown eyes. She was utterly feminine. She told me in a high-pitched musical voice that she intended to continue her university studies in Szechwan, where she had relatives. She could speak a little Szechwanese. The others, especially May-may, said Peh-gek had no chance of entering a university; all were overcrowded, were not emancipated like the Hong Kong university and seldom admitted women. This hurt Peh-gek. I was sorry for her. I tried to comfort her by telling her she was beautiful. She smiled, looked at me demurely, then laughed. At this time a woman had very little place in Chinese society. Even here in the south you could see women whose feet had been bound, and how deprived and subservient to men they were. Madame Chiang Kai-shek's 'New Life movement', which was intended to improve the status of women, had had little effect. In fact, the position of a woman in China did not improve until long after the Revolution in 1949.

The coxswain and master, chiefs and other ruffians, came out of the opium den and told the passengers they must pay 'plenty money' for protection. There was a good deal of arguing between the passengers and crew, all at the top of their voices. We watched in silent amazement. Passengers actually seemed to enjoy the bargaining; they were far more astute than the boat people, the four university students entering into the debate with gusto. Finally there was a hush, brought about by one of the male students, Choy by name. Everyone was looking at Eddy in his smart RNZAF jacket. Choy had taken the floor and kept pointing at us, laying great emphasis on our presence. The matter of paying protection money seemed to be settled; the extortionate village ruffians went back to the opium den. No more demands for money were made.

We were told that the barge would stay at the village for the night and leave at dawn. Choy explained what had happened.

'I reminded the crew and passengers that we and the foreigners had spent a long time talking at the tea house. I had found out that these three men were foreign officers being looked after by the Kuomintang Army and the Blueshirts, the Secret Police. I said if the just denials of the passengers to pay protection money delayed the journey of the foreign officers, then the Blueshirts at Hoyun would come down river to investigate. The Blueshirts would punish all the people and take all the young men for conscripts. That was enough. The mention of the word Blueshirts frightened them. They looked at you, Eddy, in the blue suit, they knew you were a foreign officer, and they gave in!'

How very clever of the Chinese student. We had told him the Kuomintang Army had helped us. The Blueshirts were not entirely his imagination. We were to learn later how terrified the people were of the Army and much more so of the Blueshirts, the Chinese equivalent of the fascist Gestapo. In fact, Choy told us, it was more than probable that the Blueshirts were watching the progress of the three foreign officers through their country, since they had agents everywhere. Eddy, overjoyed at the success his uniform had brought, began singing, 'Three German officers crossed the Rhine, parley-vous,' which he changed later to some nonsense such as, 'Three white officers crossed the river, savvy you, took the pirates from behind, savvy you!' It became our theme song for a few days.

We wandered round the village in the gathering dusk, interested to see what a village in this part of South China looked like. The students came with us, pleased with their success over the pirate attack. Peh-gek, now showing off a little after I had told her she was beautiful, walked in small mincing steps, making her, even in her coolie clothes, more sensuous than ever. Taking my hand, she daringly gave me a kiss on the cheek. Only a peck in truth, but it was very sweet. She said, 'Thank you for saving us from bad men.' She was smiling and laughing as she talked, waving her pretty hands about, so feminine. I was happy to have made such a charming friend.

Choy showed us a new house being built, saying that the man was a travelling carpenter, using local timber. The frame was joined together without nuts or screws, no metals were used. He told us how people trained in various trades travelled round to the villages to perform their work. He pointed out a travelling basket maker.

Compared with the dirty town we had been into recently, this village was clean, and the fields were neat, with winter wheat growing.

'They get two crops of rice a year as well as the wheat,' said Choy. 'It is a hard life, but the life of a peasant is the fundamental basis of life in this nation.'

The village children followed us, dressed in trousers and light-blue coats, their arms and legs looking exactly the same length. In the presence of the four students they kept fairly quiet and left us alone, chattering among themselves in tones of awe at the strange creatures invading their rural privacy. Charcoal burners, with great loads across their shoulders, came jogging from the forests, taking their loads to the barge to be shipped up the river. They made unpleasant remarks, suggesting we should return to the barge. They did not seem to appreciate sightseers in their domain.

On board we had gained in esteem. Although the other passengers knew Douglas as a doctor, because he had looked after the sick and the children, they were less sure about me because I was not in uniform, but they now treated Eddy as an important officer. Nevertheless, the majority of our friendly passengers regarded China as the centre of the world, the home of all real cultures, and we three as uncultured barbarians.

I awoke at first light, long before anyone stirred. Lying on the hard boards under the shabby rattan roof, I watched the sun's rays spreading over the distant hills. By now the sun would be up in the south-east, over the China Sea, rising on Hong Kong and those wretched prisoners-of-war. I hoped it gave them strength and hope.

Within a few minutes, the crew were up, the motor-boat engine began chugging and the barge was cast off. The river became shallower and narrower, and the boatmen had to use their long poles to push us off sandbanks, running up and down the board planks in doing so, shouting and yelling and grunting with exhaustion. The little convoy of the boat and barge crept up the river against the faster current with exasperating slowness, so much so that eventually the three of us got off and walked along the towpath. It was warm, the water was clear and inviting, and Eddy and Douglas both swam. I could not go into the water because my right hand was still in bandages. It had deteriorated steadily since the Chinese National Army medical orderly had smeared black-coloured ointment on it and was beginning to smell.

Although there was no sign of pirates, we were still in a pirate-infested area. In the early afternoon, the barge pulled into a small town called Kunyun Kok for protection for the night. It was a very old and dilapidated town, built high up on a hill. We decided to explore and climbed the many steps to the steep main street, which led to a huge market place. Immediately our arrival caused a tremendous commotion. Every child in town came running out, calling in shrill shrieks to sisters, brothers, mothers, grandmothers, even aunts and uncles, calling everyone to: 'Come and see, come and see, the foreign devils. They smell like pigs, never have you seen such big feet, such ugly noses,' repeated and repeated and best of all, 'Come and see the foreign devil with three eyes — three eyes!' There were great shouts of joy and laughter, much pushing and heaving to have a better look at the 'barbarians'. The immense curiosity we excited could not have been greater had we been visitors from another planet.

We had met this type of attention before, but this time it was frightening. The crowd was getting over-excited and very rough. We dived into a barber's shop, a filthy hole, but at least away from the shouting, pushing, poking and kicking people.

Eddy slumped into the barber's chair, not noticing the dirt around him, the grimy scissors and horrific cut-throat razors, demonstrating with his hands that he needed a shave. The noise in the street was thunderous. The crowds were pushing into the shop. The barber left Eddy, unattended and fortunately unshaven, and rushed to place a wooden bar across the door. A policeman, the first I had seen, who for some insane reason reminded me of Charlie Chaplin, arrived to control the crowd. He drew his baton and with fierce authority stepped before the door of the barber's shop. The noise was intense. Everyone wanted to see the foreign bearded devil have a shave. People pushed harder, the little policeman, crimson in the face, waved his baton and shouted. Someone must have kicked or hit him, for suddenly he lost his temper and began beating at the crowd, whacking big and small black-haired heads as hard and as quickly as he could. This infuriated the mob, and a great roar went up. The policeman was flattened against the door, the whole front structure of the shop bulging with the enormous pressure. The barber was terrified. He pushed Eddy out of the seat and ushered all of us out of the back door of the shop into a filthy little lane, a sort of running sewer, only just before the mob burst into the shop above us. We raced downhill towards the river, over the rotting garbage, running for our lives, and did not stop until we were safely aboard the barge again.

We did not dare or want to go ashore again in this dirty, smelly, fly-ridden place. It was in fact the last town in the fertile low-lying country, and was notable because the line of the Tropic of Cancer ran through it, as Eddy informed us, never saying where he had gathered this information. We were out of the tropics.

The next day was much colder. The river ran through hilly country, in bamboo and pampas grass, with mountains in the distance. After going only a short way, the motor boat cast off: it could tow us no further. Our progress now depended on being poled up the river. The perpetual incessant cries of the boatmen, up and down the side planks, became tiring and irritating: we seemed hardly to move. In the afternoon Douglas and Choy and the other student left the barge to walk to the next large town, Hoyun, and to try and hire a sampan to take us more quickly up the river. Eddy and I were left in the barge, which was poled up the river all night, looking after the fat May-may and the gorgeous Peh-gek.

There was more room on the barge now that Douglas and the two students and other passengers had disembarked to walk ahead to Hoyun, and passengers no longer had to sit bolt upright. Before they had tried to spit into the water over the heads of their neighbours. Babies were held over the side for their needs, leaving a pungent smell of urine, blended fortunately with the scent of garlic from food contained in small parcels. Eddy and I took over the forecastle for ourselves, stretching out in great luxury.

The loquacious May-may and the sententious Peh-gek joined us, two intelligent and educated young women who enjoyed instructing us in the finer points of Chinese social etiquette. May-may admonished Peh-gek for showing emotion in public. The peck I had been given hours previously burned into my cheek. Peh-gek blushed slightly, but added quickly that it was not good to shake hands or slap backs: you must shake your own hand when being introduced to a stranger. My mind went back to all the handshakes and back-slaps we had delivered to our friends Percy, Fong and Lee. Had we offended all these people?

Peh-gek, slightly aphoristic, said, 'Who is Lee? That is a common name, means pear.'

'I suppose White Jade is more distinguished,' Eddy remarked, to tease her.

May-may observed that Chinese men were seldom vulgar, coarse or brutal in their approach to women. The pirates might have molested them, but normally it was perfectly safe for young women to travel alone through the land. No one would harm them. To be more precise, Peh-gek explained that men might stare boldly at girls, or perhaps say lewd things among themselves, but you were quite safe. She then smiled, shyly, her perfectly shaped almond eyes expressing great humour. Perhaps she did not want to be so safe.

We were gliding up the clear shallow waters of the East River, the old barge being poled along step by step, the powerful muscular Hoklo boatmen grunting and groaning as they tramped up and down the sideboards under the full moon. In the bow, an armed boatman shouted out constant warnings of the closeness of sandbanks. It was impossible to sleep. Shadows formed at different times from willows and eucalyptus, or cliffs, or even from frequent small pagodas. The pale lights of river craft sailing downstream brought moments of excitement, the armed boatmen very alert lest the occupants be 'bad men'.

We sat up, the four of us, enjoying every minute of this wonderful scene, talking to each other. Eddy told them about the encounter with the nun in the hospital and how she had laughed so much at something Douglas had said to her.

'What did he say?' asked Peh-gek.

'He was trying to say we were used to any kind of hardship, a wooden bed was a luxury, we were used to sleeping anywhere.'

'Ah,' said Peh-gek, 'he must have got the tone and mono-syllable wrong. There are nine tones in Cantonese and many hundred monosyllabic noises which make up the language. The doctor does not talk through his nose enough for some words. Only a slight variation in tone pronunciation and tone changes can make all the difference between the meaning of words.' She began to shake with laughter, hardly able to keep talking, 'The doctor could have said he was used to sleeping with anyone, or even something worse, quite uninten-tionally.' May-may joined in the laughter, thinking it very funny. Eddy and I were left to guess.

May-may said the doctor should learn to write characters, then he could pass his message to anyone in China, irrespec-tive of dialect. Peh-gek, who was obviously the better edu-cated, started drawing ideographs on the deck, showing us some of those well known even to foreigners, evolved from pictorial meaning or by combining two small characters into one. Peace was a woman under a roof; discord two women under it. Going to law was made up of two dogs fighting with words. Jealousy was a woman combined with a stone. Eddy was intensely interested, trying to copy the delicate strokes made by Peh-gek.

The lesson was brought to a close by May-may offering water-melon seeds for all of us to crack between our front teeth. It was past midnight, and the crew were tired. An anchor was dropped in midstream. Armed guards took up posts at the bow and stern, and the passengers settled down. There was little noise except the gentle flop of running water against the hull. Above, the pale moon was setting, and in its place the stars lit the sky.

Weighing anchor at dawn we soon came within sight of the town of Hoyun, protected by tall stone towers, fighting towers, similar to that in which we had spent a night with the communist guerrillas.

Douglas, hair cut and clean shaven, looking very smart, even wearing his fore-and-aft cap, was at the jetty to meet us.

'Welcome to Hoyun! I am happy to offer you good food, clean barber, new boat and money!'

He came on board to say goodbye to the passengers. The children mobbed him: 'Three eyes! Three eyes!' they called with adoration. They all remembered how he had cared for them during the pirate attack. Two of the families that Douglas had looked after asked to share our boat, to which we agreed instantly because they were such friendly people. With them and the students and ourselves we would have a full load.

We had spent a week aboard this barge and had enjoyed the experience far more than we could possibly have expected and had made amazing friendships so that the process of returning the infested *meintois*, collecting our packs and saying goodbye to each passenger and crew member took up quite some time.

At last we left our friends and went into Hoyun for the usual Chinese morning meal in a restaurant.

'I've had a marvellous time,' said Douglas. 'Everything went right. Choy and I went to the boss-man, the local military governor. We had a great chat. About Hong Kong.'

He paused, looking upset, 'Oh! God, I forgot to tell you. Singapore has fallen. I can't believe it. The governor seemed very certain, said it happened on 15 February.'

'It can't possibly be true,' I said. 'They had thousands of troops there, navy and air force, I don't believe it.'

I had been stationed in Singapore for two years and had helped to build up fortifications on the island. It was meant to be invincible. Eddy was even more shattered. He had been there only recently. None of us knew, of course, about the retreat through Malaya. The last news we had heard of the Malayan battle had been on Christmas Day.

Douglas said, 'I think he must have got some radio message mixed up. Or he could have heard some Japanese propaganda broadcast.'

We agreed not to believe that Singapore had fallen.

'Anyway,' Douglas went on, 'the governor was quite a pheasant-plucker, a benevolent one, if you like. I got a lot more money, enough to hire the new boat and to keep our bodies and souls together. The boat is super. I'll take you there, but first I'll take you to my barber.'

I had the first haircut and shave. Hand clippers swathed through my golden locks close to my scalp, so close that the barber delivered a shorter haircut than I had ever had as a Gentleman Cadet at Sandhurst. I wished the terrifying Sergeant-Major Giddings of the Grenadier Guards could have seen me now. Eddy was horrified.

'The bastard won't do that to me,' he cried.

As always, a curious and inquisitive crowd, mainly of children, delightful, if dirty, round-faced Chinese children, had assembled outside the barber's shop. Choy and the other student shouted at them to go away, and we were not bothered by the crowd as we had been previously.

Next, I was shaved with a murderous cut-throat razor, very sharp, and shaved and shaved – not only my ugly stubble, but the tiny fluffy hairs on my forehead, eye-brows, my ears, and finally, terrifyingly, my eye-lids. I was thankful to be out of the chair. Choy supervised Eddy's haircut. Nevertheless, he had to go through the same trauma of the shave.

Meanwhile the spectators had gone to join a crowd on the outskirts of the town, close to a square stone-built fighting tower, where a great ceremony was to take place, traditionally performed fifteen days after New Year. At a distant temple, with lacquer pillars and beams in violently contrasting colours, blue, black, red, amber and purple, men were assembling for the dragon procession. Eventually, from the temple came the great dragon, writhing and glittering. The men held it aloft on poles as it swayed and dipped and reared and writhed in the dragon dance through the streets of the small town, round the fighting towers into the fields. The noise and explosion of fire-crackers and the banging of gongs added to the excitement; the townspeople were exhilarated, hoping no doubt that the dragon would keep them free from disease and bring good fortune for this New Year. Children were either thrilled with the dragon and its antics, or bewildered with all the commotion, awestruck and almost in tears, some tiny ones even screaming and crying. I was enthralled. This simple, village-country-town type of dragon, a rather shabby dragon truthfully, was so much more entertaining than the flamboyant dragons I was used to in Hong Kong.

We made our way to the large sampan Douglas had hired and on which he had slept the previous night. The owner and his family were away watching the dragon ceremony. The two families we had met on the barge and the students were all there, and we were allotted sleeping spaces. It was a lovely boat, the woodwork carefully scrubbed, the *meintois* new and clean, as was the rattan matting. Everyone was pleased with the vastly improved conditions.

'We are going to enjoy this trip,' said Douglas, always the enthusiast. 'It will take four days to Long Chun, then we have to leave the river and travel by truck, so they tell me. Very uncomfortable.'

I was sure we were going to make the best of these four days, judging by the jars of rice wine Douglas had collected for the journey.

18

Boatman's Family

Peh-gek and May-may congratulated us on our improved appearance, but teased me about my cropped hair. They invited Eddy and me to accompany them into the town to join in the dragon festival. Everywhere in the town there were signs of friendliness among the local country-folk. Many were strolling about the streets, their children following them, the small ones dressed in red for good luck, the parents stopping and talking to friends, taking canaries in bamboo cages for a walk. Others remained in their home-made brick houses, playing mahjong, the noise of the ivory pieces almost matching the clatter of wooden clogs on the narrow cobbled streets. Outside the doorways red strips were hung, newly placed for the dragon festival, with freshly drawn gold characters inviting good luck. A few lotus ponds and fish ponds took up more space, the fish ponds surrounded by mulberry bushes. Peh-gek said the droppings from the silk-worms were good for the fish.

May-may led us to one of the many tea-shops, which served as a meeting place for the peasants, rather like an English pub, and ordered jasmine tea and sweetmeats. Previously she had not talked much to me, being more interested in the handsome Eddy in his elegant blue suit. Now she started to question me.

'How old are you? Are you married? How many brothers have you got? Where do you live, England, London?'

Peh-gek rebuked her. 'It is bad manners to be so inquisitive.'

An old 'His Master's Voice' gramophone in the back of the tea-house was playing a high-pitched squeaky song on a cracked record, a Chinese operatic song, which she said was bad Shanghai music.

'Do you like European classical music?' Peh-gek asked.

'He only knows hymns,' interrupted Eddy.

'I don't, you clown. You only like bawdy songs. Your words of the boating song are disgusting.' Then, replying to the beautiful Peh-gek, I added, 'I love classical music, especially Chopin.'

'So do I,' cried Peh-gek enthusiastically, 'but I like the others too, Mozart, Gounod and even Beethoven. We had a good orchestra at the university. Chinese people like western type music. I could listen to Chopin all day, but have you heard Chinese songs changed into light music and dance tunes? It is very good.'

May-may, although a student at the same university as Peh-gek, did not have as much education or experience and seemed to resent her knowledge and her very good English. At times she would break into pidgin. She interrupted the conversation on music.

'Did the communists convert you to communism?'

I said that they had not, though it was an interesting experience. Our association had been with the guerrillas, brave men and women, fighting the Japanese. There was little time for indoctrination, but we were often referred to as capitalists — a huge joke, considering that all we owned were the clothes we stood up in and empty packs. 'I loved their slogans and patriotic songs,' I went on. 'The Red soldiers were happy, laughing people, unlike the dull dispirited Kuomintang lot. What do you think of the future of communism in China?'

May-may and Peh-gek looked round quickly to see who might be listening. The people within earshot looked like a bunch of happy peasant farmers, cracking melon seeds, sipping tea, playing Chinese chess and draughts, eating ginseng and noodles, oblivious of our presence. No one resembled what I thought a Blueshirt secret agent might look like, not that I really knew, of course. The children were taking the most interest in us, a small cluster of rather dirty boys and girls, staring hard at the foreigners, probably amazed to see the two Chinese women at the wooden table with us. Normally women did not frequent this tea-house. Peh-gek and May-may then held a prolonged conversation together, obviously not very happy to talk about the subject here, even though May-may had introduced it.

Eventually they explained that they themselves were not affected by the growth of communism as they were Hong Kong citizens. Seeing that I expected a better answer, they said they sensed a distinct feeling among people of a belief in an ultimate communist victory. Many things made them think so: the country's economy was in chaos, there was terrible inflation, scholarship had no real value any longer, and officials were corrupt.

'You must realise,' said the lovely Peh-gek, 'that the seeds of communism in China were sown by Sun Yat-sen many years ago — the process is an evolutionary one.'

Our talk stopped as an important-looking man approached us, wearing a European felt hat, dark blue jacket and blue trousers. He spoke politely to May-may, who introduced us.

'This is the headman, Mayor of Hoyun. He wishes to welcome you to his town.'

We stood up. Remembering our lesson on etiquette I shook my own hand, bowing slightly. Eddy copied me. We must have looked rather silly.

We thanked the headman for his welcome. He sat down on the rough wooden bench at the table and ordered rice wine. After an '*um-sing*', he began to ask questions, May-may interpreting.

'Your honourable surnames?'

May-may explained she would say, 'Humble foreigners have no surnames understandable by us. They call the one with the bad hand, To-ni and the blue suit one Ee-dee, which are their great names.'

'Where are their honourable homes?'

'Humble home is Hong Kong.'

It was getting rather tedious. The peasant farmers and other people, who had not taken much interest in us previously, now crowded round to hear the answers, especially the children. I told Peh-gek that we should go back to the sampan and asked her to thank the honourable Mayor for the wine, to congratulate him on his fine town and to wish him good luck on this dragon festival day. The Mayor was pleased. I shook my own hands again, bowed and left with Eddy and the others, who were anxious to go. It was not good etiquette for young women to sit down at tea-houses drinking wine with men; and very much worse, the thoughtless Mayor had asked if the girls were our concubines! We laughed all the way back to the boat as we plodded the narrow cobbled streets.

Temple bells, spreading joyous festival greetings, blended with the noise of children and the barking of dogs. Many odours hung about the streets, burning incense, decaying rubbish, vegetables being cooked for the evening meal. Black-wood and red-lacquered altar tables could be seen through the open doors, overhung with portraits no doubt of family elders. Delightfully coloured porcelain dishes and cups lay on tables. In the shadows a small Buddha stood. It was a different world from mine, another way of existing.

The moon was rising as we set off for the restaurant that evening. It was the first full moon after that which had helped us to escape, the same moon that was new at Chinese New Year, which we spent with the Chinese communist guerrillas and the brave inhabitants of that semi-destroyed old-walled village. I did not see it when it was new because it was raining, so tonight I made amends by bowing to it nine times, making wishes.

'What did you wish?' asked Eddy.

I did not tell him. It would be bad joss to tell. I did the right thing, my wishes were all met by the gods in the beloved moon.

At night the town looked attractive. Oil lamps lit up the stalls and tea-houses, the shops and opium dens, in an almost mystic way. It was a vivacious town, full of people shuffling along in the way country people walk, all talking at the top of their high-pitched voices at the same time, as Cantonese people do, so that nobody listens to anybody.

We sat down at a round wooden table. Choy and Douglas ordered the dinner, a very special dinner. The rice wine was poured from lovely decorated porcelain teapots into equally lovely teacups – cups, of course, with no handles, so that no one could demand right-handed or left-handed teacups. The Chinese people are so clever! It was against the law and the teachings of the 'New Life Movement' to drink rice wine because it consumed too much rice in its making, rice that should have fed the starving peasantry.

However, it was all right to drink it from teapots, so they said. Rather callous for the peasantry, I thought, but the thought did not stop us from drinking the wine. Quickly the faces round the table became flushed with the effects of the crude wine. The military governor joined us, bringing more wine, his dark features changing to maroon as he consumed the brew. The food was superb for a little country town restaurant, the vegetables especially succulent. We were all very happy, excited and talkative, making constant toasts, many '*kan-pei*' or '*um-sing*'.

'I shall make a special toast,' said Douglas, waiting for everyone to be quiet. 'To Comrade Tony and Comrade Eddy, soldiers of fortune, dear international friends – that was how they were addressed by the communists – intrepid escapers, battling through China, beaten, wounded, starved, impoverished, worn out. To you two and me: "*kan-pei*"!'

He was trying to be ironical about the pleasant journey we were enjoying. It was too much. We booed. It broke up the party and we shambled off to our comfortable new boat, Eddy singing his own version of 'Three British officers crossed the river, savvy you.'

We cast off at dawn, and were poled up the shallow river by the owner and his family. His wife and four daughters, aged from three to sixteen, were dressed in cotton blouses and pyjama trousers, each printed in pretty colours, and wore wide-brimmed straw hats. All the children had a job to do on the boat, poling or cleaning. The three-year-old even held the tiller. They were an attractive family, which never stopped working all day long. The children never complained, and seemed to enjoy all the hard work, which was all that they had. There were no toys or sweets or soft drinks to spoil them. The boat was their home. The mother poled, cleaned, washed and cooked for all of us, her family of six, the three escapers, the four students, the two families, nineteen mouths in all. The food she produced on a little charcoal stove was delicious. The whole family took great care of the boat and pride in it. In the stern, little strips of red paper with characters drawn on them fluttered in the wind, in homage to the water gods.

We made good progress. At a junction of rivers, marked by a very large pagoda, the boat took the right-hand watercourse, still the East River, actually running north-north-east. Eddy, Choy and Douglas wanted to help pole the boat, but the owner was very reluctant to allow them to do so. He said they were unskilled and might lose a pole or fall in. May-may explained that it was great loss of face to allow passengers to work, at least for the river folk to see this happening. It was also unlucky.

Eddy felt it was humiliating to watch the mother, the sixteen- and nine-year-old girls, and frequently the six-year-old, pushing at the poles to get us up the river. He explained in great detail to May-may that being a New Zealander meant that he was different from the Europeans, he belonged to a race apart, a superior race, a free and egalitarian society, men who did not like little girls being made to work for them.

May-may translated all this to the boatman, who could not understand how Eddy could be so stupid, and was a little offended because he thought Eddy implied there was something wrong with his daughters.

'Tell him he has paid for the voyage. Tell him to be thankful he does not have to work like us.'

That put an end to it.

It was interesting to hear Eddy express his opinions in this way, and also to note the impact that conditions in China had made on him. He was appalled by the terrible poverty, degrading, soul-destroying poverty that was everywhere. The students had told him that although we had travelled through rich fertile country that looked prosperous, the landlords owned everything and the peasants received only a minute fraction of the food they grew. They told him also many stories of the bullying and overpowering behaviour of the landlords and of the corruption of government officials, all of which added to the dreadful poverty of the people. Douglas and I were shocked by the poverty, but we had seen it all before in India.

The river became more beautiful as we progressed northwards to the continuous chain of mountains that disappeared into the vastness of China. Bamboo grew down to the banks of the river and the hillsides were thickly timbered with eucalyptus trees. Peh-gek sat beside me as the sampan glided over the shallow gleaming water. She asked me how I came to be wounded. I told her about the bandits' attack, that I knew, with a strange subconscious instinct, it had happened to me before, in a recurring nightmare in which the attackers had stormed over the brow of a hill in exactly the same way, how the violent blows on my unprotected head had all occurred previously in my dreams, in which I had always been killed, dropping helplessly into an empty void.

Peh-gek became intensely interested. She said, 'But they did not kill you.'

'No, they did not kill me because the dream, the nightmare, made me fight back. Because I knew I was going to be killed I fought back with terrible ferocity to save myself, fighting like a wild animal.' I went on to tell her that when I fell headlong over the cliff my flight ended as I landed at the bottom. I had stopped falling through the void. When I realised I was still alive, I knew positively that I had exorcised my evil spirit. The evil spirit had been destroyed by my violence, by the strength of my resistance.

Peh-gek was utterly astonished. She looked at me with admiration, her lovely deep almond eyes expressing wonder

and surprise. Then she said, 'Oh, how good! You did the right
thing to fight your evil spirit. It would have killed you. Your
dream was a warning to you. That is why the dream kept
coming back. There was another force, an ancestor's spirit
probably, warning you, telling you to fight the evil spirit. Did
you not know that an ancestor's spirit was helping you?'

'No, I know nothing about ancestor spirits, but I think you
must be right. Why did the ancestor spirit help me?'

'Oh, for many reasons. You are too young to die. You are
not married. You have no children who could look after your
soul, no one to give money or food to you in your after-life.'

I was not sure what she meant, but she obviously took it for
granted that there would be an after-life for me, that my spirit
would live on when I died.

'If I had been killed, what would have happened to me?'

A smile flickered across her sweet, intelligent face. She was
not convinced I was sincere. She was afraid that as a foreigner I
might be teasing her, laughing at her. She had met many
foreigners in Hong Kong and knew they were inclined to
laugh at some Chinese beliefs. It was important that I re-
assured her. I looked round the sampan, to see what the other
people were doing. The two families were in the stern, with
their children, all looking blissfully happy in the warm spring
sunshine, happy to be off that uncomfortable slow barge.
Eddy next to the families was talking to May-may, no doubt
telling her about New Zealand, a favourite topic of Eddy's,
May-may's fat, round face looking as if she did not believe a
word, almost praying that he would talk about something
else. Douglas was lying back in the bow, talking in his own
special brand of Cantonese to the two male students, Choy
and the other one named Yang, probably trying to improve
his tones, attempting to learn more words. Sitting amidships as we were, no one was interested in what we were
saying.

I said to Peh-gek, so graceful and feminine, sitting there
with the beauty of the lovely river as a background, 'I am
serious, very serious, I do wish to know about these things.
You come from an ancient civilisation which knows about the

hereafter, you respect and worship your elders and ancestors. I want you to tell me what will happen to me after I die.'

She thought for some minutes until, convinced I was not trying to tease her or make her look stupid, she said, 'We think, when you die your spirit will go into what we call the "Home of Ten Thousand Ages". Your spirit could stay there for many years, depending, I believe, on what you deserve by your behaviour on earth. Good spirits may one day travel further to the "Western Heaven", a heaven to the west of China, above all the great mountains that contain our nation in the west. Spirits may stay in the Western Heaven in great happiness for many, many years. If they are lucky, and good, after countless years they may change, change altogether, and travel in absolutely different form into what we call the "Blue Light of Ultimate Reality".'

I gently stopped her. She was getting excited, explaining all this to me with a flurry of arms. It was not entirely new to me.

'Yes, I have been told these things before, in Hong Kong,' I said. 'Is it so that it will take a very long time to reach the Western Heaven, depending on how good or bad your spirit is, and how it behaves?'

She was obviously pleased that I knew something about the subject. She replied, 'Oh, yes, many many years. This is a hard time for spirits, while they are waiting; this is the time they need comfort from the earth, by gifts from their children.'

I understood; I had seen the people making gifts of money, wrapped in red paper, and food, placing their small sacrifices on shrines, or in front of Buddhas, to save their relatives from hunger and an unhappy existence with unfriendly spirits. This also was why Peh-gek had said that I was too young to die, that I should marry and have children to look after my spirit, to help me with money, food and clothes on my celestial passage to the Western Heaven.

I said, 'Thank you, Peh-gek, for telling me these things. Who would be the ancestor who is looking after me? All my grandparents are dead.'

'Oh, it would not be your grandparents, unless they died

many tens of years ago, they would not have had time to gain any merit; it would have to be a relative far older than great or great-great grandparents. Have you been good to your ancestors?'

'No, not very, not at all in fact.'

'Then you are lucky, but it may not be your ancestor who is helping. It may be a Christian God.'

'Yes, it may well be.'

She was not only beautiful, she was very wise as well. But I cherished the thought of achieving, one day, many celestial years hence, the bliss of the Western Heaven, above those great and splendid mountain peaks of Tibet.

I heard Eddy say, irritably, 'No, New Zealanders are not all black Maoris. All Blacks are rugby footballers. Maoris are indigenous to the islands.'

'Oh! I understand, mummies are black footballs!'

The sampan was going alongside. We were stopping for a midday rest. Douglas, determined that these last few days on the river would be like a holiday, shouted, 'We'll go ashore for a drink in the tea-house. Bring your concubines with you!'

Peh-gek fell about in fits of laughter, but May-may was annoyed with Douglas; perhaps footballs, mummies, blacks and concubines were too much for her. Eddy was glad to get away from May-may.

'She understands nothing!'

'Serve you right,' I said, 'you've never stopped talking New Zealand since we left Shamshuipo.'

All the passengers left the sampan. It gave the boat-family a chance to wash down the boat and to get some rest themselves.

We were tied up near a small village, a little inland from the river. The children and dogs had noticed our arrival; the village headman came out to welcome us and offer us tea. Yong, the shy student who seldom spoke, performed the introductions. I shook my own hands. Peh-gek laughed at me. The headman led us to the one and only tea-house, a wooden shelter, where we were given cups of hot water. Choy then ordered tea, not wishing the headman to spend money on us, the poverty being very evident, and answered the headman's questions. The headman seemed to take a liking to Douglas, possibly because he looked far more fat and prosperous than the thin and lanky Tony or the robust Eddy, so that all questions concerned Douglas: what was his honourable name? how many sons had the nobleman? and so on, taking great interest in a small jar Douglas was carrying. When it was discovered it contained rice wine, the headman was delighted, sending a child off to collect some of his friends. Three toothless old cronies arrived in surprisingly quick time.

May-may and Peh-gek were not happy to join in the drinking; so Eddy and I escorted them on a stroll through the village. The village people were sitting down in their houses for the mid-morning meal. Politely they came to the doors and clapped hands at us, bowing and smiling. We smiled and waved back, but as we passed each house, great roars of laughter arose. Eddy, now a connoisseur of Chinese customs and behaviour, explained that they were laughing at the two ugly foreigners accompanied by their concubines. May-may kicked him.

'These peasant people live very sheltered lives,' said Peh-gek. 'I don't suppose they have ever seen two beautiful Chinese ladies walking out with rude and rough foreigners.'

The peasants lived a quiet life, and wished to be left alone, she explained. To them the family was all-important. They belonged to a clan; it was more important to be part of the clan than an individual. They wished to be buried in the village in which they were born. Some might go overseas, but they would return to the clan, bringing money and presents, to die and be buried close to their birthplace. They did not want warlords, civil war or other wars, the Kuomintang or any other kind of government, except that communism might relieve the burden of the landlords. All they wanted was their land, food to live on, and to live their own lives, to be born, live and die in the one place, to preserve their link with eternity.

We returned to the boat. The other passengers were all there waiting for us, the two male students looking flushed from the raw wine. The boatman and his daughters pushed the sampan away from the bank and we were away again, quietly punting up the sublime river.

Just as a superb sunset began to form, the boatman gave in to Eddy and asked him to help in the poling. Choy joined in too, telling us that the boatman wished to make sure of the haven of a village before dark lest the boat was attacked by bandits. It was almost the same story again, except that this time we made it, with the help of our strong-man polers.

The boat came to rest in a small and clean little village. Our evening meal, cooked by the mother, was superb, helped down by Douglas's supply of wine, and we enjoyed a happy evening, being regaled by the boatman with stories of the river. May-may and Peh-gek translated for us tales of pirates and bandits, of the communist army, some of whom had passed this way to join Mao Tse-tung's Long March. The communists had helped the boat-dwellers and peasant farmers and had paid for food; Chiang Kai-shek's army raped, pillaged and took anything they wanted without payment. It was surprising to hear the boatman tell us these things, especially as the students had built up a reputation for us as being under the watchful eye of the Blueshirts, the Gestapo, who would punish him for remarks such as this.

Later, Eddy, Douglas, Choy and the other student were placed on guard duty, taking it in turns through the night, armed with the boatman's shot-gun. Whoever was on guard strolled up and down the bank, changing over when the boatman told them, about every two hours, the boatman seeming to keep awake all the time. With only one usable hand, I was let off guard duty.

All safe and in one piece, the four guardsmen feeling very gallant, we sailed again at dawn. Eddy was allowed to pole occasionally. Again, at night, we tied up at a village, and were told more stories of warlords and civil war, and again our four strong men mounted guard. Rain delayed our progress the following day, and made it difficult for the young girls to use the poles. On the insistence of Eddy and others, the men were allowed to pole and eventually we tied up for the night only a few miles from Long Chun.

Before disembarking at Long Chun the next morning, I said goodbye with sadness to the boatman and his wife and daughters and the two families who had shared the boat with us.

refugees had been waiting many days for trucks to take them to Kukong, the war-time capital of Kwangtung Province. There was little doubt we would have to wait at least a week here in Long Chun, but at our expressions of despair indicated a good inn, for which he would give us money. He took Douglas back to his office and plied him with alms.

We could see the truck-loading area from where we sat in the tea-house, and the group of refugees waiting, sitting forlornly on the kerb of the dirty road with their pathetic bundles of possessions. Suddenly, three trucks drove in from the north. The refugees made a wild scramble for them and within seconds the trucks were fully laden with human freight. Quite a sizeable body of refugees was still left without transport, and the future did not look too bright for us. When 'astrakhan hat' rejoined us, however, he said that another five trucks were on the way, sufficient for all the refugees and us. Shortly afterwards, we could see the dust rising on the road running along the river bank from the north; Douglas shouted a final '*kan pei*' to the Governor, who downed his wine expertly in one gulp and then put us on the first truck in the convoy of five. We never knew if we had got our place by fair means or by the influence of the Governor and rice wine. I suspect the latter.

The vehicle was a Dodge, about five years old, heavily loaded with bags of salt, on top of which were bags of charcoal, and on top of these we perched. The students had been quick to follow us and got into the same truck, together with a large number of other people. There was room only to squat with knees up to the chin. As soon as we were on, the truck started in leaps and bounds on the very uneven road surface, throwing charcoal dust all over us. The truck was a charcoal burner, and we were sitting on its supply of fuel. Soon our faces were black, and Eddy imitated a Negro minstrel, singing 'Ole Man River'. All the black faces laughed. At least we were cheerful, even though in acute discomfort.

The driver, accompanied by a fitter and a coolie, each in only dirty singlet and brief shorts, drove with one hand on the wheel and one on the brake, speeding like a drunken cyclone, whirling up the mountain road and down into the valleys. Every time a collective groan of despair or fright or even relief sounded from the petrified passengers, the driver sang out jocularly to the fitter: '*Ka Yow! Ka Yow!*' (meaning 'Add Oil! Add Oil!'). Each time the fitter would pass him a flask of tea. I suspected the tea, or so-called oil, was laced with something much stronger.

The truck bounced in and out of huge potholes, puffing and struggling up the mountain and racing down the other side, skilfully steered along narrow razor-edged tracks on the mountain sides, overlooking great drops below. Going uphill the truck broke down frequently. The coolie would jump out with a wooden block and shove it under the rear wheel to prevent the truck rolling backwards. Fearlessly the fitter removed the cap from the boiling radiator while the coolie dashed off to collect water in a kerosene can. Then very importantly, playing to the gallery of wretched passengers, he fiddled with the engine and messed about with the charcoal burner in the rear, often refilling it and raising more charcoal dust. This drill, the same at each prolonged stop, was a great relief for the passengers, allowing them to get down and stretch their legs. The magnificent mountain scenery could be appreciated only at these halts; the external road dust and the internal charcoal dust restricted our view while in motion. We were warned to keep a good watch for there was always risk of robbery when we stopped. Wherever possible the trucks stayed in close convoy.

All along the road lay the remains of wrecked trucks, stripped of everything of value, crippled because of the stupidity of the robbers. One of the most idiotic items stolen were spare tyres, in immense shortage in wartime China, stolen not for other vehicles, but to be cut up for rubber-soled shoes, a kind of coolie sandal.

In the afternoon, while descending from a very high mountain on a particularly nasty narrow bend overlooking a ravine hundreds of feet below, a waving group of people stopped us. A truck had gone over the side. Fortunately not very far, for it had come to rest on a rocky ledge, but many had been hurt. Douglas rushed to the aid of the injured, with improvised bandages from bits of cloth and using pieces of wood from the truck as splints. Eddy, the students and everyone helped, including a woman doctor, a passenger from another truck in the convoy. The injured were carried up and placed in our truck. All the passengers squeezed somehow into the four remaining trucks, our cheerful student friends, Choy, Yong, May-may and Peh-gek, now squashed into one of the other vehicles.

Late at night, after a final steep downhill run, we arrived at a town named Linping, well over 100 miles from the start of the journey, no mean achievement over three mountain ranges on rough roads, using charcoal gas.

My diary recorded: 'When we reached our final destination last night, we were well received and given a good meal. We met Father O'Brian and talked with him until past midnight. We had very good sleeping quarters, getting single beds for the first time.' There was no mattress, of course. The bed was made of flat wooden boards covered by a bed sheet, which appeared rather dirty even in the candlelight. I dusted the bed liberally with disinfectant powder given to me by the Father, sure that even then the bed bugs and fleas would find a way to survive. The Father told me he always travelled with an oil cloth which he placed right over his bed: this made it too slippery for the bugs to crawl up on to the top of the bed. However, I did not have an oiled sheet, but I was provided with two slightly concave porcelain blocks as pillows. To me the wooden bed and the blue and white porcelain pillows were great luxury, especially the one with a glazed picture of two blue spotted lions playing with each other over a tasselled ball. Ever since I had been taken prisoner I found my thoughts concentrating on food and resting places: where would I next get food, where could I next find a refuge to sleep?

The hospitable Father O'Brian seemed very pleased to look after us. He probably longed to converse with Europeans, being lonely at this place on his own. He was an Irish Catholic missionary and had lived in the district for a number of years. Having fed us and shown us our beds, he then invited us to join him for brandy. Perhaps it was the brandy that kept us talking until after midnight. More likely it was the character of the man himself, solid and tough-looking, speaking with a slight brogue, a man of obvious courage. He had for many years shared with the Chinese people the immense hardships of their existence, the disease, the epidemics of cholera, natural disasters, the rule of warlords, civil war. He had provided a refuge for the people, open to all the people, not merely Christians. He was dedicated to his calling, a truly good man, whose experiences were well worth hearing. He spoke frequently of historical events, mentioned that we were close to the Province of Kiangsi, where the Long March began. His deep knowledge of the Chinese and of the district was absorbing. Eventually he tired, but before going to bed, he warned us of the danger of robbers on the road on which we were travelling, especially at a place he called the 'Buffalo's Back', where vehicles broke down frequently, and which had now become notorious for the robberies which had taken place.

We waited the following morning for the truck which had overturned the day before to catch up with us. In daylight Linping was an attractive town, situated on the headwaters of a tributary of the East River, nestling into the foothills of the great Kiu Lin Shan range. A part of the town had been damaged by Japanese bombing. For some considerable time we sat in the warm sunshine by the fast-flowing river watching cormorants fishing in the lower reaches. Peh-gek and Yong joined us, both rather worn out by yesterday's rough ride in the trucks.

'We have three more days of the road journey, and by then every bone in my body will have been broken,' Peh-gek said.

At last the truck which had gone over the side turned up. It did not appear to be badly damaged. Father O'Brian came to wish us goodbye as we climbed aboard and we were away, the truck creaking and groaning and swaying over earthen waves on the rough road. Before we all became covered in dust and soot, Eddy gave us a rendering of the 'Maori's Farewell', no doubt having explained to May-may that Maoris were not mummies.

Leaving the valley, we began a long uphill haul, coming at last to the area known as 'Buffalo's Back', *Ngau Bai Chek*, a very high mountain ridge. The valiant truck was forced up extraordinarily steep gradients, inclined almost as much as 45 degrees in parts, climbing 10 or 20 yards each time before stopping to generate more charcoal gas. Skilful engineers had built this road of steep inclines, bends and hairpin bends, round the side of this bleak mountain, completely bare of trees and strewn with massive boulders. The narrow ridge on which the road had been carved, no doubt by enforced coolie labour, was razor sharp at the edge. There was no room for mistakes. Despite the driver's one-handed antics on the steering wheel and his speeding, I could not but admire him for the way he handled this unwieldy, over-loaded vehicle on this section of the road, always mindful that it would lose power suddenly, splutter to a halt or boil.

Eventually, descending in low gear, we crossed the provincial border into Kiangsi Province and not long after dark stopped for the night near a walled village called Kiennan, where our road joined an old north-south highway, which may have given the village some significance in old Imperial days. Now it was crumbling, dirty and blacked out for fear of night bombing raids. Fortunately we stayed at a newly constructed wooden wayside hostel, close to a tea-house and many ambulant pedlars. We slept on a bed of wooden planks, large enough for three of us, with wooden pillows, now very familiar to us.

I rose at sunrise and had a look round. We were in mountainous country, almost all of which had been terraced for cultivation. Not one single piece of land seemed to have been left untilled or unterraced. It made you feel that the whole of China consisted of terraced fields, mile after mile of cultivated, irrigated terraces. Of course it was just an illusion, but the sight of so many people working in the fields was by no means an illusion. Always there were people working, people in big straw hats and simple clothes, ploughing with buffaloes, digging, planting, always increasing the size of the cultivated land, the good earth, repairing and extending the thousand-year-old terrace and irrigation system, working to provide food for the ever increasing population, more important to sustain the family, the great everlasting peasant family. These were the people who irrespective of rulers, invaders, regardless of natural or man-made disasters, overcame all with phoenix-like resilience, absorbed all to keep the family together, to keep the very life of China going.

We had only just touched the southern tip of historic Kiangsi Province, historic because of all the momentous events that took place here in the 1930s, resulting in the Long March and eventually the Revolution, the People's Republic of China. It was in Juichin, in south-east Kiangsi, not far away, that in 1931 Mao Tse-tung was elected chairman of the All-China Soviet Government. That great soldier, Chu Teh, was the military commander. The land was taken from the landlords and given to the peasants. Then late in 1933 Chiang Kai-shek launched a great anti-communist war. The Red bases in Kiangsi and Hunan were besieged and blockaded. The slaughter by the Kuomintang was horrific; they claimed to have killed or starved to death a million people in Kiangsi alone. The Red Army suffered 60,000 casualties; the peasants fought to the death for their land, knowing that the landlords would return with the Kuomintang.

The Red Army decided to withdraw to another base and concentrated near Yutu, not far from where I had spent the night at Kiennan. I could imagine that great army assembling in this countryside, ill-equipped, ill-fed, not only soldiers but peasants, women and children, young and old. No mercy would be offered by Chiang's armies. Then, on 16 October 1934, a memorable date, they advanced westwards and south-wards, breaking through the blockading lines of fortifications into Hunan and Kwangtung. Thus began the epic Long March, one of the greatest feats in military and social history. The army covered some 6,000 miles in just over a year — an astonishing speed at which to cross mountain ranges and rivers, fighting battles on the way, evading or eluding the enemy, occupying cities — so that the Reds could continue the fight against the Japanese and Kuomintang from Shensi, in the north-west. They left behind peasant red guards to continue the guerrilla fighting. From these scattered forces originated the guerrillas who had befriended us in the Japanese-occupied territories.

On the way into Kiangsi, on the part of the journey into and out of Kiennan, I had seen many derelict fortifications, forts and entrenchments. These had been some of the lines of fortifications built in Kwangtung to blockade the Reds inside Kiangsi and were the fortifications which the gallant Red Army had broken through. I was travelling on the very path tramped by this amazing Red Army.

The assembly and grouping of the Red Armies had been accomplished by night, swiftly and secretly. The main forces of Red Troops, about 90,000 men, were on the march for several days before the Kuomintang became aware of troop movements. As a professional soldier, I could not understand how a concentration of troops as large as this could possibly have been achieved with the primitive communications available at that time. To my knowledge they had little radio communications, if any, while land telephone lines would have been insecure. They must have relied on messengers, horse-borne messages travelling great distances at a gallop.

Almost the whole of the Red Army had been assembled and grouped into formations near Yutu, and had advanced, without warning, taking the Kuomintang completely by surprise, overrunning the enemy troops and occupying their positions, giving the Red Army access to the roads leading south and west. It must have been a spectacular advance, but the fighting must have been horrific, the slaughter terrible. Terrible too, that this fighting was civil war, people of the same nation killing each other.

As we travelled onwards to Kukong I thought constantly about these fearful happenings, the cruelties, the agony of the wounded, the appalling encounters between massive

19

The Long March

Long Chun turned out to be a small, well-kept town, with wide tree-lined streets, lotus ponds, tea shops and restaurants. At the official, administrative building in the centre of the town the Military Governor met us at the door, almost as if he had been waiting for us. As all our movements in every town had been followed invariably by a thousand eyes, the Governor might well have been warned of the arrival of three strange Europeans and come out to see for himself. He was tall in his austere grey-blue tunic and was justly proud of his fine astrakhan hat. Douglas invited him to take tea with us. It may have been Douglas's monocled appearance, his quaint Cantonese, or the immediate request from a total stranger to take tea, but whatever it was, the Governor burst into uncontrolled laughter. As always there were plenty of bystanders. They joined in the hilarious laughter also. Children cried to others to watch the fun. Douglas then complimented the Governor on his hat. The Governor roared with pleasure at this well-placed flattery, shook Douglas's hand violently, and waving the crowd aside, led us to a nearby tea-house. Douglas ordered tea and dumplings, and in a moment of instinctive daring ordered rice wine, to be served from teapot to teacup, surreptitiously.

Little did we know that the Governor had a reputation for being universally unhelpful, but also for being very partial to rice wine. As the wine flowed he became genuinely interested in us. He kept his cherished hat on while his features became more and more flushed. At first he told us that a long queue of opposing forces. The valleys through which we travelled must have been full of ghosts, of spirits whose owners had been cut off in the prime of life, who would have little chance of ever reaching paradise.

20

An Inn and a Monastery

From Kiennan, on a much improved road surface, we sped down into the valley of a tributary of the North River. We had crossed the watershed between the East and North Rivers. The morning meal was taken at wayside stalls in the pretty village of Weng Yuan, where peach and orange blossom, grown especially for the Lunar New Year in large round wooden tubs, decorated the circular doorway of a small temple, together with chrysanthemum and gladiolus, which grow all the year round. It was obviously a rich agricultural valley, and all kinds of vegetables — white cabbage, flowering cabbage, Chinese spinach, sweet peppers, Chinese kale and others — were on sale in the market.

Following this attractive valley downstream for many miles we came to a wide road, the main highway, in fact an old Imperial highway which ran north from Canton to Peking. The truck turned north at the road junction and stopped shortly afterwards at a river crossing, where pedlars were dispensing tea and cakes. An old and beautiful stone bridge spanned the river, built on pillars formed to look like boats facing the current, a type of ancient boat that carried courtiers and mandarins and officials on their way to the Imperial Palace by this Imperial highway. The truck crossed the bridge and climbed once more into the mountains.

The mountain roads were again nerve-racking; narrow, winding and primitive. The charcoal-burning truck frequently stopped, the wooden block jammed under the rear wheel to prevent it rolling back down the steep gradient, while we waited for the gas to build up again. My injured hand had begun to throb with some sort of infection, and I was running a temperature. Large numbers of Chinese soldiers seemed to be on the move, marching along in single file at the side of the road and weighted down with rifles, packs and blankets. A line of shuffling coolies followed behind, with further bundles of supplies at each end of bamboo shoulder poles. We passed a long line of gaunt and ragged men roped together, like animals. I was told they had been rounded up in towns and villages for forced enlistment but had not yet been supplied with uniforms. I saw a coolie collapse from exhaustion on one precipitous stretch of mountain road and an armed soldier push him over the cliff edge with his rifle butt. Life in China was cheap, and we were all upset by the incident.

At last we arrived at the large village of Yungyun, which had been badly damaged by bombing. The driver took us — covered in bruises, charcoal and road dust, and desperately tired — to an inn where the surly innkeeper said there was no room. The students were not at hand to act as our interpreters this time, for their truck had been left miles behind with a burst tyre.

Douglas, resilient as ever, forced the insolent innkeeper to listen to him, saying that one of us was sick and must have a room, for which we would pay a good price. A crowd assembled, small children squeezing through and pulling at our sleeves. Many offered the innkeeper advice, or tried to translate Douglas's Cantonese, for a local dialect confused the speech of these people. Gaining no positive response from the innkeeper, Douglas then explained we were foreign military officers, guests of the Chinese National Army, and demanded a room, just *one* room, with one big bed for the three of us.

Immediate exclamations and translations came from the crowd. The innkeeper bowed, shook his own hands, and told Douglas politely that he did after all have a spare room in the inn for us, but only a very humble room, not good enough for the noble foreign military officers; that was why he had said there was no room at the inn, but if we wished he would show it to us. Standing aside he waved us into the building and up a flimsy staircase, to a large cubicle on the floor above. The room contained a large wooden bed, of the sort we had become so used to, big enough for the three of us, but without a mattress, with a dirty cloth over the boards, and porcelain pillows on which an enterprising artist had painted a soporific scene of two green and brown loving ducks under a flowering magnolia tree.

It suited us well. Perhaps the innkeeper was not so unpleasant as he had appeared. He told Douglas he thought we had wanted three rooms, that foreigners must have rooms to themselves, and could not sleep all in one bed. After the camouflaged earthen hideouts in bushes, the concrete Chinese graves, the flea-infested straw and the bug-ridden wooden beds that we had slept in for the last months, it never occurred to us that we should be expected to sleep in anything but one bed. So, the innkeeper's loss of face restored, Douglas paid handsomely for the room, with a show of largesse. The happy, beaming man then pointed out a red lacquered barrel in the corner, sealed with a lid, and under the bed a delicately coloured porcelain bedpan in the shape of a duck. Seeing that we were satisfied, the innkeeper gave us a packet of anti-bug powder, bowed respectfully, almost a kowtow, and shuffled backwards out of the room. We were in, we had a room for the night, we even had a basin and water in which to wash, a thunderbox, a potty and a candle light.

The inn was a dirty, gloomy place, which had suffered bomb damage. We walked into the dimly-lit cobbled village street and found a restaurant, which was full of people eating and playing Chinese chess, spitting sunflower seeds on the floor. A curious mob followed us. A shabby, thin waiter in worn singlet and shorts beckoned us in. Seating ourselves at a filthy marble-topped table, Douglas asked the waiter to clean the table and bring tea. The man wiped down the table with a disgustingly soiled wet rag and brought green tea. Douglas immediately waved him away in anger, demanding the owner be brought. The customers of the overcrowded restaurant strained to see what was happening, trying hard to listen.

Douglas spoke sharply to the owner, better dressed in blue jacket and trousers, an obsequious individual who bowed and apologised at once, dried the table with a clean cloth and brought highly scented tea flavoured with petals of jasmine.

'We will get to Kukong tomorrow evening,' said Douglas. 'You will have to go into hospital, Tony, to have that hand fixed. Father O'Brian told me there is a good mission hospital there with an Irish surgeon, qualified at Dublin no doubt. So this could be the last night we shall be together. Let's make the most of it!'

He called for the servile owner again. Together they pondered over the menu, the owner explaining and making suggestions, customers now standing round us offering advice. Douglas enjoyed ordering Chinese food; I always loved the way he did it, with such expression and waving of hands. In due course many splendid dishes and superbly cooked fried rice arrived. Having eaten very little all day on the grimy old Dodge truck, we set to with a vengeance, Eddy now an expert with chopsticks, holding them like a courtier in an Imperial court at the top of the sticks, not half-way down like a coolie. The rice wine, poured from a teapot, as was customary, glowed with a rich smoothness on the palate. We were happy.

'I had no idea the trip would turn out like this,' Eddy remarked. 'Do you remember how you tried to put me off, Duggie? You asked me what could I provide, and I said, "two strong fists"!'

We laughed. It was just as well he had joined us. Those two strong fists and arms had saved our lives.

On the wall at the back of the restaurant a picture had been painted of many mountain peaks, snow-covered, nestling into celestial, iridescent clouds: it was the Western Paradise. Through the haze of rice wine I wondered if the spirits of us three would find bliss there together in eternity. Having surmounted our willow pattern bridge, would we be eating Chinese food perpetually in sublime bliss, Douglas doing the ordering?

The customers had gone. A policeman came in. Like the one

who saved us in the barber's shop, he too reminded me of Charlie Chaplin. It must have been his fearsome baton, or an air of pathos about him. He said there was a curfew in the village; we should return to the inn. Douglas offered him a teacup of wine, which he drank greedily. It was time for us to go.

Sliding down the steep, slippery mountain road from Yungyun, the truck swirled and skidded round blind corners, the horn going full blast, pedestrians jumping out of the way. At least the driver was enjoying himself, if no one else was. The driver had become a friend, and had joined us for a brief toast in the restaurant the night before adding more oil to his constitution. He was anxious to show us things on the way and to make our journey more comfortable and enjoyable. He did not have to try. I was exulting in the warm humidity of spring sunshine under a blue sky dotted with cumulus and nimbus clouds, crossing and recrossing the cascading rivulet by narrow old bridges and temporary wooden ones. It was so thrilling and lovely that I forgot entirely that I was still travelling through a battlefield, the early route of the Long March, brushing aside youthful ghosts and unhappy spirits, possibly crushing human bones built into the roadway, in our hideously mad rush down the charming valley.

A halt was called at the attractive but sleepy town of Wushek, on the banks of the North River at a junction of the road and railway, a railway line running from Canton to north China, now with the sleepers and steel tracks removed to impede an advance by the Japanese.

At last we had reached the great North River, the Peh Kiang, a wide gentle river with many varied types of craft on it, some under sail, others powered by chugging motors, a river which flowed southwards in endless curves to join the great West River, the Si Kiang, west of Canton. After all this travelling to get away from the Japanese, we were still only 130 miles, as the crow flies, north of Canton, Japanese-occupied territory extended at least 40 miles north of Canton.

We were less than 100 miles from the enemy and within easy bombing range. A small buffer area held by Communist guerrillas separated the Japanese from the Chinese National Army, which, in any case, did not want to fight. If the Japanese wished to extend their territory, they needed only to make a concerted drive on the guerrilla forces that stood against them.

At Wushek the North River wound gently through a large fertile valley, where two crops of rice a year could be grown, due to the adequate water supply from the river. In the fields the tireless peasants were cultivating such crops as sweet potato, yam and soyabean. On the lower hill slopes a variety of citrus trees were growing, also lychee. The market for all this produce was Kukong, our destination.

It was delightful travelling up this beautiful valley on a good, hard-surfaced road in our ramshackle truck, as it roared like a fierce dragon left over from a dragon ceremony through hamlets and villages. People waved to us, or scuttled out of the way in the nick of time, no doubt believing that the mythical devil following close behind must be angry at being run over and was therefore in hot pursuit of us. Fat sows and piglets with curly tails dashed grunting and squealing off the road at our noisy approach. Cackling chickens and hordes of ducks with their long-poled duck-master flapped out of danger. Huge silver carp leaped right out of a large pond, as if to see what all the fuss was about.

We drew up by the stone steps of a large monastery. The driver said he would wait an hour or so if we wanted to look over it. On either side of the red lacquer entrance-gate stood two enormous stone figures, looking like griffins in their ferocity. A young monk with shaved head and wearing a long saffron robe offered to show us round.

The monastery had been in existence for more than a thousand years, but recently it had been restored to its former glory. Inside the gates we passed through a paved courtyard, decorated with peach and orange trees which were in blossom in their huge stone tubs. The monastery was built in tiers or terraces, on each of which stood a separate temple, dedicated to a great god, or to a former monk or great man, surrounded always by stone Buddhas.

The whole place gave me a feeling of immense peace and tranquillity. The young monk, quickly sensitive to my feelings, led us to the Lao Yeh (Venerable Father) a dear, gentle old man with a wrinkled shaved head, in the same saffron robe as the other monks, eyes twinkling with interest and kindness and perhaps curiosity, looking very hard at the monocle when Douglas appeared. The Lao Yeh gave us a blessing and took us to the main temple to show us the bodies of three embalmed and deified priests, many hundreds of years old, lying there for eternity, in perpetual peace. Beyond the temple stood a beautiful newly-renovated pagoda, highly coloured, and with a great gong, which the abbot said could be heard for fifty 'li' around. He showed us old, very old camphor trees, which he said had been dead for many years, dead during all the troubles in China, the revolutions, warlords and civil wars, but when the war with Japan had commenced the tree had bloomed again. The legend was that when these trees came to life China would become great and united again, and regain its splendour. In fact, China did become united only seven years later, as the People's Republic.

'At 3.30 in the afternoon,' my diary states pedantically, 'we reached Kukong.' I dreaded the arrival. Ever since I had left the barbed wire of the prison camp I had been free, free from authority, answerable to no one, on my own. Except for a happy early childhood in India, I had lived a life under constant discipline, at boarding schools, at Military College, in the Regular Army, often harsh and stringent discipline, petty and exasperating, a stifling form of oppression. Ever since the escape I had been happily free from this imperious domination. In Kukong, the wartime capital of Kwangtung and the main capital of South China, there was bound to be some British official who would start issuing orders. Kukong meant a return to authority and bureaucracy.

We dismounted from the old Dodge truck at the Kuomintang Customs post, a barrier of sandbags laid across the road. Untidy sentries with long bayonets attached to their rifles were standing in faded sentry boxes, while Customs clerks occupied drab wooden huts placed in front of the massive stone grey walls of the ancient city. The Customs officials received us politely, bowing and welcoming us to their city, in reality to China itself. Our names were recorded; we had now officially entered China. Hitherto we had been passing through a frontier area, and no one had taken any official notice of us. It was an easy and pleasant entry into China, even though it had taken a long time and much travelling.

Fond goodbyes were said to our fellow travellers, charcoal-black in the face, and to the intrepid driver, the ostentatious fitter and the overworked coolie. All of us were grateful to have completed the road journey and still be in one piece. Grateful for their help and cheerful company on the boat and road journey, I thanked the students, May-may, Yong and Choy, and gave the graceful and lovely Peh-gek a kiss, in return for the one she had given me so sweetly days ago, only a little farewell kiss, not wishing to offend her prevailing sense of propriety.

A friendly Customs clerk led us through huge city gates to an hotel, a large and grimy three-storey building, where we met Mr Lockwood of the YMCA, a kind and helpful man, who arranged our accommodation and a meal. Hotel servants carried a galvanised iron tub of hot water into my single room. A mattress was provided on the bed. That night I would be alone in comfort. Or so I thought. With horror I discovered that I was covered in bites from head to foot.

21

Last Supper

Kukong city had come alive. Hundreds of feet, some bound in tiny black satin shoes, some in soft leather shoes or sandals, others in wooden clogs, shuffled, scraped and clattered along the paved streets in thunderous uproar. Men in loose, sombre Chinese suits, women in black pyjama trousers and white or blue jackets, sped along shouting at each other like hundreds of shrill chirping cicadas. Some stopped to do *tai chi* exercises. Everyone was going to work. Canaries in cages were being taken out for morning air. Bicycles and tricycles wound their way between the hurrying pedestrians, angry red-faced drivers screaming loudly to force a passage. Lean rickshaw coolies in scant singlets and shorts bawled obscenities to force their loaded carriages through the mob, their wealthy passengers — well dressed, grave businessmen in European felt hats, pretty women, with fresh peach-red faces, in brightly coloured dresses — snobbishly oblivious of the noise and fuss. Cars, buses and trucks weaved their course dangerously through the swaying crowd, with horns blaring. It was pure babel. Kukong city had come alive with a bang.

With a bang also came officialdom. A young Englishman in the Colonial Service rapped loudly at my door and entered without waiting to be asked. He had been in Hong Kong, learning Chinese, but had evaded capture.

'Your escape is classified as secret. You are not to disclose how you did it.' The tone was imperious, pompous. 'You are to be regarded as distressed British subjects, fugitives, not escapers — for security reasons you understand.' I could have kicked him in the teeth, the ass.

Naturally, I understood that I was not to disclose any information which might jeopardise the attempt of other prisoners-of-war to escape, but after all our experiences and the long journey to freedom on our own initiative, the remark by my visitor could have been better phrased. I accepted the role of a distressed British subject, perhaps I was always a rather distressed and humble subject, one who 'only knew hymns' as Eddy put it; but I objected strongly to the suppression of the word 'escapers'. A considerable number of Europeans, military people and civilians, had got out of Hong Kong before the capitulation in a Motor-Torpedo-Boat with Admiral Chan Chak. Others who for various reasons were not placed in prisoner-of-war or civilian concentration camps had also got away. Strictly all these people should be referred to as 'evaders': they had evaded capture. There was all the difference between evading capture and getting away from a prisoner-of-war camp through barbed wire or from a civilian concentration camp under armed guard; these were the 'escapers'. I felt strongly about the use of these words. I was proud to have *escaped* from a Japanese prison camp, and said so.

'Lindsay Ride is here, arrived this morning from Chungking,' I was informed. I knew the First World War veteran well, a Queenslander by birth, Dean of the Faculty of Medicine at the University of Hong Kong, Commander of the Hong Kong Volunteers' Field Ambulance. He was a man for whom I had a deep liking and regard.

'I must see him, at once,' I said.

Picking up my pack I collected the others and we set off behind the Colonial Service official who strode stiffly through the throng without looking to left or right. In the spring sunshine we came quickly to the great North River, crowded with all types of craft, sampans, barges, power-driven boats, houseboats. In one of the spacious houseboats tied up alongside the bank we found Colonel Ride. He met us with his warm, gregarious, Australian manner even though he was tired after the long journey from Chungking.

'Congratulations, many congratulations,' he said, with a welcoming smile. 'Oh, well done, well done indeed, all three of you.' Then, shaking my left hand, 'Good on you, Tony, good on you!'

It was marvellous to see him again. He was genuinely pleased that we had escaped, following his example. I told him that his escape had caused no fuss and no repercussions in the camp, so we had decided finally to go too.

Lindsay Ride had escaped from Shamshuipo two weeks before us, with three Volunteers. They had taken a different route from ours through the New Territories, where they had been picked up quickly by guerrillas, making much faster progress than we had, not going near the communist camp. He had already travelled to Chungking where the British Embassy had authorised him to set up an organisation to help other prisoners to escape from Japanese camps. It sounded an interesting assignment; I wanted to hear more, but he was tired and had much to do, and Douglas wished to get me into hospital. Before we left we were given money, accountable to the 'Distressed British Subjects' imprest account.

The Methodist Mission Hospital was an imposing cluster of two-storey buildings surrounded by carefully kept lawns and gardens full of roses, dahlias, snapdragons, carnations. We climbed the white-washed steps, at the top of which stood a steward boy of serious face, impressive in a long sky-blue gown, black velvet shoes and black silk cap, who led us into the drawing room. Doctor Moore and his wife were having afternoon tea in a beautiful room, set out tastefully with Chinese carpets and rattan furniture. Tall french windows were open on to the verandah. I felt completely out of place and embarrassed. I was dirty, my hand stank with infection, I hardly liked to sit down. The place was so clean, and Dr Moore so smart in grey coat and tie and white trousers. The Moores were at once kind and sympathetic to any awkwardness, interested in our adventures, especially in Eddy, whom we had left behind on the houseboat. Mrs Moore was herself a New Zealander.

After tea Douglas returned to the houseboat while Dr

Moore took me into the hospital and put me into a small ward by myself. A sweet little Chinese sister in white starched dress and hat unbound my swollen hand.

'How long ago did this happen?' Dr Moore asked.

'Seven weeks.'

'What did you put on it?'

'Potassium permanganate. A Chinese army medical orderly put some black ointment on it many weeks ago, but mainly Duggie washed it in potassium permanganate.'

The smell was nauseating. The sister turned up her nose.

'It's gone a little bad,' said Dr Moore. 'It's such a long time since it was cut open that it may not be possible to join the tendon up again. I'll ask Gordon King to have a look.'

He spoke in Chinese to the sister who sent a nurse off to fetch him. Dr King had evaded capture in Hong Kong and was staying in the hospital for a few days on his way through China. He was a gynaecological surgeon, from Western Australia. He examined the wound.

'It's a bit crook,' he said. 'You'll have to open it up to see how far the tendon has slipped. It's a pity the wound is so infected.'

'All right,' said Dr Moore, 'we'll do the best we can, Captain Hewitt. We'll operate tomorrow afternoon.' He gave the sister some instructions and left with Dr King, saying, 'Come and join us for dinner when you are ready.'

The sister put some powder on the wound and dressed it. The hand was very sore, but the sister, with her tiny Chinese hands, was very gentle and did not hurt. A nurse, in light blue dress and cap to match, brought hot water and helped me to wash and clean up, so that I felt better in the Moores' house at dinner, even in my filthy clothes.

The serious number-one steward boy, now in immaculate long white gown, orchestrated the serving of dinner with smooth efficiency; he and the other stewards slid noiselessly round the table in their satin shoes. No alcohol appeared on the table. After dinner we listened to the wireless, and heard disturbing news of Japanese advances in the Philippines, Burma, Java and Sumatra. Singapore had indeed fallen over a month ago. Even Darwin had been bombed. It was all very gloomy and I was glad to get back to the ward and snuggle down in pyjamas in my comfortable hospital bed.

Next morning the Matron came to see me. She was young and attractive, and wore big round glasses which suited her intelligent face.

'How is it?' she said.

'Not bad.'

She called the sister and had a look at the cut. I felt ashamed to smell so badly. The sister re-dressed the wound and took my pulse and temperature.

'The operation will be this afternoon. Please stay here and keep quiet. You must not drink or eat anything.'

I replied, rather formally, 'Thank you Matron, I understand.'

She smiled and left me. She was so nice, but said so little, asked no questions.

The operation was successful and the tendon joined up, a clever piece of surgery after it had been separated for so long. It left a scar seven inches long, which I showed off for many years to come. I was grateful to Dr Moore, a remarkable man, a devoted Methodist Missionary who was to be forced out of China by the Revolution and went to Hong Kong to work among the poor and under-privileged and the drug addicts, the people who needed him most.

The lack of medical attention in the seven weeks since my hand had been cut had caused it to become septic. The wound was very painful, but the little Chinese sisters and nurses who laughed at me so much could not have shown more patience or taken greater and gentler care of me. There was no penicillin in those days and septicaemia had to be dealt with by sulphonamide drugs, the supply of which in wartime China was scarce. They could be used only for the worst cases. I found out that almost the last tablets the hospital possessed were being given to me. When I asked Dr Moore not to give me any preference, he said he would rather use them now than amputate the hand. Just before the last tablet was swallowed the sepsis began to subside.

I was floating through lovely racing cirrus clouds, stretching my hands out to catch them, surfing over waves of clouds, Eddy flying astride huge air force wings, Douglas gliding along, arms and legs stretched, waving a pair of chopsticks in one hand and holding an enormous jar of rice wine in the other. We were on our celestial way to the Western Paradise. The heavens were piled high with fried rice, immense dishes of pork, beef, chicken, duck and monstrous plates of vegetable. We had completed our odyssey, we had arrived at last; I was so happy, laughing to myself, rolling about with joy . . .

A sister and the Matron were shaking me. 'You are throwing yourself out of the bed laughing so much. You must be quiet.'

I looked up into the Matron's smiling eyes. 'I was in heaven, the Western Paradise.'

The Chinese sister giggled and asked, 'Was it good?'

'Marvellous! Lovely clouds, so much food!'

'You are a little delirious, Tony. You are not going to the Western Heavens. You are not a Buddhist. You are staying here in a Christian hospital.'

I opened my eyes again and saw a white shape and large white veil about me. 'You look like an angel,' I said, and then added glibly, to show I was not quite so delirious, 'An angel of mercy!'

'You have been shouting and making the nurses giggle. Wherever did you learn that kind of Cantonese?' the Matron said with a happy chuckle.

'In a Buddhist monastery,' I lied, daring to call her Constance.

'No wonder all the staff scream with laughter at you!'

I was all too aware of the difficulties of speaking Cantonese, of getting the nine tones right. I once had a tutor in Hong Kong, an old Mandarin type of man, who wore the Imperial style of gown and silk skull cap, and had a scraggy beard of only a few long hairs. Often, when I simply could not get a word right, I longed to pull out one of those hairs. But he was a dear, kind old man, who tried so hard with the barbarian. He used to bring along a tuning fork and a very pretty girl to sing the tones in a lovely high-pitched voice. Unfortunately, I did not learn the language well for my attention was too taken up with the beautiful singer.

Constance told me that when I asked the nurse for water I had been using the word-tone for horse. The staff thought I must be delirious and confused about the Year of the Horse.

'If you're not careful,' Constance warned with a laugh, 'they'll take you at your word and bring a horse into the ward.'

Lying in that comfortable hospital bed, I became almost bewitched by the singing I heard coming from the river, from the lower reaches below the town, not far from the hospital. It was a lovely lilting song, which I heard again and again. I asked the nurse what it was.

'That is the river boatmen,' she said. 'That is the song they sing as they paddle their boats on the river. It is called "Peh Kiang Boat Song".'

She hummed it. She did not know any words to it. I loved it, and have never forgotten it. It is always associated in my mind with Kukong.

Constance helped me through the sepsis delirium, often re-dressing the hand herself. She brought Douglas and Eddy to my bedside when she would not let others disturb me.

Douglas told me he had volunteered to go back to Waichow to set up an organisation with the guerrillas to get more prisoners out of the camp, and that Colonel Ride had accepted him. Waichow had been occupied three times already by the Japanese; they would make mincemeat of an escaped prisoner if he were captured again. I could not bear the thought of it, but I admired Douglas for doing it and congratulated him.

Eddy was to be sent to Chungking and then to India. The Moores invited him to a farewell dinner in their spacious house. Lindsay Ride came too, and Constance took me along on the first evening I was allowed out of the hospital. Eddy was not quite so boisterous or raucous as he had been at Chinese New Year or on the East River, but he was all the same in good heart. In the acetylene lamp-lit room, dressed in his newly-cleaned airforce uniform, he looked very handsome. I knew I was going to miss him greatly. Before he left the party, he sang, as I knew he would, the 'Maori Farewell'.

Eddy's departure broke up our threesome. It was the end of the 'bridge with three men', the mystical bridge we had used as our highway to freedom. The crossing had been a wonderful adventure.

Shortly afterwards Douglas went south to Waichow. He came to see me before he left, very pleased with life, having had a Chinese tailor make a splendid new uniform, thin green twill cloth jacket and trousers, very Chinese-looking. It was a relief to see the end of the ridiculous pantaloons and the dirty battle dress blouse. But I was sorry to see him go, concerned at the danger he was facing and sad because his departure meant the ultimate break-up of our threesome; from now we were just three individuals, three escapers, on our own in the vast expanse of China. I would miss him, but I envied him as well.

After a week or so, the hand needed to be dressed only once a day and I was free to go out with my arm in a sling. I would walk with Constance over the hill behind the hospital and through the woods and orchards. A Chinese tailor made me a thin cotton suit, rather like a suit of pyjamas. I could not afford a smart uniform like Douglas's, nor did I want one. My Chinese pyjama suit had no badges of rank or any of that nonsense. I was still free.

Frequently Constance took me to meals and prayer meetings with other missionaries who were devoted to helping the Chinese people. Many had suffered great hardships and frightening experiences, but thought nothing of it. Their houses and those of all foreigners were sited together in one area outside the city, rather like the 'cantonments' outside cities in India. I never ventured into the great Chinese city of Kukong; there was no need.

Sometimes I took Constance to a Chinese restaurant. She would order the meal for me in her perfect Cantonese. I had never been so happy. Often we crossed the river by sampan to visit other people, lovely trips over a river filled with song. The haunting tune of the Peh Kiang Boat Song was ever with me. But one day I would have to go. I would be sent to India or the Middle East or even England, so far away from Kukong,

Figure 2 The author's Chinese passport

where Constance had to remain, in wartime China. Separation brought about by distance and war was insurmountable. In this terrible war there was no permanency, no discernible future. In the infantry, I had little chance of surviving; so many of my contemporaries had been killed already. I knew

Figure 3 The author's Chinese identity card

these things but never spoke of them. I spent my time being happy and just living for the day. It was unforgettable, and I wanted it to go on for ever.

Then one day came a telegram from Chungking: 'WHEN WILL HEWITT BE FIT TO GO TO INDIA?' Colonel Ride suggested I took the evening train. I went despondently to General Chu, the military governor, for a passport with which to travel through China. Sensing my reluctance to go, he said he could not let me have a passport so quickly. Ride then suggested I might leave the next day and break my journey to Kweilin by visiting a British Military Mission on the way.

The passport was still not ready on the following day, a Friday. 'You come Monday,' the General said. Monday was the 13th. It would be. But at least we would have two more days together. Constance did not work and we spent the whole of Saturday together, making every minute ours. Ride thoughtlessly invited me to lunch in his houseboat on Sunday. As soon as I could after my lunch I joined Constance and in the evening we went to another missionary's house for Communion. So on that last day we were never alone.

Early next morning a passport photograph was taken. I walked for hours with Constance in the garden until the passport, identity card and railway tickets were delivered by the hospital clerk. At five I left the hospital with Constance and took a sampan across the river to the railway station. The train left at 6 p.m. on 13 April 1942.

22

Western Heaven

There was nothing I could find to soothe the pain. I looked round at the carriage, a comfortable, modern, first-class sleeping compartment. I would have been more at home in third class. What did it matter? I could not look out of the window with the blinds drawn; the train was blacked out against air attack. I gazed at my new rice-paper passport, with my silly face stuck on to it, surrounded by Chinese characters I could not understand. My identity card at least gave me a name in two characters 侯 活 which had been chosen for me in Kukong, and which somehow kept me in touch. I could not sleep. A steward brought me a meal of chow-fan.

It was 250 miles due north to Hengyang. After a long climb we glided down the valley of the Lei Shui, some of which I saw as it got light, a huge terraced and highly cultivated valley. It was cold and raining at 7.30 a.m. when I got off the train. I called for a rickshaw. Here in Hunan province Cantonese was not spoken, but bystanders anxious to offer advice understood 'Melican' and directed the gaunt driver to the American Mission Hospital. We moved slowly through the narrow streets of this ancient ugly city, attracting little notice. The people were used to strangers; the place was full of soldiers and foreigners. A long bridge spanned the convergence of the Lei Shui with the Siang Kiang, a big river running northwards for 200 miles to flow into the great Yangtze Kiang.

I stayed that night with an American doctor and his wife and four children. It was the doctor's thirty-fifth birthday and I was welcomed to the family celebrations.

I did not feel refreshed at five the next morning, trying to find my train in the blacked-out station. A railwayman pointed out a waiting train in the West station, but an army officer stopped me boarding it and demanded to see my passport and tickets. He then took me to the East station and insisted that I should enter the train standing there and sit down. I felt sure he was mistaken, and that this train would simply take me back to Kukong. When the officer left, I showed my tickets to a number of people who would not attempt to help. Either they were anti-foreigner or frightened of the military. I scrambled out of the carriage, ran back in the darkness to the other station and jumped into the first train just as it left.

I tried to talk to the passengers in the crowded third class compartment into which I had tumbled so hurriedly. They all stared back at me as if suffering from shock at the unwelcome arrival. I wanted someone to tell me when we got to the village of Lichiaping, where I had to get off. There were no station names in roman letters. All I knew was that the journey would take three and a half hours. My watch had been taken by the bandits. None of the sullen passengers had a watch that I could see. I jumped up at each halt to peer out, much to the annoyance of the grumpy sleeping passengers. Then at last I saw the slight figure of a Chinaman dressed in British army uniform standing beside the railway line, and got out.

'Movement Control, 204 Commando, Sir!'

He was a private in the Royal Army Service Corps. I could have kissed him, I was so pleased to be out of that train. There was no motor transport and the camp was twelve miles away, but he had a rickshaw standing by. I asked him to tell the rickshaw to wait, and invited him to join me for a meal in the very dirty village tea-house. He was delighted and helped order tea and food; he was anxious to tell me about himself, his important job of meeting all trains and despatching those who descended from them into rickshaws. He had been enlisted in Singapore. I knew where his home was on the island, a link which made us friends. He was worried about his parents and family. They kill all Chinese, he said. He was lonely and wanted someone to talk to. He could not understand the local Hunan dialect and was bewildered at being in China, stuck in this outlandish place.

The rickshaw coolie was young and strong. He had to be, to pull the old hard, solid-wheeled cart up and downhill on the rough roads. It started well, for I was a source of interest for passers-by, bringing prestige for the coolie. But when we began to climb a long hill I got out to walk, and this made him furious, obviously losing face because his passenger regarded him as too weak to pull the rickshaw. He dealt with my strange behaviour by shouting and yelling to all and sundry, no doubt telling them what a stupid barbarian I was to pay to ride in a rickshaw and then to walk. After all, I had hired the thing, so why not use it, irrespective of any human feelings I had for the driver? Anyone who has sat in a rickshaw for four hours, in an old unsprung hard-wheeled rickshaw at that, not like those in Hong Kong with pneumatic tyres, behind a sweating coolie on a bumpy road paved with great blocks of limestone 1,000 years old, and probably not repaired since then, will understand why I wished to walk.

At last we came to the town of Kiyang and passed through a splendid stone gateway. As I rode through the streets, people gathered in doorways, calling out to the coolie, who replied at length. Some of what he said must have been complimentary, for the people often clapped hands and bowed politely in welcome.

Beyond the town I found the military mission quartered in a group of rambling farm buildings. It was strange after my long journey to see British soldiers again. There were Australians also. They were there to train Chinese National Army soldiers in commando tactics and to lead them in raids. They had little success. It must have imbued a loss of face to be taught by foreigners, especially by foreigners with little experience of fighting compared with that of the Chinese. The disasters at Hong Kong and Singapore did nothing to help matters.

At the railway station the following evening, I had another meal with my recently-met friend, the Chinese private soldier in the RASC, who put me into a second class compartment on the night train to Kweilin, the capital of Kwangsi province, about 200 miles to the south-west. The train followed the route taken in 1934 by the Red Army on the Long March, by the First Front Army of Mao Tse-tung and Chu Teh from Kiangsi, where it was joined by an army group from Hunan. I tried to picture that amazing cavalcade rolling and sweeping across the land, thousands upon thousands of men — some soldiers, some unarmed peasant porters — women and children, all except the tiny children with bamboo poles across their backs, carrying loads in their endless rhythmic step; mules and donkeys laden with everything portable or of value, stripped factories, all kinds of machinery, arsenals, silver dollars. It must have been like a martial exodus of Israelites from Egypt. Yet these people, this ant-like horde, were to bring about a Great Revolution that would change their nation into a People's Republic.

As it became light an astonishing landscape was revealed, extraordinary limestone mountains jutting sheer out of the earth as if beckoning to the heavens, some at strange angles forming numerous caves. A river wandering through the rocks, with cormorants fishing in it, added to the strange beauty of the place.

A handsome man of Miao race, with silver buttons on his vest, met me at Kweilin and offered to carry my pack. We walked happily into the city like friends, neither knowing where we were going, unable to speak a common language. At last a police officer took me in charge and handed me over to the Lok Kwan Sair, a foreigners' hostel. Immediately I had dumped my pack in my suite — bedroom, sitting room and bathroom, at 55 Chinese dollars a day — I walked along the main street to the Eurasia office to book a seat on an aircraft to Chungking. Colonel Lee, a procrastinating Chinese gentleman in charge of such matters, politely refused to commit himself to a date on which I might fly, blaming air raids and other events, and advising me to enjoy myself in the beautiful city. I did not care about the delay, as long as I could remain solvent.

Despite the Japanese bombing, which occurred almost daily, life in Kweilin continued as vivaciously as ever. The city was described as the 'Paris of South China'. It was not unlike Saigon in Indo-China, referred to as the 'Paris of the Orient', which I had visited before the war. Both cities were gregarious by nature, with wide tree-lined boulevards, sidewalk cafés and many restaurants. In Kweilin the cafés and restaurants were full of an amazing assortment of people of every race and colour — escapers and evaders from many parts of China; people with names like Trechencho, a charming Russian doctor, Elsie Fairfax-Cholmondeley and Israel Epstein, both left-wing journalists; and British Army staff officers, pompous, frustrated, bewildered at Chinese ways. Pitiful refugees struggling for a new way of life mingled in the streets with the permanent citizens, cheerful and friendly Kwangsi people, and foreign businessmen representing great international companies, as well as missionaries of many different denominations. I was introduced to a Chinese lady who was related to the famous Soong family and who was anxious to show off her relationship by giving me a letter of introduction to Dr H.H. Kung, the Finance Minister, husband of Ai-ling Soong. I looked forward to meeting a descendant of Confucius.

The same lady took me along to meet the Commander-in-Chief of Nationalist forces in Kwangsi province, General Chang Fat-Kei, known locally as the 'iron general'. The General, small and obviously very strong, with hard eyes, dressed smartly in a grey uniform buttoned up to the neck and wearing white kid-gloves, seemed a little surprised that I was not in anything that resembled a uniform. He asked questions about the fall of Hong Kong, wanting to know in detail the strength of our forces in the fighting. He was critical about the number of prisoners the Japanese had taken in Hong Kong, and even more so about those taken in Singapore.

'Chinese soldiers do not surrender,' he said flatly.

I may have looked a little sceptical. To convince me he added, 'China is fighting twenty-nine Japanese army divisions. We have been fighting for five years. We have not been conquered, even by twenty-nine divisions, because we do not surrender. Hong Kong was taken by one division, Singapore by two, Java by one.'

There was nothing for me to say. The General smiled at me, congratulated me for escaping and shook my bandaged hand.

Our good name as fighting allies was restored a little when we heard that, on 18 April, United States aircraft had hit back at the Japanese mainland, with bombing raids on Tokyo, Nagoya, Kobe and Osaka.

I could have stayed in Kweilin for ever, but the fastidious Colonel Lee found a seat for me on an aircraft. The Japanese gave me a final farewell salute by bombing the airfield just before I boarded the overcrowded Junkers aircraft which was to convey me to Chungking. Even with people and baggage filling the corridor between the seats, the intrepid Chinese pilot produced sufficient acceleration to lift the machine off the ground, and we were away, flying through low clouds over the mountain ranges to the wartime capital of China.

Two years after my stay in Kweilin, the Japanese captured the city and sacked it, committing the most vile atrocities, just as they did in the same year in Kukong, destroying the Methodist Mission Hospital, driving out Dr and Mrs Moore. Constance Green had left before the Japanese arrived.

The aircraft landed on a long sandbank in the middle of the shallow river. It was an astonishing descent into the bowels of the river, great cliffs soaring high on either side, on the banks of which stood the enormous city of Chungking, built mainly on a promontory between the convergence of the mighty Yangtze and another big river, the Kialing Kiang.

I gazed up at the towering cliffs and the steps leading up the bank, almost five hundred of them. The wharf was crowded with sweating coolies and multitudes of boxes and bales. Everyone seemed to be shouting at each other. I decided to walk up the steps, but two Huakan men pestered me so much that I was forced to sit in their chair and be carried shamefully up the hundreds of grimy steps, weaving our way through swarms of people and hosts of dangerous bamboo poles attached to heavy loads.

At the summit I selected what I thought looked the most intelligent rickshaw coolie that I could find, instructing him in Cantonese, Malay, Hindustani and English to take me to the British Embassy. After a very slow journey through crowded streets in which the inhabitants lived in appalling squalor, I arrived at the British Military Mission. The Embassy was on the other side of the river, so the rickshaw coolie had done well.

I met the British Military Attaché almost immediately, a Major-General Bruce, a most friendly Gurkha, and was given a room in a bungalow at the Embassy on the other side of the river. From my bedroom there was a splendid view of the Yangtze. At night, in almost a full moon, the scene had great beauty, but by day the river water looked jaundiced and unattractive, churned by the ceaseless activity of swarming river traffic.

I disliked Chungking intensely. It was a grim and ugly city, which had been damaged severely by bombing. Suddenly I was glad to be leaving China, almost three and a half months after I had escaped from Hong Kong.

At the airstrip on the long sandbank surrounded by the golden waters of the river, I boarded a US Army DC3 troop carrier. The well-tuned twin engines pulled the heavily laden aircraft gracefully off the airstrip and we flew smoothly up the valley of the great Yangtze, west for some way and then south, with the high snow-covered mountains of the Taliang Shan range on our right wing. In 1935 the Long March had proceeded this way in the opposite direction, over daunting rugged country. At Kunming, we collected three US Army Air Corps pilots who had made a forced landing in China after a bombing mission over Japan. They too had a high opinion of the communist guerrillas who escorted them to the Chinese Nationalists.

It was too noisy in the aircraft to talk. I stared down at the Burma Road, the only overland supply route available to China (closed since the Japanese capture of Burma) which

twisted and turned over mountains and valleys. We crossed a
southern bend of the Yangtze, and later the rivers Mekong,
Salween, and the headwaters of the Irrawaddy and Chindwin.
Flying north of the Naga hills, the aircraft descended into the
valley of the Brahmaputra and landed in Assam. Frozen stiff
from the long flight at high altitude, I stepped out on to the
sub-continent of India, the land of my birth, which I had left at
the age of ten. The return had little emotional effect on me at
first: I was too cold to think. Even the memory that the waters
of the Brahmaputra came from the Himalaya and Tibet, and
so virtually from the Western Heavens, made little impression
on me.

From there it was a shorter hop to our final landing at Dum
Dum, notorious because a bullet of that name covered in beef
tallow was one of the causes of the Indian Mutiny in 1857. I
followed the US pilots into the airport shed and straight
through Customs, without anyone taking notice of us. Standing about in the shed was a British officer in stiff-peaked cap,
starched shirt and absurdly wide shorts, hose-tops, polished
boots, and highly polished Sam Browne belt. EMBARKATION
STAFF OFFICER was emblazoned on his arm band, and he looked
stupid and pompous. If I reported to him I would be put into a
transit camp and that would be the end of my freedom. I still
had some of the Chinese money given to me as a 'distressed
British subject', part of which I had converted into rupees. I
decided to stay free a little longer, and jumped into the airport
bus which drove into Calcutta through streets of hideous
poverty and overpowering smell, to deposit me at the imposing Great Eastern Hotel.

I walked happily up the whitewashed steps, carrying my
little Red Cross bag containing a towel with Chinese characters on it wishing me 'good luck', razor, toothbrush, soap and
a few clothes. In my smart Chinese pyjama suit without any
badges of rank, I approached the Parsee at the reception desk
and asked for a room. He looked me up and down in
disgust.

'Have you baggage?'

'Yes,' I said, indicating my Red Cross bag.

He let out a snort. 'That is no good. We do not accept guests without baggage.'

I was furious. As a child I had never liked Parsees. They thought themselves superior to Hindus. I felt like giving him a Churchillian gesture, but instead wandered into the hotel bar. Sitting there was an officer I knew well.

'Hello Colonel!' I said.

He looked up in surprise. 'Oh, hullo — good God, it's you Tony, wherever have you come from?'

'I have just walked across China.'

'Have you, by gad — I have just walked across Burma!'

It was a farcical Stanley-Livingstone meeting. He did not say another word. He just sat there slumped into his chair, holding his whisky glass. He looked desperately tired, perhaps he was too tired to speak. Then a great shout came across the room.

'Tony! Tony! How did you get here?'

It was Freddie Guest, an officer in my own Regiment who had evaded capture in Hong Kong, leaving by sea with a Chinese Admiral before the capitulation. He filled me with drinks, 'burra pegs', and took me in to dinner in the luxurious hotel dining-room, still clutching my Red Cross bag. We were joined by a US Air Force officer by the name of Whitney, a son of the US Ambassador to India, who was sharing a room with Freddie. I told them I had been barred from staying in the hotel.

'Don't worry about that,' Whitney said, 'we have three beds in our room. You can have the spare.'

The next morning the hotel manager upbraided me for sleeping in the hotel without signing in. I did not argue, or pay for the night's lodging. I simply transferred my custom elsewhere, to the Grand Hotel just down the street, where a pleasant Hindu clerk accepted me willingly and politely.

I found my way to Fort William, a monstrous edifice dating back to the days of Clive. I had no great wish to re-join the army after enjoying so much my journey as a free man through China, but thought perhaps I had better report. The British and Gurkha military policemen at the main gate took

no notice of me as I walked past in my pyjamas. The interior
was depressing. Everywhere there were notices in abbrevia-
tions, S.S.O., G.S.O., A.Q.M.G., etc. I did not want to enter
any office, or to speak to any of the officers, many of whom
were hurrying about with important-looking documents.
Then, suddenly, I saw another notice: FIELD CASHIER. I went to
the desk of a pleasant Bengali babu who possessed a deep-
black, shiny face.

I told him about myself, told him how wonderful it was to
be in the land of my birth, talked Hindustani to him, and made
a friend of him. Eventually he asked me how much I needed. I
felt rather like that villain Wong at Grassy Hill, when Douglas
had asked him how much he wanted and he had replied,
'Perhaps $100'.

'Perhaps 1,000 rupees!'

'Of course!' said the kind cashier, handing it over to me. I
ran out of that ghastly fort like a small boy just given his
pocket money.

I stayed on in luxurious splendour in the Grand Hotel,
enjoying my self-appointed leave. When at last I reported
again to the Fort, I was informed that I had been posted to an
infantry battalion on the Assam border, which was busy
engaging the Japanese. I had no intention of going to that
battalion or to the Assam border. Hastily acquiring a railway
warrant through a friend, I took the train to Delhi, thirty
hours to the west. A kind Englishwoman at Maidens Hotel
did not object to my dirty Chinese pyjama suit or my Red
Cross bag in lieu of baggage, and even suggested I should
spend the day in bed while the dhobi washed, starched and
ironed the suit, which I did. On the following day, smartly
attired as a respectable Chinese gentleman, I reported to
the Military Secretary, a friendly and amused Major-
General.

I was given a letter from General Wavell, then Commander-
in-Chief in India, congratulating me 'on the skill and determination that you displayed in effecting your escape from
Japanese hands', and was posted to the 1st Battalion, The
Lancashire Fusiliers, in Cawnpore. It was a happy choice; I

NEW DELHI.

16 June, 1942.

Dear Hewitt

I am writing to congratulate you on the skill and determination that you displayed in effecting your escape from Japanese hands.

The conditions must have been hard and difficult and I am glad to think that you surmounted them in order that you might be able to continue your full share in the prosecution of the war.

The fact of your escape and the spirit you showed will be placed in your records.

Yours sincerely

A.P. Wavell

General,
Commander-in-Chief in India.

Captain A.G. HEWITT,
    Middlesex Regiment,
        Attached 1st Bn. Lancashire Fusiliers,
            CAWNPORE.

Figure 4 Letter from General Wavell

had visited them in Shanghai five years previously and had many friends in that old and famous regiment.

A pleasant gharri wallah drove me through the squalid streets of Cawnpore city to the spruce, tree-lined roads of the cantonments, past the grisly well into which the mutilated bodies of European women and children had been dumped in the Mutiny, to Wheeler Barracks, named after the General savagely murdered in the Indian Mutiny. I was met by a young Adjutant who took me to an enormous white-washed bungalow standing in its own spacious grounds, with servants' quarters detached. There I was introduced to my bearer, a tall and extremely handsome old Pathan covered in medal ribbons, the second bearer, washman, gardener and sweeper. A woman in purdah and children stayed in the background. I had acquired an instant household!

The Colonel drove up in horse and trap, groom balancing on a step behind him, and took me to dinner in the Club. We sat at a table on the lawn under the great stars of the Indian sky. The Colonel told me I was to command a detachment of B, D and HQ companies and take them to the hills.

'Tomorrow you will have to get some uniform made up. By the way, from tomorrow you will be a Major. Get crowns, not pips.'

I was to command 400 men, half the battalion. Furthermore, I was being sent to the Himalaya, those glorious mountains close to the Western Paradise, like the ones on hundreds of scrolls all over China. It was too good to be true; those Christian and Buddhist Gods, the ancestors, the spirits in pagodas to whom I had bowed, all were working for me.

The combined efforts of the rotund and jovial Quartermaster and the Regimental Tailor soon had me kitted out. I had some difficulty, however, with the Indian Paymaster, a pedantic Bengali babu, from whom I tried to extract six months' back pay.

'Oh, Sir, I must refer this to Command Paymaster, Hong Kong!' he exclaimed.

The Colonel took the salute at the Guard Room as I led my new command out of the barracks for the railway station. The red glow of first light was spreading over the grey-green Mother Ganges and the band played the regimental march, 'The British Grenadiers', 400 steel-edged boot heels hitting the ground at the same second, 400 bare right arms in exactly the same controlled swing. We marched as only a battalion of long-term regular soldiers can march. I was thrilled, altogether forgetting my desire to remain a free man. I had been born to this life in this land.

As soon as the Fusiliers had entered the long dusty troop train, I set off with the transport trucks, laden with supplies for the detachment. It was a very different journey from the one over the mountains in China. We sped along the straight flat roads of the Plains, past the famous Residency at Lucknow, besieged in the Mutiny for eighty-seven days and still showing signs of the bombardment, the Union Jack that was never lowered flying bravely in the wind. The colourful life of the Great Trunk Road had hardly changed from the days of Kim and his Lama, searching for the River of Life. Still there were the holy men and fakirs, the beggars and pedlars; bullock carts meandering across the road, drivers fast asleep; half-starved horses pulling gharris and carts; mules and donkeys carrying excessive loads; old forts and palaces, temples and mosques. People in the fields and villages, some sheltering under huge banyan and mango trees from the sun, women in gaily coloured saris, old pensioned soldiers wearing campaign medals, waved and salaamed to the British troops as we drove past. It was intensely hot and dusty.

Some distance past Bareilly the convoy halted for the night at one of the many military camp sites along the road, and I slept on the hard parched earth under an enormous full moon again. At dawn we drove on, the country becoming greener. A huge, highly-decorated elephant being led down the road delayed our journey for a while. Suddenly hills appeared straight out of the plain, and we were climbing through lovely wooden country. Before long we were 3,000 feet high. Strawberries were for sale. At 4,000 feet, peaches and apricots were being offered.

Climbing up the twisting, hair-pin bends, we drove

through the hot-weather hill station of Naini Tal and on to our destination, Ranikhet, surrounded by cool and beautiful pine forests. You could not see much through the haze, even though I was now 7,000 feet above sea-level. A cloud of dust and heat haze and black rain clouds hid the great mountain range of the Himalaya. Then, awesomely, without warning, the monsoon broke with violent lightning and deafening thunder. The rain came down in cascades, pouring out of the heavens by thousands of gallons. All night it rained. But by dawn it had stopped, and then suddenly the whole gigantic range of the Himalaya became visible, standing out in splendid vivid glory. Although many mountain ranges, interspersed with rhododendron-filled valleys, separated me from the magnificent 25,000 foot peak of Nanda Devi, it seemed to be almost on top of me, the air was so pure and clear.

I was on the threshold of the Western Heaven. The superb snow-covered mountains, shrouded by strips of racing cirrus cloud, stood close to me, in exact replica of pictures in China. This was the final signal that my adventure with China had come to an end.

Perhaps one day, with luck, I might be reunited with Duggie and Eddy in the Western Paradise and be granted the privilege to escape to the Blue Light of Ultimate Reality.

Postscript

After the three of us went our separate ways in Kukong, Eddy achieved his objective — 'Chungking or bust' — and returned to the war in Egypt, North Africa, Malta and Sicily, finishing as a Squadron Leader with a mention in despatches and eight medals to his credit, including the Military Cross. His was one of the only two MC's awarded to the RNZAF in the Second World War.

Eddy wrote to me often after the war, cheerful and humorous letters, enclosing relics of our adventure. He married and had a son and a daughter, and managed an advertising business until his untimely and accidental death in 1956 at the age of 39.

Douglas returned to Waichow for a few months to set up the British Army Aid Group for Colonel Lindsay Ride, and then rejoined the Indian Army. He was soon into battle in Burma, commanding a field ambulance in the Arakan and during the prolonged advance to Mandalay and Rangoon, finishing the war in Java, in the rank of full Colonel. He also received the Military Cross and a mention in despatches. Finding peacetime soldiering in Malaya tedious, he resigned his commission and studied psychiatry in California before returning to take up private practice in Hong Kong. He is married and has two sons (both doctors) and a daughter.

After serving in India with the Lancashire Fusiliers, I travelled by sea via Australia and the United States to England, where I rejoined my Regiment. I had been continuously overseas for more than eight years. All the same, I was almost immediately despatched to France for the Northwest European campaign, finishing the war on the Baltic.

I remained in the army and attended the Staff College at Camberley. With the exception of two tours of duty in England, I then served again overseas in command and staff appointments in Sierra Leone, The Gambia, Germany, Austria, Norway and Ghana. After that I became Military Adviser to the British High Commissioner in Canberra and then Deputy Commander of Singapore District, retiring with the rank of full Colonel, an MBE and a Military Cross.

I organised a number of international medical conferences throughout Australia before settling in Queensland, where I now live with my wife, Elizabeth, who has a son, Mark Weedon.

Over the years since our adventure in China, I have made many visits to Hong Kong, and reminisced over champagne (not rice wine) with Douglas. I often saw Sir Lindsay Ride on these trips, and attended his funeral in Macau, on which occasion I met Constance and her husband.

I never saw Percy Davis again, although a journalist once put me in touch by telephone with a communist guerrilla chief, but it is doubtful if he was the original Percy.

The King's and Regimental Colours, buried at Flagstaff House during the battle, were never found despite a number of searches.